HORACE MANN-LINCOLN INSTITUTE OF SCHOOL EXPERIMENTATION

# CAREER PATTERN STUDY

*monograph two*

_____

# THE VOCATIONAL MATURITY
# OF NINTH-GRADE BOYS

Donald E. Super *and* Phoebe L. Overstreet
*in collaboration with*
Charles N. Morris
William Dubin
Martha B. Heyde

*Bureau of Publications 1960*

_____

TEACHERS COLLEGE   COLUMBIA UNIVERSITY   NEW YORK

© 1960

**TEACHERS COLLEGE, COLUMBIA UNIVERSITY**

LC: 60–12516

Manufactured in the United States of America

# Foreword

The Career Pattern Study is an attempt to do no less than to conceptualize the field of vocational development. This monograph, which analyzes the vocational maturity of ninth-grade boys, lays the groundwork for the study of career development during the succeeding adolescent years.

The present monograph contributes not only to the construction of a theory of vocational development—this being the main purpose of the longitudinal study—but also to the enlightenment of school practice. While, as the authors point out, the findings must still be considered tentative, they nevertheless clarify the nature of the educational problems associated with the making of prevocational and vocational decisions during the early high school years.

The Career Pattern Study is one of a number of research projects of various types being carried on in the Horace Mann–Lincoln Institute of School Experimentation. It is our hope that through such research the basic nature of the problems of education may be revealed, and that the need for the continuing experimentation which must accompany education may be made clear. The present study is a significant contribution to this end.

Arthur W. Foshay

v

# Preface

In many school systems, as boys and girls enter the ninth grade they are called upon to choose among several different curricula. While it is true, of course, that these are educational choices, they are also vocational; for different curricula lead to different kinds of occupations.

How ready are boys and girls, on leaving the eighth or entering the ninth grade, to make such choices? Have they reached a stage of development at which they can know themselves well enough to make such decisions? Are their aptitudes, interests, and personality traits sufficiently developed? Are their vocational aspirations sufficiently stable? Do they know the world of work and of education sufficiently well? It is questions such as these that this monograph seeks to answer, even while recognizing that the answers provided at this time can be only tentative.

This is the second in a series of publications by the staff of the Career Pattern Study, a longitudinal research project concerned with vocational development. Planning for the study and the initial phases of the project have been described in the first monograph *(Vocational Development: A Framework for Research)*. The present monograph reports the results of the first year of research, and is based primarily on data from a group of 105 boys who were in the ninth grade of high school when the study began.

In the following pages, the theoretical framework of the study is summarized; the subjects, their school, and their community are described; the research procedures and instruments are also described; and the findings are presented and discussed. The monograph has two primary aims: to explore the validity of certain constructs concerning vocational maturity, and to present information about the maturity of vocational behavior in the group of ninth-grade boys studied. From our findings, we have drawn implications for education, which are discussed in the final chapter.

Although this monograph has been written by the two authors whose names appear below, others have contributed materially to its development: *in the initial planning of the study,* Junius A. Davis, Martin Hamburger, Harold L. Henderson, Charles S. Nicholas, and Albert S. Thompson; *in field work,* Harry Beilin, Junius A. Davis, Martin Hamburger, George R. Hudson, Charles S. Nicholas, Albert S. Thompson, Alice S. Hayes, and Charles F. Warnath; *in conceptualization,* Alvin J. Bernstein, John O. Crites, Raymond C. Hummel, Jean Pierre Jordaan, Helen P. Moser, Albert S. Thompson, and Charles F. Warnath; *in instrument development and data analysis,* David Cohen, Max Dubrow, William McC. Eastman, Patricia A. Gross, Harold L. Henderson, Margaret Herbert, George R. Hudson, Robert L. Jacobson, John F. Kinnane, Perin M. Mehenti, Charles S. Nicholas, Herbert W. Nolte, Joseph Sturm, William P. Wolk, and Malavalli Yoganarasimhiah. Their imprint is clear in the text, and our indebtedness to their continuing interest and devoted work is great. Thanks are also due to David L. Schneider, Career Pattern Study secretary, who typed our manuscript, and to Alfred L. Webersinn, who assisted in the preparation of data for statistical analysis.

In particular, we would like to express our sincere appreciation of our collaborators in the preparation of the monograph, Drs. Charles N. Morris, William Dubin, and Martha B. Heyde, whose long-term participation in this study and whose help in dealing with statistical problems and in the criticism of the manuscript have been invaluable; and of Dr. Robert L. Thorndike, who gave earlier drafts of the first six chapters of the manuscript a critical reading; and of our colleagues in the Horace Mann-Lincoln

Institute of School Experimentation who, under the leadership first of Dr. Stephen M. Corey and then of Dr. Arthur W. Foshay, have reacted to our plans, our methods, and our findings as we have shared them in staff meetings over the past several years.

The field work of collecting data for this study was financed largely by the Horace Mann–Lincoln Institute of School Experimentation, with the support of a grant from the American Philosophical Society. Subsequent support has come entirely from the first-named Institute. Our indebtedness to both sources is hereby gratefully acknowledged.

The cooperation of a number of school officials and other community leaders in Middletown, New York, and vicinity is also gratefully acknowledged. We are especially indebted to Mr. Ralph L. Shattuck, Mr. Frederick F. Singer, Dr. Herbert Smith, Mr. Daniel Finch, Mr. Robert G. Walker, Mr. Boyd Swem, Mr. Douglas Swartz, Mr. Fred Germain, Jr., Dr. Edwin H. Miner, and Mr. Walter Kennett.

Our research could not have been carried out without the cooperation of the boys who participated in the study. To them we owe a special and a continuing debt of gratitude.

*July 1959*

Phoebe L. Overstreet
Donald E. Super

# Contents

xi

# CHAPTER I

# A Conceptual Framework

In this monograph, the maturity of the vocational behavior of a group of ninth-grade boys studied by the staff of the Career Pattern Study is described.[1] The conceptual framework for this research is presented in detail in another publication (Super et al., 1957). Basic concepts are discussed briefly in this chapter, as background for the presentation and discussion of the research findings in the following chapters of the monograph.

## THE DEVELOPMENTAL FRAME OF REFERENCE

Making vocational decisions and adjusting vocationally are processes—that is, they are a series of related behaviors rather than a limited number of discrete acts, and they are behaviors which change with time, generally in the direction of increasing complexity and greater specificity. These processes may, therefore, appropriately be studied from a developmental frame of reference. The development of vocational behavior does not take place independently of development in other areas. For example, the development of physical strength and coordination, of intellectual

---

[1] Vocational behavior is defined as any interaction between the individual and his environment which is related to work (Super, Crites, Hummel, Moser, Overstreet, & Warnath, 1957, p. 3).

1

capacities, of special aptitudes, and of interests all have important implications for vocational development.

Behavior consists of making responses to stimuli at any specific point in time, while development is a general term for the processes of growth and learning which take place over a period of time, providing the individual with a behavioral repertoire (Super et al., 1957, p. 36). Through growth and learning, the behavioral repertoire increases and changes; behavior becomes more complex and also more differentiated, and the developing individual becomes more capable of responding to environmental demands in an efficient and independent manner. With increasing age during childhood and adolescence and into adulthood, the individual acquires the capacity to make not only a greater variety of responses but also more appropriate responses to stimuli impinging upon him. His potential for behavior (the repertoire of behavioral acts he can perform or of behavioral acts which he could perform if required) becomes greater as physical structures and physiological mechanisms mature, as psychological capacities grow, and as new behavior is learned and old behavior is eliminated or is practiced and perfected. Development is a continuous process, with the ability to perform new behavioral acts largely dependent on capacities for behaviors which have already developed.

### Behavioral Demands

Because of the extension of the behavioral repertoire with increasing age (at least until adulthood is attained), more is expected of the individual as his age increases. Furthermore, different kinds of behavior are expected of individuals at different stages of their development. Behavior which may be considered appropriate and adequate at one point in time may be considered inappropriate and inadequate at another point in time: the total behavior of a typical two-year-old is appropriate when the child is two years old, but seems inappropriate if manifested at age ten.

As individuals become socialized members of the society in which they live, they must meet the behavioral demands of that society. They must become capable of doing what that society requires in order that the society be maintained as a functioning whole. These required behaviors vary with the particular society.

They also may vary within a society. Differentiation of required (or expected) behavior occurs in relation to differentiated social roles or groupings based on such variables as sex, age, or social status within the hierarchy of the total group. But all societies do tend to set up certain behavioral demands (requirements, expectations).

Different students of behavior use different terms to denote the concept of behavioral demands. Sears speaks of expectancies for action:

If one thinks of maturation in respect to its social implications, of course, he is at once led to an influence that has nothing to do directly with physical change but is a stimulus by-product of it. As the child takes on new characteristics, his parents expect new things of him.

. . . behavior is in part a function of the *expectancies for action* expressed to the individual by others. The parents' expectancies obviously change not only because of physical changes in the child but also because of their realization that he is learning new things. (Sears, 1957, pp. 151–152)

Gesell and his associates state: "The organism must gather up and activate a heritage of potentials in response to a surrounding culture. This is the developmental task of the individual." (Gesell, Ilg, & Ames, 1956, p. 16) Havighurst has emphasized the developmental task concept, which he defines as follows:

A *developmental task is a task which arises at or about a certain period in the life of the individual, successful achievement of which leads to his happiness and to success with later tasks, while failure leads to unhappiness in the individual, disapproval by the society, and difficulty with later tasks.* (Havighurst, 1953, p. 2)

The tasks which must be mastered vary at different stages of development, with changes in the individual and in the demands of society. Havighurst (1953) has described developmental tasks typical of different periods within the life span: infancy and early childhood, middle childhood, adolescence, early adulthood, middle age, and later maturity. Some of the tasks of infancy and early childhood, according to Havighurst's formulation, are learning to walk, learning to talk, learning to control elimination, forming simple concepts of physical and social reality. Some of the tasks of adolescence, as described by Havighurst, are achieving a masculine or feminine social role, achieving emotional independence of parents, and selecting and preparing for an occupation.

Important in the developmental task concept is the idea that successful achievement of earlier tasks is influential in determining the ease or difficulty with which later tasks are mastered.[2] If this idea is correct, one should be able to predict success with future developmental tasks from success with earlier tasks. The work of Havighurst and his students offers some evidence to confirm this proposal. In a study by Schoeppe and Havighurst (1952) (using, however, only a small number of cases—fifteen boys and fifteen girls), ratings of achievement on five developmental tasks at three age levels (ten, thirteen, and sixteen) were correlated. All except one correlation were significant at the .01 level, and the remaining correlation was significant at the .05 level. It should be noted that these were ratings on the performance of similar tasks at different points in time, as the hypothesis tested was that "good achievement on a developmental task at one age is followed by good achievement on similar tasks at subsequent ages" (Schoeppe & Havighurst, 1952, p. 340). It should also be noted that the ratings for ages ten and thirteen were made at the same time as those for age sixteen, so there is a possibility that the ratings were contaminated.

Although the developmental task concept may be useful as a frame of reference for prediction, it does not per se constitute an explanation of behavior. However, the concept does serve at least partially to explain the orderliness, the patterning, of emerging aspects of individual behavior within a society. In the process of socialization, individuals are required to learn how to deal with much the same tasks at much the same points in time. For example, they must learn how to walk, to speak, to control elimination processes, to accept their sex role, to deal with subordinate-superordinate relationships, to become independent and self-maintaining, and to nurture others. Although individuals may learn somewhat different ways of handling these tasks, they all must try

[2] The success-with-developmental-task concept may be considered a specific instance of the generalization that an efficient way to predict future behavior is to examine past behavior.

to handle them. They generally acquire some knowledge of the preferred way of dealing with the required tasks within a particular sub-culture. The overt expression of aggressive, hostile impulses, for example, may be more freely permitted within one sub-culture than another, but the necessity of having to handle such impulses is common to both sub-cultures, and the way in which the impulses are handled will tend to be similar within each sub-culture. Anderson has stated the situation well:

If the stimulation for learning is set by the culture in such a way that all growing individuals meet similar stimulation at the same ages, an orderly progression is produced which, from the developmental point of view, is superimposed upon the development that is in the person by virtue of his biology. The classical instance is the imposition of the first grade upon children at six years. (Anderson, 1957, p. 42)

### Life Stages

Cultural stimulation of certain kinds of behavior at certain age levels (which may be conceptualized as the imposition of developmental tasks by society) will result in the appearance of particular kinds of behavior at different age periods or life stages. What must be mastered at a particular point in time depends on the life stage of the individual.

Various writers have described life stages in somewhat different ways. Havighurst's classification of parts of the life span from infancy through maturity has been given above. The classification used by Charlotte Buehler is the one adopted by the Career Pattern Study. Buehler, on the basis of work done in Austria and published in 1933, has described five life stages (growth, exploration, establishment, maintenance, and decline) and has indicated the activities and problems most characteristic of each stage.[3]

Miller and Form (1951) have described life stages from the point of view of work characteristics. They also distinguish five stages (preparatory work period, initial work period, trial work period, stable work period, and retirement period), which to some extent parallel those proposed by Buehler, although theirs were developed from a different frame of reference. All work lives do not show an

[3] Because Buehler's work is discussed in some detail in the first Career Pattern Study monograph (Super et al., 1957), the discussion is not repeated here.

orderly progression from one work period to another. The later work periods may never be entered by some workers, as Miller and Form have demonstrated in their research. Their formulation is intended to point out the kinds of periods into which working lives may be divided, not what necessarily occurs in every case.

Ginzberg and his associates (Ginzberg, Ginsburg, Axelrad, & Herma, 1951) have traced the process of occupational choice through stages based on the characteristics of choice or the presumed determinants of choice. According to their point of view, the individual tends to make his choices with emphasis upon different factors at different age levels. Their approach was developmental, and is described by them as follows: "Our basic assumption was that an individual never reaches the ultimate decision at a single moment in time, but through a series of decisions over a period of many years; the cumulative impact is the determining factor." (Ginzberg et al., 1951, p. 27) Three periods in determination of occupational choice were identified by them: the period of fantasy choices (between ages six and eleven approximately); the period of tentative choices (during adolescence); and that of realistic choices (early adulthood) (Ginzberg et al., 1951, p. 60). The period of tentative choices was divided into four stages, based on the factors given most consideration in occupational choice-making at that stage (interests, capacities, values, and, finally, a transition stage, when the focus is shifted from these primarily subjective factors to reality conditions).

Although Ginzberg and his associates did not use a developmental task frame of reference, the shift in the choice-making process from an unrealistic, fantasy approach to an increasing cognizance of reality considerations, which they hypothesized and to some extent demonstrated, can be conceived as a response to societal demands. Increasingly mature behavior is expected with increasing age; reality orientation is indicative of maturity; therefore, increasing reality orientation is expected with increasing age.

## CAREER PATTERN STUDY CONCEPTS

The various descriptions of the life span from a developmental frame of reference, as just presented, suggest an expected move-

*idea that occupations will change rapidly with technological change and therefore individual must be able to change easily to fit a new occupation? How does this jibe with stabilization? Is this*

ment in vocational development from change to stabilization and from fantasy to reality.

## Postulates

Influenced by these concepts, the Career Pattern Study has organized its research framework around the following postulates:

1. Vocational behavior, like other behaviors, develops over time, through processes of growth and learning which provide the individual with a behavioral repertoire.
2. Vocational behavior develops from less complex and less effective behavior to more complex and more effective behavior with increasing age from childhood well into adulthood.

    2a. Vocational behavior becomes increasingly reality-oriented.

    2b. Vocational behavior becomes more specific, less general.
3. As the individual becomes capable of increasingly complex vocational behavior, he becomes ready to progress from one life stage to another.

    3a. Each life stage makes characteristic demands upon the individual.

    3b. Acquiring the behavioral repertoire required to cope with the behavioral demands of a particular life stage (i.e., the vocational developmental tasks of that life stage) is prerequisite to success in handling the behavioral demands of the next life stage.

    3c. Progression from one life stage to the next depends on a combination of readiness for more complex vocational behavior and encountering the societal demands of the next life stage.
4. The vocational development of an individual may be evaluated with reference to the maturity of his vocational behavior. This may be done on a normative basis following—

    4a. A determination of the vocational developmental tasks characteristic of each life stage.

    4b. A determination of the behaviors engaged in by individuals who are coping with the same developmental tasks.

    4c. A qualitative evaluation of the presumed complexity and effectiveness of such behavior.
5. The more highly developed the behavior, the more effective it

will be.  Vocational maturity is, therefore, a predictor of vocational adjustment.

6. Vocational behavior is the result of a variety of determinants.[4]

   6a. Some determinants, such as intelligence or socioeconomic status, are more important than other determinants.

   6b. Determinants vary in importance from one life stage to another.

   6c. Determinants interact in affecting vocational behavior.

7. Vocational behavior is not entirely subsumed under a dealing-with-vocational-developmental-task classification.[5]

## Vocational Maturity and Vocational Adjustment

The Career Pattern Study is concerned not only with observing and describing vocational behavior but also with assessing such behavior from two related, but conceptually distinct, frames of reference: vocational maturity and vocational adjustment.

The development of vocational behavior through different life stages may be evaluated by assessing the vocational maturity of the individual.  Such an assessment can be made by either of two methods, depending on the purpose of the assessment.  The behavior of the individual may be compared with 1) the behavior to be expected from one in his life stage as determined by his age (VM I), or 2) the behavior of others dealing with the same developmental tasks as those with which the individual under consideration is dealing (VM II).  In either comparison, normative data upon which to base the assessment are required; it should be stressed that vocational maturity is an operational, normative concept and as such does not involve value judgments.

Vocational Maturity I (VM I) is defined as the life stage in which the individual actually is, as evidenced by the developmental tasks with which he is dealing, in relation to the life stage in which he is expected to be, in terms of his age (Super et al., 1957, p. 57, p.

[4] The construct *determinants of vocational behavior* is a general term referring to attributes of the individual as well as to characteristics of the environment.  Obviously, behavior is engaged in by a person in an environment.  The individual is not a passive recipient of stimuli, but actively interacts with his environment.  For further discussion of this point see Blau, Gustad, Jessor, Parnes, & Wilcock, 1956; Super et al., 1957; and Super & Bachrach, 1957, Chapter VI.

[5] For example, many of the acts a worker engages in (such as the details of work performance that time-and-motion studies observe) are vocational behaviors, but they can hardly be called dealing with vocational developmental tasks.

132). To establish standards for evaluating VM I, the vocational developmental tasks characteristic of each life stage must be identified.

Vocational Maturity II (VM II) is defined as maturity of behavior in the actual life stage (regardless of whether it is the expected life stage), as evidenced by the behavior shown in dealing with developmental tasks of the actual life stage compared with the behavior of other individuals who are dealing with the same developmental tasks (Super et al., 1957, p. 57, p. 132). To establish standards for evaluating VM II, variations in behavior in dealing with the developmental tasks of each life stage must be identified, and the frequency of the behaviors manifested must be noted.

The aspects of development evaluated by measurement techniques appropriate for VM I and VM II are somewhat different. Nevertheless, either of these two approaches to assessing vocational maturity will give an indication of the extent to which an individual's repertoire of vocational behavior has developed, by showing the life stage which he has reached or by showing how he is dealing with developmental tasks in comparison with others dealing with the same tasks.

Vocational behavior may be evaluated in terms of its outcomes, as well as in terms of maturity. Essentially, evaluation of the outcomes of vocational behavior is evaluation of integrative vocational adjustment. Integrative vocational adjustment is defined as the extent to which vocational behavior results in the accomplishment of a vocational developmental task with long-term satisfaction to the individual in meeting socialized objectives (Super et al., 1957, p. 67). It is hypothesized that success is required as one basis for satisfaction, because success is an important means (at least within the middle-class culture) of self-realization and because it is also important to society (Super et al., 1957, p. 67). Integrative vocational adjustment, therefore, has two aspects: satisfaction and success.

### THE NEED TO ASSESS VOCATIONAL MATURITY

The concept of vocational maturity has important implications for counseling practice. Presumably, the best time for an individual to begin to deal with a vocational developmental task is when he is ready to begin (assuming that societal demands are somewhat flexible in their time requirements). Before a behavioral act can be performed, a repertoire of appropriate behavior must be present. Dysinger's concept of "vocational readiness" as a construct analogous to reading readiness is, we feel, a very apt one (1950). Havighurst has characterized this concept of readiness as "the teachable moment."

When the body is ripe, and society requires, and the self is ready to achieve a certain task, the teachable moment has come. Efforts at teaching which would have been largely wasted if they had come earlier, give gratifying results when they come at the *teachable moment,* when the task should be learned. (Havighurst, 1953, p. 5)

When the individual is ready to begin vocational planning, he will presumably do so more effectively than when, in terms of his vocational development, he is not yet ready. Therefore, it would be helpful in vocational and educational counseling to be able to ascertain the vocational maturity of students and clients, particularly of those in the early phases of the exploratory stage, in junior and senior high school. Furthermore, if normative data indicating the vocational behavior typical at different life stages were available, atypical vocational behavior could be recognized more readily. This would be of assistance in identifying those most in need of special help and in diagnostic work with individuals.

The concept of vocational maturity has other important implications for education. School systems in this country are so organized that some anticipatory or actual vocational decisions have to be made at the end of junior high school or at the beginning of high school. The individual student usually has to decide among different curricula, such as college preparatory, general, or vocational. Other decisions must be made during the high school years, for instance, whether to remain in high school, to change curricula, to continue education beyond high school. These educational decisions influence the student's subsequent vocational career by limiting future educational and vocational choices. If a boy has decided to drop out of high school at sixteen, then marries at nineteen, it is unlikely that he will ever complete high school, go to college, and prepare for a profession. If a student has attended a vocational high school, he will have difficulty in being admitted to a private liberal arts college. If a person has learned the trade of carpenter and worked at it for a number of years, he probably will not subsequently retrain for work as a machinist. Obviously, educational and vocational decisions have to be made sooner or later, and many decisions are the right ones for the persons concerned. But time is wasted if unwise educational and vocational choices have been made, necessitating attempts at correction later. Especially in years of political and social crisis, it is important to the individual and to society that time and resources not be wasted in unnecessary educational or vocational floundering.

Granted, then, that the educational decisions required of a young person at about the age of fourteen have an important bearing on his later occupational history, it is pertinent to ask whether he is ready to make the decisions typically required at that age. Is his vocational maturity sufficient for him to be able to deal adequately with the choice-making tasks with which he is faced? If he has to make a choice before he is ready to make it, what will happen? What can be done to increase readiness for decision-making among those who are not ready?

To answer these questions, information concerning the vocational maturity of young people in the American culture is needed. Studies of vocational development can provide normative data concerning vocational behavior at different age and grade levels. When such basic data are available, obtained from an adequate sampling of the population, educators will know more clearly whether the educational system as now organized requires appropriate choice-making tasks of its students, at appropriate times, or whether some revision in educational practice is needed.

Young people should be ready to make the step-by-step choices that are called for as they progress through school, so that the vocational choices they eventually make will be appropriate for them, conducive to their personal satisfaction and to their success as productive members of society. To attain this goal, more research-derived knowledge of the developmental sequence of vocational behavior and of the determinants of vocational behavior is needed.

## CAREER PATTERN STUDY RESEARCH

The Career Pattern Study is attempting, through its research program, to increase knowledge of vocational behavior by testing empirically its hypothetical constructs concerning vocational development. At this stage the focus of this research is on construct validity; later studies of the same boys, using longitudinal data, will examine the predictive validity of our constructs and thus further refine them.[6]

In discussing construct validity, the Committee on Technical Recommendations for Psychological Tests and Diagnostic Techniques has written:

The clinician interested in construct validity has in mind an admittedly incomplete construct, the evidence for which is to be found roughly in such-and-such behavioral domains. The vagueness of the construct is an inevitable consequence of the incompleteness of current psychological theory, and cannot be rectified faster than theory grows and is confirmed. At a given stage of theoretical development, the only kind of prediction that can be made may be that certain correlations should be positive, or that patients who fail to conform to a group trend should be expected with considerable frequency to exhibit such-and-such an additional feature, or the like. . . .

The correlation or measure of discrimination obtained in studying construct validity is not to be taken as the "validity coefficient," . . . Studies of many such predictions, possibly involving quite independent components of theory, will in the mass confirm or disconfirm the claims made. (1954, p. 15)

It is anticipated that the tentative statement of theory presented in Monograph 1 and briefly reviewed in this chapter will undergo modification as the study progresses. The testing of the validity of the constructs may well lead to changes in our formulations. Furthermore, because the underlying theoretical constructs are still being modified, the degree of refinement of the constructs will vary at different stages of data collection. The first monograph of the Career Pattern Study, on the theoretical framework, was written

[6] This section of the chapter is largely based on a paper prepared by Charles N. Morris.

after data collection had begun, though before the data for the present monograph were fully analyzed. Preliminary statements of theory had been made in unpublished Career Pattern Study working papers, which were later published in modified form (Super, 1953; Super, 1954; Super, 1955). However, decisions about the sample of subjects, the kinds of data to collect, and the methods of data collection were made before the proposed theoretical constructs were clearly formulated. These research decisions also reflected, of course, the practical requirements and limitations of the research situation.

Another objective of the Career Pattern Study is to develop, on the basis of its hypothetical constructs, measures indicative of current, or predictive of future, vocational behavior. In this monograph, an analysis of the vocational behavior of boys in the ninth grade is presented in some detail. However, because all of these data were obtained when our subjects were in the ninth grade, studies of the predictive validity of these data are not reported here. Such findings will, of course, be presented in subsequent monographs, when information obtained in follow-up studies will be related to the data collected at earlier periods. The reader should keep in mind, however, that the indices of vocational maturity presented in this monograph have as yet been analyzed neither for their predictive validity nor for the developmental trends they may reveal. These are still cross-sectional, not longitudinal, data; they are data about vocational behaviors which we assume (for the present) to be indicative of vocational maturity. Whether they actually are will be ascertained by further research, using additional data from our own follow-up studies to observe developmental trends, and, ideally, cross-validating the findings on other samples.

New samples of subjects, as well as more refined measures, will be required for a more rigorous assessment of theoretical constructs and for more precise tests of predictive validity. Additional studies of vocational development using subjects other than those of the Career Pattern Study should be made, in order more fully to establish the validity of the concepts we have explored.

# CHAPTER II

# Ninth-Grade Boys in Middletown

Decisions were necessary, at the outset of the Career Pattern Study, on the scope and design of its research; decisions concerning the time span and location of the study, as well as the age and sex of its subjects.

## SCOPE OF THE STUDY

It was the aim of the study to observe the vocational behavior of a group from relatively early in the vocational choice-making process until a time when the careers of many in the group should be stabilized and the patterning of their careers should generally be clear.

It was decided that the study should be limited to boys, to control the data in respect to sex differences, because the work lives of men tend to differ from the work lives of women (Super, 1957; Jersild, 1957, Ch. 15). Boys who were enrolled in the eighth and ninth grades of the Middletown, New York, public schools during a substantial part of the first year of the research project were selected as the subjects of the study.

### Time Span

Boys at these grade levels were chosen because they were already faced with, or soon would be faced with, the task of preparing to

14

make vocational choices. The Career Pattern Study has been observing the group periodically from this rather early phase of the exploratory stage of vocational development and will continue to do so throughout a twenty-year period (until the subjects are about thirty-five years of age and presumably well along in the establishment stage of vocational development).

### Subjects

There were 138 boys in the eighth-grade group and 142 boys in the ninth-grade group during the first year of the study. The two grades were located in different schools, because the Middletown school system included one junior high school for grades seven and eight (Memorial Junior High School) and one high school for grades nine through twelve (Middletown High School). The ninth-grade group may be considered more representative of the school population of Middletown and the immediately neighboring communities than the eighth-grade group, because Middletown High School served all pupils from Middletown and nearby residential areas who attended public school, as well as a number of pupils from neighboring rural areas. Through the eighth grade, some children attended rural schools or a Roman Catholic elementary school instead of attending the public schools of Middletown, but Middletown High School was the only high school in the community; there was no local parochial high school nor rural high school. Accordingly, the ninth-grade group served the Career Pattern Study as the main source of data, and the eighth-grade group was used as a source of additional cases for special purposes. All of the data used in this monograph (except for control-group data) are based on work with the ninth-graders or their families. Further information concerning them is given in a later section of this chapter entitled The Freshman Class of 1951–52.

### Location

It was decided that the community in which the study was to be conducted should be one with diversified industry and with a population of 20,000 to 50,000. A community having these specifications would provide opportunities for a variety of occupations and yet would not be so large as to make studies of its occupational distribution impractical for a comparatively small staff of research workers. Distance from New York City was another factor considered in the selection of a community for the study: a city within a few hours' drive of New York was preferred, for convenience of travel from the project's home base at Teachers College, Columbia University. Several towns of adequate size met these requirements; Middletown, New York, was the one selected.

The cooperation of the community was, of course, vital to the study. Contacts with appropriate community leaders (the superintendent of schools, members of the Board of Education, the principals of the Junior and Senior High Schools, the secretary of the Chamber of Commerce, and the president of the Orange County Community College) brought support for the proposal to conduct the study in Middletown.

### THE COMMUNITY OF MIDDLETOWN

Middletown is located about sixty-five miles northwest of New York City, in Orange County, equidistant from the Hudson and Delaware Rivers, fairly near the borders of Pennsylvania and New Jersey. It was the second-largest town in the county, with a population of 22,586 according to the 1950 Census. (Newburgh, the largest town in Orange County, had a population of 31,956 in 1950.) Middletown served as a shopping center for the surrounding rural area and for smaller communities in the vicinity. Nearby is the county seat, Goshen (population 3,311 in 1950), which may be better known than Middletown, though much smaller, as it was for many years the home of the Hambletonian Stakes.

In 1950 the population of Orange County was 152,255. No town in the county except Middletown and Newburgh had a population exceeding 10,000; the third largest town in the county (Port Jervis) had a population of only 9,372 persons, and the remaining towns in the county had less than 5,000 inhabitants each.

Middletown had its beginnings with the purchase of land in the area by two prospective settlers about 1756. A small settlement developed and the village of Middletown was incorporated in 1848. It was incorporated as a city in 1888. During its early years, Middletown grew slowly, with little industrial development.

Early in the 1840's, however, a group of businessmen in Middletown induced the Erie railroad to go through the town, by financing the building of the road from Goshen to Middletown. For five years (from 1843 to 1848) Middletown was the terminus of the railroad and during that time became the main shipping center of Orange County *(Golden Jubilee, 1888–1938)*. Industries were attracted and by 1956 there were 36 industrial establishments *(Middletown, N.Y., Wallkill, Goshen Directory, 1956)*. Much of the industry was light, such as the manufacture of cosmetics, clothing of various kinds, pocketbooks, and shoes, and was therefore suitable for the employment of women as well as men.

The population of Middletown was 87 per cent native-born; the small groups of foreign-born were mainly Italian, German, English, and Irish in origin *(Middletown, N.Y., Wallkill, Goshen Directory, 1956)*.

*Population Characteristics from Census Data*

The population of Middletown expanded rapidly from 1870 (the first year in which census data for the community were collected) through 1890. By 1900 the rate of expansion of the population had begun to decrease, and the current trend appears to be a leveling off at a very gradual rate of population increase. Trends in population growth in Middletown have differed from those in New York State as a whole from 1870 until the 1930–1940 period, when both showed a decrease in rate of population growth, probably as an effect of the depression (see Figure 1). Currently, the rate of population growth in Middletown is below state and national figures.

Data from the 1950 Census which are helpful in describing the population of Middletown are given in Table 1 through Table 7. From an examination of these tables, characteristics of the population of Middletown as compared to those of New York State as a whole and of the United States are evident.

From an examination of Table 2 it is apparent that the population of Middletown in 1950 was somewhat older, on the average, than that of New York State or the United States. The median age in Middletown was higher. Furthermore, Middletown had a smaller percentage of persons in younger age groups (through 44

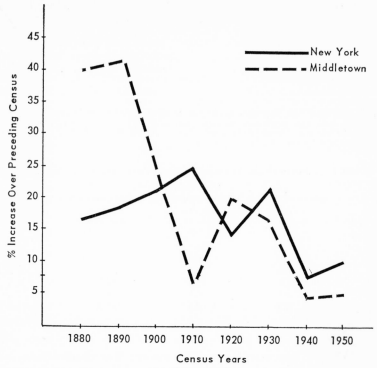

*Figure 1.* Comparison of Trends in Population for Middletown and New York State*

* Data from United States Department of Commerce, Bureau of the Census, *Census of population: 1950*. Vol. 2, Part 32, Table 1, p. 6, and Table 4, p. 9.

years) and a larger percentage in older age groups (45 years and above) than the state or country as a whole.

Middletown did not differ appreciably from New York State as a whole or from the United States in the median number of school years completed by persons twenty-five years of age and over (9.5 years for Middletown as shown in Table 3). However, a smaller percentage of persons in this age group in Middletown had completed at least four years of high school or at least four years of college than in New York State as a whole. These educational differences may be due to the age differences discussed in the preceding paragraph: higher education is less frequent among older persons, due to different patterns of education at different time periods. Fur-

TABLE 1. Population in 1950

|  | Total | Urban |
|---|---|---|
| Continental United States | 150,697,361 | 96,467,686 |
| New York State | 14,830,192 | 12,682,446 |
| Orange County | 152,255 | 81,142 |
| Middletown | 22,586 | 22,586 |

Note.—Data from New York State Department of Commerce, *New York State Business Facts, Mid-Hudson Area, 1954 Supplement* (hereafter cited as *N.Y.S.B.F.*), p. 3; and United States Department of Commerce, Bureau of the Census, *Census of Population, 1950*, Vol. 2, Part 1 (hereafter cited as *1950 Census, 2:1*), Table 58, p. 105.

TABLE 2. Percentage Distribution of Population by Age (1950)

| Age (in Years) | Continental U.S. (Median Age: 30.2) | New York State (Median Age: 33.7) | Orange County (Median Age: 34.1) | Middletown (Median Age: 40.9) |
|---|---|---|---|---|
| Under 5 | 10.7 | 9.2 | 9.1 | 7.7 |
| 5–14 | 16.2 | 13.4 | 13.4 | 10.8 |
| 15–24 | 14.6 | 13.4 | 14.4 | 10.1 |
| 25–44 | 30.0 | 31.7 | 28.4 | 27.5 |
| 45–54 | 11.5 | 13.6 | 12.6 | 14.3 |
| 55–64 | 8.8 | 10.2 | 10.8 | 13.5 |
| 65 and over | 8.2 | 8.5 | 11.2 | 16.0 |

Note.—Data from *N.Y.S.B.F.*, p. 3; and *1950 Census, 2:1*, Table 37, p. 89.

TABLE 3. Educational Level of Persons Twenty-Five Years and Over (1950)

|  | Median No. of Sch. Yrs. Completed | Percentage Completing at Least— 4 Yrs. High School | 4 Yrs. College |
|---|---|---|---|
| United States | 9.3 | 33.4 | 6.0 |
| New York State | 9.6 | 36.1 | 7.7 |
| Orange County | 9.0 | 30.6 | 6.0 |
| Middletown | 9.5 | 31.8 | 6.1 |

Note.—Based on 20 per cent sample. Data from *N.Y.S.B.F.*, p. 2; and *1950 Census, 2:1*, Table 44, p. 96.

TABLE 4. Percentage Distribution of Employed Workers in Civilian Labor Force (1950)

|  | United States | New York State | Orange County | Middletown |
|---|---|---|---|---|
| Private Wage and Salary Workers | 71.2 | 77.4 | 69.8 | 71.2 |
| Government Workers | 9.8 | 9.8 | 12.4 | 16.6 |
| Self-employed Workers | 17.1 | 12.3 | 16.5 | 12.0 |
| Unpaid Family Workers | 2.0 | 0.5 | 1.3 | 0.3 |

Note.—Data from *N.Y.S.B.F.*, p. 4; and *1950 Census, 2:1*, Table 53, p. 101.

TABLE 5. PERCENTAGE DISTRIBUTION OF EMPLOYED PERSONS BY
OCCUPATIONAL GROUP (1950)

| Occupational Group | United States | New York State | Orange County | Middle-town |
|---|---|---|---|---|
| Professional, Technical and kindred workers | 8.7 | 10.7 | 8.7 | 10.2 |
| Farmers and Farm Managers | 7.7 | 1.7 | 4.6 | 0.2 |
| Managers, Officials, and Proprietors, except Farm | 8.9 | 11.0 | 9.6 | 12.1 |
| Clerical and Sales workers | 19.3 | 24.2 | 16.9 | 21.4 |
| Craftsmen, Foremen, and kindred workers | 13.8 | 13.9 | 14.1 | 12.6 |
| Operatives and kindred workers | 19.8 | 21.0 | 25.4 | 24.3 |
| Private Household workers | 2.5 | 2.4 | 2.5 | 2.4 |
| Service workers, except Private Household | 7.6 | 9.3 | 9.0 | 12.7 |
| Farm Laborers and Farm Foremen | 2.6 | 1.1 | 3.8 | 0.5 |
| Laborers, except Farm and Mine | 6.1 | 4.6 | 5.4 | 3.6 |

Note.—Data from *N.Y.S.B.F.*, p. 5; and *1950 Census, 2:1,* Table 53, p. 101.

TABLE 6. PERCENTAGE DISTRIBUTION OF EMPLOYED MEN AND
WOMEN BY OCCUPATIONAL GROUP (1950)

| Occupational Group | United States | | New York State | | Middletown | |
|---|---|---|---|---|---|---|
| | MEN | WOMEN | MEN | WOMEN | MEN | WOMEN |
| Professional, Technical and kindred workers | 7.3 | 12.3 | 9.8 | 12.4 | 8.1 | 13.8 |
| Farmers, and Farm Managers | 10.3 | 0.7 | 2.3 | 0.2 | 0.4 | 0.0 |
| Managers, Officials, and Proprietors, except Farm | 10.7 | 4.3 | 14.0 | 4.1 | 16.6 | 4.0 |
| Clerical and kindred workers | 6.4 | 27.3 | 9.4 | 32.3 | 6.7 | 21.5 |
| Sales workers | 6.4 | 8.5 | 7.7 | 6.8 | 9.1 | 9.4 |
| Craftsmen, Foremen, and kindred workers | 18.6 | 1.5 | 19.1 | 1.8 | 18.8 | 1.6 |
| Operatives and kindred workers | 20.0 | 19.2 | 19.7 | 23.1 | 22.1 | 27.6 |
| Private Household workers | 0.2 | 8.5 | 0.2 | 7.1 | 0.2 | 6.1 |
| Service workers, except Private Household | 5.9 | 12.2 | 9.0 | 9.7 | 11.6 | 14.5 |
| Farm Laborers, unpaid Family workers | 1.5 | 2.0 | 0.2 | 0.3 | 0.0 | 0.0 |
| Farm Laborers, except unpaid, and Farm Foremen | 3.4 | 0.8 | 1.2 | 0.2 | 0.7 | 0.1 |
| Laborers, except Farm and Mine | 8.2 | 0.8 | 6.4 | 0.5 | 5.4 | 0.4 |
| Occupation not reported | 1.1 | 1.8 | 1.1 | 1.4 | 0.4 | 0.9 |

Note.—Data from *1950 Census:* Vol. 2, Part 1, Table 53, p. 101; and Vol. 2, Part 32, Table 28, p. 67, and Table 35, p. 107.

TABLE 7. PERCENTAGE DISTRIBUTION OF EMPLOYED PERSONS BY
INDUSTRIAL GROUP (1950)

| Industrial Group | United States | New York State | Orange County | Middle-town |
|---|---|---|---|---|
| Agriculture | 12.2 | 3.0 | 8.7 | 0.8 |
| Mining | 1.7 | 0.2 | 0.1 | 0.0 |
| Construction | 6.1 | 5.3 | 7.0 | 5.3 |
| Manufacturing | 25.9 | 30.3 | 27.2 | 23.5 |
| Transportation, Communications and Utilities | | | | |
|   Total | 7.7 | 8.9 | 9.5 | 11.7 |
|   Railroads, Ry. Express | 2.5 | 1.9 | 4.4 | 6.1 |
|   Trucking, Warehousing | 1.2 | 1.2 | 1.4 | 1.2 |
|   Other Transportation | 1.5 | 2.9 | 1.1 | 0.8 |
|   Communications | 1.1 | 1.5 | 1.3 | 1.4 |
|   Utilities | 1.4 | 1.5 | 1.4 | 2.1 |
| Wholesale–Retail Trade | | | | |
|   Total | 18.8 | 21.2 | 18.1 | 24.4 |
|   Retail | 15.2 | 16.3 | 15.1 | 19.7 |
| Financial, Insurance, Real Estate | 3.4 | 5.8 | 2.3 | 2.4 |
| Business, Repair Services | 2.5 | 3.1 | 2.7 | 2.5 |
| Personal Services | | | | |
|   Total | 6.2 | 6.6 | 6.7 | 6.8 |
|   Hotels | 0.9 | 1.2 | 1.4 | 0.9 |
| Entertainment and Recreation | 1.0 | 1.3 | 0.8 | 0.8 |
| Professional and Related Services | | | | |
|   Total | 8.3 | 9.7 | 12.9 | 17.8 |
|   Medical | 2.9 | 3.8 | 5.1 | 12.4 |
|   Educational | 3.7 | 3.3 | 5.7 | 3.2 |
|   Other | 1.7 | 2.5 | 2.1 | 2.3 |
| Public Administration | 4.4 | 4.6 | 4.0 | 4.0 |

Note.—Data from *N.Y.S.B.F.*, pp. 6–7; and *1950 Census, 2:1,* Table 55, p. 103.

thermore, figures for New York State are affected by inclusion of figures from New York City.

Information about the distribution of employed workers is given in Table 4. In 1950, Middletown had exactly the same percentage of persons employed as Private Wage and Salary Workers as the United States as a whole (71.2%), but less than New York State (77.4%). Middletown had an appreciably higher percentage employed as Government Workers (16.6%) than did New York State or the United States (9.8% for each). Middletown tended to resemble the figures for New York State in the percentage of workers who were self-employed (12.0% for Middletown and 12.3% for

New York), but had a smaller percentage than the United States (17.1%).

Occupational groups into which the employed are classified are shown in Table 5. None of the differences between percentages for Middletown and for New York or the United States were greater than 5.1 percentage points, with the exception of farm occupations. As one would expect, farm occupations were represented more extensively in figures for the nation as a whole than in figures for Middletown, which was an urban community even though located in a rural region. It may be concluded, therefore, that the occupational distribution of the employed in Middletown was much like that of the state in which it is located and also like that of the country as a whole.

A somewhat larger percentage of the employed were women in Middletown than in New York State or in the United States as a whole (36.2% as compared to 31% in New York State and 28% in the United States). Correspondingly, a somewhat smaller percentage of the employed in Middletown were men (63.8% as compared to 69% in New York State and 72% in the United States as a whole). (Table not reproduced. United States Department of Commerce, Bureau of the Census, 1950, Vol. 2, Part 1, Table 53, p. 101; Part 32, Table 28, p. 67, and Table 35, p. 107.)

In Table 6, the percentages of employed men in various occupational groups are shown, as well as the corresponding percentages of employed women. Excluding farm occupations, the two occupational groups for which the percentages of men employed in Middletown diverged most noticeably from the percentages for the United States as a whole were Managers, Officials, and Proprietors, in which the percentage of men employed in Middletown exceeded the national percentage by 5.9 points, and Service Workers, in which the percentage of men employed in Middletown exceeded the national percentage by 5.7 points. None of the differences between numbers of men employed in the various occupational groups in Middletown and in New York State exceeded 2.7 percentage points. A smaller percentage of the employed women in Middletown were Clerical Workers than in the United States as a whole (5.8 percentage points less) and a larger percentage were Operatives (8.4 percentage points more). The situation was similar when the occupational distribution of women in Middletown was compared to that in New York State: fewer Middletown women were employed in clerical work (10.8 percentage points less) and more were employed as Operatives and Service Workers (4.5 and 4.8 percentage points more, respectively).

Table 7 shows the percentages of total employed persons in various industrial groups. Omitting Agriculture and Mining, which would not apply to Middletown, comparisons can be made between the percentages of employment for industrial groups in Middletown, in New York State, and in the United States. The percentages for Middletown did not differ by more than 5 points from the corresponding percentages for New York or the United States, with these exceptions: Middletown had fewer persons employed in Manufacturing than did New York (a difference of 6.8 percentage points); Middletown exceeded New York and the United States in persons employed in Professional and Related Services (Total) and in Medical Services by over 8 percentage points; Middletown exceeded the United States by 5.6 percentage points in Wholesale and Retail Trade. The figures for professional services were influenced by the number of persons employed in medical services in Middletown, in which a state mental hospital was located. The comparatively larger number of persons employed in wholesale and retail trades may be attributed to the fact that Middletown served as a shopping center for the neighboring rural areas, as pointed out earlier in this chapter.

The median income in Middletown in 1949 ($2,932) was only slightly less than that for New York State ($3,055) and was somewhat more than that for the United States ($2,619). (Table not reproduced. United States Department of Commerce, Bureau of the Census, 1950, Vol. 2, Part 1, Table 57, p. 104; New York State Department of Commerce, 1954, p. 9. Data based on a 20 per cent sample.)

In summary, data from the census closest in time to the year of our first contact with the Career Pattern Study subjects indicate that in most respects examined Middletown did not differ very much from state or national trends. It did tend to have a somewhat older population, somewhat more women employed, and somewhat fewer men employed than the nation as a whole.

Consistent with the conclusion that Middletown did indeed seem to be a rather average American community in various respects are findings from E. L. Thorndike's study (1940) of *144 Smaller Cities*.[1] Thorndike gathered data about 144 United States cities of 20,000 to 30,000 population. Twenty-four items were covered, in categories presumed indicative of the general "goodness of life" in a city. Categories explored were Health (for example, infant death rate, general death rate), Education (for example, per capita public expenditure for teachers' salaries), Economic and "Social" (for example, average wage of factory workers), Creature Comforts (for example, per capita domestic installations of electricity, number of telephones), and miscellaneous items such as literacy. One credit was given for each of the twenty-four items in which the specific city was better than the ordinary city,[2] and a penalty of one was given for each item in which it was worse; the algebraic sum for each city was obtained. Middletown received a score of zero.

## MIDDLETOWN HIGH SCHOOL [3]

At the time of our first year of work in Middletown (1951–52), twelve hundred students were enrolled in the high school. There were sixty-one teachers and an administrative staff consisting of the principal, the vice-principal and dean of boys, and the dean of girls. Middletown High School has a Guidance Department, at that time staffed by a director who also served as a counselor, one additional full-time counselor, and one part-time counselor, who was also a classroom teacher. The dean of boys and the dean of girls also worked with the Guidance Department as part-time counselors. The school had its own library and a librarian. A nurse, a dental hygienist, and a doctor were also on the staff (the latter two on

1 It should be noted, however, that Thorndike's findings are based on 1930 data, and their applicability to the 1951–52 situation is unknown; they do suggest that Middletown has been a "middle town" for some time.

2 The ordinary city's score was defined as the median score of 295 cities with a population of over 30,000.

3 The discussion in this section is based largely on material in *The Blue Book*, Middletown High School, 1951–1952, published by the Student Council, and on discussion with Mr. Boyd R. Swem, Director of Guidance, the Middletown Public Schools.

part-time). Twenty-six members of the staff had Bachelor's degrees, thirty-five had Master's degrees, and one had a Ph.D.

Courses were offered in the following fields: English, Latin, Modern Languages, Mathematics, Science, Social Studies (more recently termed Citizenship Education), Art and Mechanical Drawing, Commercial, Homemaking, Music, Industrial Arts, Vocational Agriculture, Dress Design and Garment Construction, Health, and Physical Education.

Students of varying levels of ability were admitted to Middletown High School. In 1951–52, courses in all required subjects were offered at two levels of difficulty: Regents and non-Regents. The non-Regents courses were less demanding.

There were various student organizations and activities, such as Student Council, a school newspaper which frequently won awards in the Columbia Scholastic Press Association competition, a yearbook, a variety of clubs (for example, Art Club, Le Cercle Français, Future Farmers of America, Junior Red Cross, National Honor Society, National Thespians, Science Club, Woodwork and Ceramics Club), intramural sports, interscholastic sports for boys (such as football, baseball, basketball, soccer, tennis, bowling, and track), and several musical organizations (including orchestra, band, *a cappella* choir, and glee club). Participation in extra-curricular activities was recognized by a point system, which led to awards by the Student Council for graduating seniors who had accumulated a certain number of points.

### THE FRESHMAN CLASS OF 1951–52

All 142 boys in the ninth grade of the Middletown High School were interviewed and tested as part of the Career Pattern Study, but the statistics to be presented in the following chapters of this monograph are based on 105 of the boys, not on the total group.

### Total Group and Core Group

This group of 105 boys, called the core group, was selected from the total group on the basis of having a maximum number of scores on the various indices of vocational maturity discussed in later chapters. Any individual lacking four or more scores used in the computation of the indices of vocational maturity was eliminated from the core group, in order to minimize the instances in which scores would have to be assigned on a chance basis for statistical treatment. It was considered preferable to eliminate 37 cases in our total group who lacked data on four or more of the forty-seven vocational maturity variables used in the first intercorrelational analysis, than to include all the cases, with the attendant necessity of using a number of arbitrarily assigned scores.[4]

The determination of the core group was made entirely on the basis of presence or absence of vocational maturity scores; presence or absence of scores on other variables which were studied in relation to vocational maturity scores (referred to as *correlates* and described in Chapter V) was not considered in this connection. Since failure to have particular vocational maturity scores was attributable to various reasons, it was not felt that any bias would be introduced into our sample by this procedure of determining the core group. For example, many of the vocational maturity scores were derived from interviews. Very few boys in the total group missed one or more of the interviews, but a few recorded interviews had been accidentally erased from the tape, or part of a recording was not sufficiently clear for transcription of the interview. In some such cases data were not available to score a particular boy on a particular variable. Even within our core group some scores were missing on nine of the forty-seven vocational maturity measures (see App. A).

To check the assumption that our sample of 105 cases was not significantly different from the total group of 142 cases, comparisons of the core group with the total group were made. The results of these comparisons are shown in Tables 8 and 9. None of the critical ratios nor of the chi squares was statistically significant. Therefore, it may be concluded that the core group was like the total group in the respects shown, and that no bias was introduced by our procedure for selecting the sample used in the statistical analysis of the data.

From an examination of Table 8, it is evident that our subjects

[4] Scores on twenty indices of vocational maturity (to be described in the next chapter) were studied statistically, but part scores as well as total scores were used in analyzing the data. Thus, forty-seven vocational maturity measures were included in the first correlational analysis.

TABLE 8. Core Group Compared to Total Group

| Characteristic | Mean | | Standard Deviation | | Critical Ratio [a] [b] |
|---|---|---|---|---|---|
| | CORE | TOTAL | CORE | TOTAL | |
| IQ | 102.47 | 102.50 | 10.33 | 11.80 | 0.00 |
| School Achievement | 76.30 | 75.94 | 6.44 | 7.03 | 1.09 |
| Age in Months | 171.70 | 172.04 | 10.28 | 11.34 | .33 |
| Socioeconomic Status | 4.50 | 4.51 | 1.26 | 1.35 | .15 |
| Adjustment | 119.29 | 119.40 | 11.66 | 8.10 | .05 |
| Vocational Aspiration Level | 3.02 | 3.04 | 1.43 | 1.42 | .28 |

[a] A formula for comparing a subgroup with a total that contains the subgroup was used (McNemar, 1949, p. 88).
[b] A critical ratio of 1.96 is necessary for significance at the .05 level, two-tailed test.

TABLE 9. Additional Core–Total Comparisons
(Chi Squares)

| Characteristic | Core–Total | Needed for Significance at .05 Level |
|---|---|---|
| Birth Order | .03 | 3.8 |
| Broken–Unbroken Homes | .91 | 3.8 |
| National Origins of Parents | 3.74 | 16.9 |
| Urban—Rural Residence | .07 | 3.8 |
| Work Experience | .69 | 3.8 |
| Educational Aspirations | 3.73 | 7.8 |

may be described as an average group of boys. Their mean IQ was slightly above 100. The average socioeconomic status of their fathers' occupations was not far from 4, the middle of the seven-point scale which was used in rating occupations.[5] On a test of general adjustment, the average score of the Middletown High School ninth-grade group (119.4) was exactly the same as the average reported by Rotter for a group of fifty-seven male college students classified by their instructors as adjusted (Rotter & Rafferty, 1950, Table II, p. 9).[6] The Middletown ninth-graders' average on this test was quite close to the average of 55 boys in a high school in Ohio (mean 120.9, standard deviation 17.7), reported by Rotter and others (Rotter, Rafferty, & Lotsof, 1954).

[5] For details concerning these and other variables see Chapter V.
[6] Rotter's college group was scored by criteria in the College Manual, while the Career Pattern Study group was scored by use of unpublished scoring criteria for high school boys. The authors wish to express their appreciation to Dr. Rotter for making his scoring criteria for the high school level available to them.

Detailed information concerning the age of the 105 boys in the core group is given in Table 10. As of September, 1951, when they entered ninth grade, their average age was fourteen years, four months, but there was a wide range in age (from twelve years, eight months to seventeen years, six months). The group cannot be considered homogeneous with respect to age, as is evident from an examination of Table 10. Therefore, when reading the descriptions of vocational maturity and vocational behavior in the following chapters, it should be kept in mind that they are drawn from the behavior of boys in the ninth grade, regardless of age, not exclusively from the behavior of fourteen-year-olds or some other strictly defined age group.

TABLE 10. AGE OF INDIVIDUALS IN CORE GROUP
(September 1, 1951)

| Age Interval | Number of Boys |
|---|---|
| 12 years, 6 months–12 years, 11 months | 5 |
| 13 years, 0 months–13 years, 5 months | 7 |
| 13 years, 6 months–13 years, 11 months | 21 |
| 14 years, 0 months–14 years, 5 months | 41 |
| 14 years, 6 months–14 years, 11 months | 12 |
| 15 years, 0 months–15 years, 5 months | 12 |
| 15 years, 6 months–15 years, 11 months | 3 |
| 16 years, 0 months–16 years, 5 months | 1 |
| 16 years, 6 months–16 years, 11 months | 0 |
| 17 years, 0 months–17 years, 5 months | 2 |
| 17 years, 6 months–17 years, 11 months | 1 |

## Core Group and Control Group

The preceding section makes it clear that the core group selected from our total ninth-grade sample for intensive statistical analysis was like the total group in the several comparisons of important characteristics which were made. In evaluating the adequacy of the core group sample as representative of the Middletown High School male freshman population, a comparison with a different group of entering ninth-graders is useful. Therefore, the comparisons reported in Table 11 were made between the core group and another group (referred to as the control group).

The control group consisted of 173 boys who entered the ninth grade of Middletown High School in September, 1950, the year preceding the year in which the Career Pattern Study sample entered the ninth grade of the same high school. Data concerning the control group were obtained from the high school cumulative records. Only three boys in the control group were siblings of the boys in the core group.

TABLE 11. CORE GROUP COMPARED TO CONTROL GROUP

| Characteristic | Mean | | Standard Deviation | | Critical Ratio [a] |
|---|---|---|---|---|---|
| | CORE | CONTROL | CORE | CONTROL | |
| IQ | 102.47 | 99.53 | 10.33 | 11.19 | 2.30 |
| Age in Months | 171.70 | 174.53 | 10.28 | 12.21 | 2.06 |
| Socioeconomic Status | 4.50 | 4.55 | 1.26 | 1.31 | .30 |
| Vocational Aspiration | | | | | |
| Level | 3.02 | 3.17 | 1.43 | 1.52 | .83 |
| School Grades | 76.30 | 74.93 | 6.44 | 7.05 | 1.63 |

[a] A critical ratio of 1.96 is necessary for significance at the .05 level, and of 2.58 at the .01 level, two-tailed test.

Slight but statistically significant differences in age and intelligence were found between the two groups. The small amount of difference is of little practical significance, however. The core group was almost three months younger and had an average IQ about three points higher than the control group. The core group made slightly higher grades, on the average, than the control group did, but the difference between the two means was not statistically significant. It may be said, therefore, that the core group was rather similar to the control group in the characteristics which were compared.

GENERALIZING FROM CAREER PATTERN STUDY DATA

This chapter has presented information about the community where our study was conducted, about the high school in which much of the data were gathered, and about the boys who were the subjects of the study. We conclude that the boys in the core group, who were the source of data for the detailed analyses to be presented in subsequent chapters, were a representative sample of the entire group of ninth-grade boys from which they were drawn and were generally similar to ninth-graders who attended Middletown High School in another year, with whom they were also compared. An important question still remains to be answered: How representative are the boys in the Career Pattern Study core group, or the

Middletown ninth-grade boys they represent rather well, of other ninth-graders in the United States; and to what groups, therefore, may the findings presented in this monograph be generalized?

Obviously, the findings may not be generalized to girls, because these data are based only on research with boys. This is the only part of the answer to the question posed in the preceding paragraph which may be given with considerable assurance. It is probably accurate to state that the findings are applicable to other samples of ninth-grade boys in Middletown High School, if studied within a period of a few years and if studied by the same methods.[7] However, no cross-validation of our findings has been attempted. It may be accurate to say that the findings may be generalized to ninth-grade boys in other high schools in towns of similar size in New York State, and possibly the Northeastern States, though again we cannot be sure of this without replication.[8]

The possibility that the generalizations we make from these data are more broadly applicable within this country than to a sample exactly like the Career Pattern Study core group is, of course, a possibility which we would like to entertain. The comparisons of Middletown with New York State and the United States suggest this may be justifiable. However, we cannot claim that this is so on the basis of any cross-validational data, because there are none.

For convenience of discussion in later chapters, we shall sometimes write in general terms about our findings, but the reader should keep in mind the fact that we are actually referring to what we have found typical of this group of 105 boys in the ninth grade of Middletown High School, Middletown, New York, during the year 1951–52.

---

[7] It should be noted that our study was begun during the Korean War. Our subjects were, of course, too young for military service, but the draft laws then in effect, and the experiences of some of their older siblings, may have had an effect on their early vocational planning. If the study had been postponed until a time of peace, it might have been impossible to undertake it for many years; although the Korean War is over, the "cold war" has so far continued throughout the period of the Career Pattern Study.

[8] It would be more precise to specify towns with a rather slow rate of population growth, since Middletown appears to have stabilized in this respect, as discussed earlier in this chapter. Communities of similar size to Middletown but with recent rapid growth in population may not be comparable (see Kluckhohn, 1950, pp. 387–389). Whether the citizens of such communities, especially the ninth-grade boys, are more similar to those of Middletown than are the communities themselves is another question.

# CHAPTER III

# Indices of Vocational Maturity

The concept of vocational maturity was considered in the first monograph of this series (Super et al., 1957, pp. 56–64), following earlier discussions by the senior author (Super, 1955) and independent treatments of the subject by Dysinger (1950) and by Norton (1953a, 1953b). Although the concept is by no means new to practicing counselors, nor to educators and psychologists doing research in vocational guidance, little attention has been given to it and little effort has been spent in constructing measures of vocational maturity.

In planning this study, it was therefore considered important to devote a substantial amount of time to developing both a theoretical framework for and measures of vocational maturity. Monograph 1 of this series (Super et al., 1957) reported much of our thinking concerning theory. It has been restated more briefly in Chapter I of the present monograph. We shall therefore limit the presentation in this chapter to a brief statement of our rationale for the selection of indices of vocational maturity and to a more extended discussion of their construction.

## CONCEPTUALIZATION AND SELECTION OF INDICES [1]

Three concepts taken from developmental psychology contributed to the formulation of our theory of vocational development and to

[1] We are indebted to Alvin J. Bernstein and Charles F. Warnath, for the first formulation of a rationale for selecting indices of vocational maturity and for a preliminary list of possible indices, as well as to Joseph Sturm for an evaluation of the textbook literature on maturity.

the construction of indices of vocational maturity. These are the principles that 1) development proceeds from random, undifferentiated activity to goal-directed, specific activity, 2) development is in the direction of increasing awareness and orientation to reality, and 3) development is from dependence to increasing independence. Since our concept of vocational maturity is normative (see Ch. I), development is examined in terms of behavior characteristic of a given life stage.

Guided by these principles, a list of characteristics and behaviors which might reveal vocational maturity in early adolescence was drawn up and reviewed by staff and seminar members. Considerations of conceptual adequacy, such as logical relevance to vocational development and appropriateness to the ages or life stages of the Career Pattern Study subjects, as well as considerations of usefulness and of measurability were applied. Sometimes one of these considerations indicated including an index which would have been discarded on the basis of another. When this happened, judgments had to be made as to which consideration was more important.

Consistency of preferences, for example, was an aspect of vocational behavior which seemed worth studying because it is clearly relevant to vocational development, is practically useful in vocational counseling, and can be readily ascertained. But questions were raised as to the appropriateness of consistency of preference indices to the age group being studied. At age fourteen, having a sequence of varied preferences may result in becoming oriented to a number of occupations and hence may be more appropriate than being consistent in wanting to enter one particular occupation (which could represent a fixation on an inappropriate field). Since vocational counselors tend to make use of consistency of vocational preferences in counseling, this index was included despite doubts as to its conceptual adequacy at age fourteen. It seemed important to ascertain the significance of consistency of vocational preferences, by relating it to other presumed indices of vocational maturity (to test its construct validity) and by relating it to later measures of vocational maturity and adjustment (to test its predictive value), even if only to explore the adequacy of consistency measures at this grade level.

The logically refined indices of vocational maturity were then classified according to type, with five categories or dimensions emerging, as described in Monograph 1 (Super et al., 1957, pp. 60–63). Following is the list of dimensions and indices which preliminary work suggested as feasible.

### DIMENSIONS AND INDICES OF VOCATIONAL MATURITY

Dimension    I. *Orientation to Vocational Choice*
      *a.* Concern with choice
      *b.* Use of resources in orientation
Dimension   II. *Information and Planning about the Preferred Occupation*
      *a.* Specificity of information about the preferred occupation
      *b.* Specificity of planning for the preferred occupation
      *c.* Extent of planning activity ♦
Dimension III. *Consistency of Vocational Preferences*
      *a.* Consistency of vocational preferences within fields
      *b.* Consistency of vocational preferences within levels
      *c.* Consistency of vocational preferences within families (fields and levels)
Dimension IV. *Crystallization of Traits*
      *a.* Degree of patterning of measured interests
      *b.* Interest maturity
      *c.* Liking for work
      *d.* Degree of patterning of work values
      *e.* Extent of discussion of rewards of work
      *f.* Acceptance of responsibility for choice and planning
      *g.* Vocational independence ♦

[2] The measure Extent of Planning Activity was originally a component of Vocational Independence. Intercorrelations among the seven original components of Vocational Independence indicated that the first two components (Acceptance of Responsibility for Choice and The Extent of Planning Activity) did not appear to belong with the others (Cohen, 1958, p. 43). Therefore, these two components were dropped from the Vocational Independence index. Extent of Planning Activity was used as a separate index, and was assigned to Dimension II. Acceptance of Responsibility for Choice was used as one component of the index Acceptance of Responsibility for Choice and Planning (see Dimension IV).

[3] As a result of preliminary statistical work, the Vocational Independence index was renamed Independence of Work Experience and was placed in a new Dimension V. Former Dimension V (Wisdom of Vocational Preferences) thus became VI, with all its indices. The revised organization is shown in Table 12 (p. 51).

Dimension V. *Wisdom of Vocational Preferences*

      *a.* Agreement between ability and preference

      *b.* Agreement between measured interests and preference

      *c.* Agreement between measured interests and fantasy preference

      *d.* Agreement between occupational level of measured interests and level of preference

      *e.* Socioeconomic accessibility of preference *(Super and Overstreet, 19*

The methods used in computing these indices are described in Appendix A. As we have pointed out elsewhere (Super et al., 1957, p. 64), these dimensions and the indices believed to measure them are strictly hypothetical and were proposed that they might be tried out. It will be shown later in this chapter and in Chapter IV that the scheme needed revision, both on the basis of the further work on theory which took place as the study progressed and also on the basis of evidence obtained concerning the interrelationships of our measures. Thus theory guided experimentation and experimentation modified theory.

## METHODS OF MEASUREMENT

Methods of measurement for the possible indices listed were considered next, taking into account the fact that data for the ninth-grade boys had already been collected. This fact of course imposed some restrictions on methods, but fewer than might have been the case if the staff and seminar group which originally planned the data collection had not had the same theoretical orientation and practical interests as the staff and student group planning the indices. Actually, the membership of these two groups was overlapping.

In some instances the data already existed in the form of objective measurements. For example, the Interest Maturity Scale of Strong's Vocational Interest Blank provided a method of assessing the maturity of the measured interests of these fourteen-year-old boys. Other indices could readily be computed by relating some one objectively ascertained item to another. A boy's IQ could be related to the intellectual level characteristic of men in a given occupation, in order to obtain a measure of the wisdom of his vocational preference. The wisdom of his preference could also be judged on other grounds, for example, by relating measured interests to preferences or socioeconomic status to preferences. In still other instances no readily usable measure was avialable for the ninth-graders, but one could be constructed from questionnaire or interview material.

Thus, data for some of the measures were obtained from standardized instruments or other rather objective sources, while data for other measures were obtained from content analysis of typescripts of the recorded interviews. The sources of data for the various indices are given in the following sections of this chapter, and the indices are described in a later section, when their reliability is discussed.

## *Indices Derived from Standard Measures*

All of the indices of Dimension III, Consistency of Vocational Preferences, were objectively processed, although they made use of interview data. Preferences were elicited in interviews (Super et al., 1957, Appendix C, Interview IV); the degree of consistency of several preferences, according to a revision of Roe's occupational classification (Moser, Dubin, & Shelsky, 1956), was expressed in discrepancy scores. Thus, if a boy indicated in the interview that he wished to be either a mechanic or an engineer, he had a zero score (no discrepancy) for consistency of fields, since both occupations are technical, but a score of two (inconsistent) for consistency of level, derived by subtracting the occupational level rating of engineer from that of mechanic (see Appendix A).

Three indices of Dimension IV, Crystallization of Traits, made use of standard methods: Degree of Patterning of Measured Interests employed an adaptation of Darley's classification of scores on Strong's Vocational Interest Blank; the Interest Maturity score on the same test served as an index, as indicated previously; and the number of significantly high or low scores on a locally constructed Inventory of Work Values was used to assess Degree of Patterning of Work Values.

For Dimension V, Wisdom of Vocational Preferences, all indices were constructed from standard types of data. Indices of wisdom of preference in relation to ability, interest, and socioeconomic status have already been described; still another index related interests as measured by Strong's Blank to fantasy preferences, and one index used a measure of discrepancy between the Occupational Level score on Strong's Blank and the level of the individual's preferred occupation converted into similar terms.

### Indices Derived from Interview Data

All of the scores on indices of Dimensions I and II and the last four listed in Dimension IV were derived from interview material by what were essentially content-analysis methods. The concept of Orientation to Vocational Choice, Dimension I, while not exactly unfamiliar, is one which has merely received passing mention in the literature and practice of vocational guidance. Before it could be measured it was necessary to define it and to describe behavior in which it might be revealed; next, the interviews with our ninth-grade boys were examined to ascertain whether or not a content analysis might provide indications of orientation to vocational choice.

Dimension II, Information and Planning about the Preferred Occupation, is a more familiar concept and has been more fully exploited in the literature, but because of the wide range of educational and occupational objectives which characterized this group of subjects, no objective measure of these types of behavior had been included in the battery of tests. It was therefore necessary to find some way of judging these from the discussions of preferences and plans in the interviews, the fourth interview with each boy having been constructed to elicit such discussion (Super et al., 1957, pp. 122–123).

In the case of Dimension IV, the concepts of Vocational Independence, Liking for Work, Extent of Discussion of Rewards of Work, and Acceptance of Responsibility for Choice and Planning are not entirely unfamiliar in the field of vocational guidance, but they have not been refined and they have not been measured. It was found possible to assess these concepts by analysis of parts of the first, second, and fourth interviews with the boys in this study (Super et al., 1957, pp. 117–119, pp. 122–123).

### Constructing an Interview-Based Index

Each proposed index whose measurement was to be based on interview data was assigned to a committee of staff and seminar members. The task of these committees was to outline the index, drawing on the literature of vocational psychology, vocational guidance, developmental psychology, education, industrial sociology, and other relevant disciplines, and on the counseling and teaching experience of its members. Since their professional experience varied considerably in extent, type, and situation, these contributions were important: they included high school teaching and counseling, vocational counseling in colleges and community agencies, and industrial personnel work, sometimes over periods of several years. The outline of each index was discussed at some length in the project seminar, sometimes undergoing several revisions and re-examinations. In the process, transcribed interview protocols were examined in order to obtain actual examples of the kinds of behavior believed to illustrate each type and level of vocational maturity in the ninth grade and to make sure that appropriate data would be available in the interviews.

The index of Concern with Choice may be used to illustrate this method. A committee broke down the proposed index into three (originally four) components: 1) Awareness of the Need for Choice, 2) Awareness of Factors in Choice, and 3) Awareness of Contingency Factors. Two of the three components were further divided, into presumed elements. In the case of the first component, Awareness of the Need for Choice, these elements were (*a*) Need for Immediate Choices (e.g., algebra vs. general mathematics), (*b*) Need for Intermediate Choices (e.g., college vs. technical institute vs. apprenticeship vs. a semiskilled job), and (*c*) Need for Ultimate Choices (e.g., a life work, specialties within a profession, etc.). Each of these elements was then examined in order to ascertain what kinds of behavior might exemplify it, and interview transcripts were read to provide illustrative material; these behaviors were then classified on *a priori* basis according to presumed maturity, that is, according to their appropriateness as methods of coping with the specific developmental tasks in question.

Each of these three elements was rated on a scale of from three to six points; the rating assigned was based on the highest-rated excerpt. For example, the scale for Concern with Immediate Choices ranges from "No mention of concern" to "Mentions steps for implementation of immediate choice." The intermediate steps represent behaviors and attitudes which are judged to fall in between these two extremes of showing no concern and of doing something about a concern.

The second component of the index of Concern with Choice, Awareness of Factors in Vocational Choice, illustrates a second type of procedure for analyzing the interviews in assessing vocational maturity. This component consists of 21 items, each of them a factor which should be considered in making a vocational choice: e.g., aptitudes, interests, cost of training, etc. The interview analyst scans the interviews and excerpts statements revealing awareness of the importance of these factors; the raw score for this component (and for others of this type) is the sum of the different factors mentioned.

Since different numbers of items enter into the various elements and components, raw scores (ratings or number of items mentioned) are converted into T-scores (normalized because of the correlational studies planned) and the index score is the sum of the T-scores: thus equal weight is given to each of the lesser parts of the index. Although differential weighting might be justified, it was considered that at this time there is no basis for giving differential *a priori* weights; in due course, when predictive validity data are available, empirical differential weighting may be defensible.

Procedures similar to the one just described for Concern with Choice were used in the construction of the other interview-based measures (see Appendix A). After these outlines of indices and the related scales devised for scoring interview excerpts had been subjected to criticism on theoretical and logical grounds by staff and seminar, they were then tried out in inter-judge reliability studies. Two or more of the participants in the work just discussed acted as judges, scoring a number of interview transcripts with the manuals that had been developed. The percentage of agreement was ascertained for the excerpting and the classification of excerpts, as well as the correlations of the two sets of scores. The details of most of this work are reported in theses by Sturm (1958), Nolte (1956), Wolk (1958), Cohen (1958), and Yoganarasimhiah (1957). Final modifications in each index and scoring manual were made in the light of the reliability studies, and the scoring methods were made final. Indices, it was decided, would be subject to further revision after studies of internal consistency and intercorrelations were completed.

### Sources and Treatment of Data Used in the Indices

The instruments used to collect the data, and the procedures used in the data collection, are described in some detail in the first monograph on the Career Pattern Study (Super et al., 1957, Chapter VII and Appendices). Those that are most relevant to this phase of the study are the Personal Data Blank, the Otis Quick-Scoring Test of Mental Ability (Gamma), the Strong Vocational Interest Blank (slightly modified for use at the eighth-grade and ninth-grade levels), the Work Values Inventory (locally developed by the senior author), the Life Planning Questionnaire (devised by Martin Hamburger to secure both realistic and fantasy expressions of vocational preferences and statements of vocational expectations), and a series of semi-structured interviews designed to survey the boys' experiences and attitudes in school, in out-of-school activities, in the family, and in educational and vocational planning. The interview outlines are shown in Appendix C of our first monograph. A number of other instruments were used for other purposes; they are listed in Appendix B of the first monograph, and some are described in Chapter V and Appendix B of this monograph because they provide data on variables which were studied in relation to vocational maturity measures.

The largest separate unit of measurement of vocational maturity, analogous to a test score, was termed an *index*. Some of the indices were composed of part scores termed *components,* which were summed to obtain one total score. Some of the components were also made up of part scores, termed *elements.* Elements were the smallest separate units of measurement. As previously described in this chapter, indices that appeared to assess separate but presumably related aspects of vocational maturity were grouped into *dimensions*. The dimensions served as broad categories for classification but did not themselves have specific scores.

In statistical treatment of the data, frequency distributions were made of the raw scores on the smallest unit for each measure (element, component, or index). From these distributions, the raw scores were converted to $T$ scores.[4] Where index total scores were obtained from part scores, the $T$ scores of the part scores were summed.

## EVALUATION OF THE TENTATIVE INDICES [5]

The proposed indices of vocational maturity were evaluated by studies of their reliability and of their interrelationships.

### Reliability

The reliability of the tentative indices of vocational maturity in the ninth grade was the subject of various types of study. A reliability check was not considered as important for the indices based on standard types of measures as for those based on interview data, since the reliability of the former has been established in other studies. The degree of reliability which characterizes interest inventories, intelligence tests, and vocational preferences at this age level is well documented. Consistency of preferences, often used as an index of reliability, was itself an index being studied. It is true that when discrepancies between two such data are used to yield an index of vocational maturity, their unreliabilities are compounded: thus the consistency indices combined the relative unreliability of several statements of preference; the wisdom indices combined the relative unreliability of vocational preferences

---

[4] The $T$ scores with a mean of 50 were reduced to single digit scores with a mean of 5 (except for indices IIA, IVA, IVB, and VIA). (Raw scores, not $T$ scores, were used for indices IB and VIB.)

[5] The following discussion of reliability draws heavily from a working paper prepared by William Dubin, and the statistical data in Tables 12 through 17 were computed under his immediate supervision as a Career Pattern Study staff member.

at age fourteen with the relative reliability of intelligence test scores at that age.

In the case of indices based on interview material, it was considered sufficient to establish inter-judge agreement of reliability of excerpting in the first indices developed and to demonstrate inter-judge reliability in scoring every index from interview protocols.

Recognizing the possibility of obtaining spuriously high correlations between indices if the same interview excerpts were repeatedly used in more than one index, care was taken in the drafting of manuals, in selecting sample excerpts, and in training exercises, to avoid multiple use. A critical examination of the scoring manuals after they had all been completed, with multiple use in mind, and a review of a sample of the statements excerpted in scoring the indices, led to the conclusion that differential rather than multiple use had been generally achieved.

The determination of reliability involves obtaining two measures, either simultaneously by two different instruments (whether tests or persons) or successively by the same or similar instruments. As Cronbach (1947) points out, the assumption is made that the trait is constant (the individual does not change) and that the process of measurement does not affect the trait (experimental independence).

In the study now being reported, most of the measures have been taken only once. This means, in Cronbach's terminology, that only in rare instances could we ascertain the coefficients of stability, stability and equivalence, and self-correlation for the indices which concerned this study. But coefficients of equivalence could be obtained for some of the indices, using inter-judge agreement and odd-even methods. For example, the interview-derived indices were based on statements excerpted from interviews by judges, and classified or scored by these judges. Therefore, inter-judge agreement in excerpting and classifying or scoring could be ascertained and viewed as evidence of reliability (equivalence), for inter-judge agreement involves simultaneous observations of a unique event. In this type of instance, the equivalence was that of judgments, that is, the reliability of judges using manuals as instruments.

Interview excerpts can also be scored on an odd-even basis, when the excerpts are recorded with this in mind, to obtain another type of measure of the reliability of an index. This appears at first glance to be another coefficient of equivalence (equivalence of two halves of a test and hence of two simultaneous observations). However, it is actually in some instances a coefficient of equivalence and stability, for it measures not only the equivalence of two halves of a scale as used by one judge, but when ratings were based on material from more than one interview in the series, it also measures the stability of the interviewee's behavior over a time span. The type of recording needed to compute odd-even reliability coefficients based on individual items was generally not done in this study, but the reliability of indices having a number of elements could be ascertained by treating element scores as items in a test and correlating scores obtained from odd with those obtained from even items. As is frequently true in psychological measurement, the assumption of experimental independence may not have been met.

Each of these methods of estimating the reliability of our data has its limitations. The inter-judge agreement method treats the judge's responses to the boys' statements as the items, not the statements themselves: this check does not show whether or not the basic data, the statements themselves, are stable. The use of the odd-even method involves the assumption that the items, which may be either statements or elements in this study, are comparable. Such an assumption is dubious when the items correlated are actually sub-test scores (elements), because our elements were developed as presumably related but somewhat unique variables, each of which was thought to constitute an important and distinctive aspect of vocational behavior. For example, Awareness of the Need for Immediate Choices was presumed to be related to Awareness of the Need for Intermediate Choices, but the relationship was not expected to be very high. These two elements of the first index's first component can hardly be considered in the same manner as items in a verbal reasoning test or in a test of introversion.

We were nevertheless interested in reliability coefficients for our measures, however limited, and present the coefficients that were obtained in the following paragraphs.

IA. CONCERN WITH CHOICE.—The index of Concern with Choice consists of three components: the first, Awareness of the Need for Choice, has three part scores (elements) relating to immediate, intermediate, and ultimate choices; the second has one score, the total number of factors to be considered in vocational choice that were mentioned by the individual; and the third has four part scores (elements), consisting of types of contingency factors. The scoring manual is shown in Appendix A.[6] It was possible to treat the eight part scores as test items, viewing the index as a test, and thus ascertain the odd-even reliability of the index. As was previously pointed out, this involves the assumption that the elements measure the same thing, whereas actually they are believed to involve related but distinct aspects of Concern with Choice. The obtained odd-even reliability coefficient of .34, corrected to .57 by the Spearman-Brown formula (significant at the .01 level), is probably an underestimate of the reliability of Index IA since part scores (elements) are treated as items. It therefore seems acceptable for research purposes. The inter-judge reliability, when two judges scored the interviews of thirty boys by independently excerpting and classifying interview statements, was .78.

IB. USE OF RESOURCES IN ORIENTATION.—The index Use of Resources in Orientation was designed to assess the use made by the subject of resources in his environment for orientation to the world of work.[7] The index has no part scores, only a total score, the sum of the number of resources mentioned. No internal consistency measure of reliability was possible here. Inter-judge reliability in scoring was ascertained. Two judges scored ten boys, by independently excerpting and classifying statements; the inter-judge rank-order correlation was .79.

IIA. SPECIFICITY OF INFORMATION.—This index consists of four components, the components reflecting the amount of information a boy had about the requirements, duties, conditions of work, and

[6] This index was developed by Max Dubrow (1959) and Joseph Sturm (1958).
[7] This index was developed by Robert L. Jacobson, Helen P. Moser, William McC. Eastman, and Phoebe L. Overstreet. Most of the work was done by William Eastman.

opportunities in his preferred occupation.[8] Odd-even reliability could be computed based on these four components, but with the same dubious assumptions as in the case of the first index, and with the particular defect that only four component scores were used to sum up a number of observations on the amount of information a boy had about his preferred occupation. Scoring was so handled as to permit the use of items (excerpts). The uncorrected odd-even reliability coefficient was .79, and the corrected $r$ was .88; the inter-judge reliability (two judges scoring twenty cases) was .79.

IIB. SPECIFICITY OF PLANNING.—This index consisted of nine components, constructed to represent the various stages of education and vocation for which planning may be done by a ninth-grader.[9] The number of components was reduced to eight because one component (Alternative High School Plans) did not receive any scores. The eight remaining elements and their total were included in the matrix of intercorrelations discussed in this chapter. Subsequently, further changes were made in this index, which are noted in Chapter VI.

Odd-even reliabilities based on the components might be computed for this index, but were not. Inter-judge reliability, determined by the independent excerpting and scoring of interviews with twenty boys by two judges, was found to be .82.

IIC. EXTENT OF PLANNING ACTIVITY.—As indicated earlier in the chapter, this measure had formerly been a component of the original Vocational Independence index developed by Cohen (1958), but was used as a separate index when the latter was refined. The scoring manual for Extent of Planning Activity is shown in Appendix A. The scale was designed to assess the extent to which resources outside the subject's family were used in planning. Using the original seven-component measure, the rank-order correlation between the Vocational Independence scores assigned twenty subjects by two judges was .81, and the product-moment correlation was .84. Inter-judge reliability in scoring was not computed for each separate component.

8 Developed by Herbert W. Nolte (1956).
9 Developed by William P. Wolk (1958).

IIIA. CONSISTENCY OF VOCATIONAL PREFERENCES WITHIN FIELDS.—
Occupational preferences expressed in interviews were classified
according to fields, after the Career Pattern Study modification of
the Roe Scale (Moser, Dubin, & Shelsky, 1956). Multiple preferences which fell in the same field were perfectly consistent, while
those which fell into different fields were inconsistent. The fact
that as many as four preferences were used gave a scale of four
steps. The number of observations was too limited to permit the
computation odd-even reliabilities. The objective nature of the
categorizing assured inter-judge agreement.

The measure Consistency within Fields, as well as the other
two consistency of preference measures (Consistency within Levels,
Consistency within Families), are themselves, of course, essentially
reliability measures, measures of the reliability or consistency of
the preferences of individuals. To have a measure of the test-retest
reliability of the consistency of preferences indices used in this
study, it would be necessary to have four statements of each individual's preferences, two of which would yield one consistency
index and two of which would yield another. The two consistency
indices could then be correlated. The questions eliciting these
statements of preferences should be so phrased as to make the responses to the second pair of questions equivalent to the responses
to the first pair of questions. In this study, the several statements
of preference could not be paired in this way, for they were not all
first, or pairs of first and second, preferences. Thus no test-retest
measure of the reliability of our consistency indices could be obtained.

IIIB. CONSISTENCY OF VOCATIONAL PREFERENCES WITHIN LEVELS.—
Preferences were also classified according to level, using the modification of the Roe Scale, the difference between the highest and
lowest level preferences providing the consistency score. The scale
consists of five steps. No reliability measure could be used, for
reasons given above.

IIIC. CONSISTENCY OF VOCATIONAL PREFERENCES WITHIN FAMILIES.
—This index consists of the sum of the scores on the two preceding
indices. Ascertaining its reliability presented the same problems
as it did for the two indices from which it was derived.

IVA. DEGREE OF PATTERNING OF MEASURED INTERESTS.—This index consists of the classification of boys according to whether or not they have a primary interest pattern as shown by Strong's Blank, using an adaptation of Darley's method (Darley, 1941; Mehenti, 1954). No method of ascertaining the reliability of these pattern categories is known, other than retesting, and here we had only one test. Perhaps it suffices to know that the broad categories with which we are dealing (that is, the classification according to the patterning of interests) are based on scores from scales which in some cases have reported average reliabilities of about .67 for boys aged sixteen to seventeen (Darley and Hagenah, 1955, p. 38, from Taylor, 1942). The inter-judge reliability of the categorizing done in this study was found to be perfect.

IVB. INTEREST MATURITY.—This index consists of the standard scores on Strong's Interest Maturity Scale. Reliability has not been checked for this group, the IM Scale having been found reliable in other studies. Strong reported an odd-even reliability of .93 for college seniors and a retest reliability after one year for college freshmen of .76 (1943, p. 78, p. 261).

IVC. LIKING FOR WORK.—The index of Liking for Work used data from interviews.[10] Excerpts dealing with work attitudes were rated on a five-point scale. Scoring of excerpts was not recorded in such a way as to permit obtaining odd and even scores. Inter-judge reliability, with two judges scoring twenty cases, was found to be .80.

IVD. DEGREE OF PATTERNING OF WORK VALUES.—The Work Values Inventory administered to the ninth-grade boys was scored for fifteen values. The number of scores significantly above or below chance levels was obtained for each boy, to yield a measure of patterning. The test-retest reliability of the Work Values Inventory for twenty-five boys in the eighth grade was ascertained by Hana (1954); he obtained a rank-order correlation of .81.

IVE. EXTENT OF DISCUSSION OF REWARDS OF WORK.—This is an interview-based index,[11] in which relevant content was excerpted

10 Developed by Malavalli Yoganarasimhiah (1957).
11 Developed by Malavalli Yoganarasimhiah (1957).

and rated on a three-point scale. Odd-even reliability was not computed because of the limited number of items. Two judges scored 20 cases; inter-judge reliability was .96 (rank-order correlation).

IVF. ACCEPTANCE OF RESPONSIBILITY FOR CHOICE AND PLANNING. —This interview-derived index consists of three parts, involving choice, educational planning, and vocational planning.[12] Excerpts were scored on scales of six, four, and four steps, respectively. Scoring mechanics made obtaining odd-even reliabilities impossible. Inter-judge reliability in scoring 30 cases was .85.

VA. INDEPENDENCE OF WORK EXPERIENCE.—The interview-derived index which was first called Vocational Independence, with seven components, was renamed Independence of Work Experience when the intercorrelations of the part scores showed that two components did not belong in the scale and that the remaining five components clearly dealt with work experience only.[13] Inter-judge reliability was found to be .84, using the method of two judges independently scoring twenty cases.

VIA. AGREEMENT BETWEEN ABILITY AND PREFERENCE.—This index assesses agreement between the individual's intelligence and the intelligence required for his preferred occupation, as described in Appendix A. The mechanics of deriving it made using any of the existing formulas for checking reliability inapplicable. While it is true that the reliability of the final score is a function of the reliability of intelligence tests and of preferences, combining the two makes obtaining a coefficient impossible without readministering both instruments.

VIB. AGREEMENT BETWEEN MEASURED INTERESTS AND PREFERENCE. —Again, the use of an agreement measure, and the fact that no adequate check on the reliability of the preferences could be applied, precludes ascertaining the reliability of this index.

---

[12] Developed by David Cohen, Max Dubrow, and Helen Moser.
[13] Developed by David Cohen (1958).

VIC. AGREEMENT BETWEEN MEASURED INTERESTS AND FANTASY PREFERENCE.—The lack of means for establishing the reliability of the fantasy preference (one observation) precludes checking reliability for this index. The dichotomous scores (agree or disagree) are not quite evenly divided, 61 of the 105 boys having fantasy preferences which agree with their measured interests, and 44 having fantasy preferences which disagree with their measured interests.

VID. AGREEMENT BETWEEN OCCUPATIONAL LEVEL OF MEASURED INTERESTS AND LEVEL OF PREFERENCE.—This index was scored dichotomously on the basis of a comparison of the boy's actual score on the Occupational Level scale of the Strong Vocational Interest Blank and the OL score of the occupation for which the boy had expressed a preference in the interviews. An OL score equal to or above the mean OL for the subject's preferred occupation, minus one standard deviation, was considered indicative of agreement. An OL score falling below the occupational mean minus one standard deviation was considered indicative of disagreement. This method is more satisfactory than a simple difference score, since it takes into account only differences which are likely to be practically significant, but it does not lend itself to reliability tests. The distribution of these dichotomous scores is about even, a slight majority, 56, of the 105 boys having measured levels of interest which place them well below the level of their preferred occupations.

VIE. SOCIOECONOMIC ACCESSIBILITY OF PREFERENCES.—In this index the level of each boy's first preference was converted into a score on Warner's occupational scale (Warner, Meeker, & Eells, 1949), revised by Hamburger (1958), as was the level of the parent's occupation, yielding a discrepancy score for the boy's preference and parental occupation. But since no suitable reliability coefficient could be found for parental occupation, or even for the boy's preference as ascertained in this study, no quantitative estimate of the reliability of this index was possible. Small discrepancies (none, or only one step on the scale) were found in 45 cases, while larger discrepancies (two or more steps on the scale) occurred in 60 cases.

CONCLUSION CONCERNING RELIABILITY. We concluded that the indices of vocational maturity were reliable enough for use in the study of group trends at the ninth-grade level. If the reliabilities are in error, the two odd-even reliability coefficients obtained (corrected $r$'s of .57 and .88) probably underestimate the reliability of the indices based on interview data, by incorrectly assuming the identity of elements, while the nine inter-judge reliabilities that were computed (rhos of .78 to .96) err in evaluating judgment methods and judges rather than data. No comparable measures are available with which to compare the reliabilities of the measures we have constructed.

*Interrelationships among Measures*

In Chapter I, it was pointed out that the focus of our research is on construct validity. Manifestations of vocational maturity must be measured in order to study the construct. The adequacy of the measures of vocational maturity must, therefore, be explored as an aspect of validation of the construct. Information concerning reliability of our vocational maturity indices has been discussed in the preceding section of this chapter. In this section, interrelationships among the various measures are reported. We have hypothesized that all of the measures should have some amount of positive interrelationship to be considered measures of vocational maturity.

Interrelationships among the measures of vocational maturity were studied by correlating part scores (elements or components) with total scores within an index,[14] by correlating part scores of one index with total scores of other indices, and by correlating all index total scores with each other. Because some of the indices do not have part scores, part-total correlations could not be computed for all measures. Results are reported in Tables 12 through 17.[15]

In Table 12, the column headings are the two indices of Dimen-

---

[14] Each part score was subtracted from the total score of which it was a part before coefficients of correlation were computed.

[15] As is apparent from an examination of the scoring manuals for the measures of vocational maturity in Appendix A, high scores on most, but not on all, of the measures are in the favorable direction. For indices IIIA, IIIB, IIIC, IVA, IVC, and VIE, low scores are more favorable than high scores. For consistency in reporting results in the tables, signs of correlation coefficients involving these variables have been reversed when necessary.

sion I, and the elements or components of Index IA. (Index IB has no part scores.) Index total scores, arranged by dimension, provide the headings for the stub listings. The entries in the field are, therefore, the correlations between indices, components, or elements of one dimension, on the one hand, and total scores on all other indices, on the other. The correlations of components and elements with their total index score are set in boldface type, to facilitate examination of the internal consistency of indices. Coefficients of correlation are reported in the same manner in Tables 13 through 17.

DIMENSION I.—Table 12 makes it clear that Index IA, Concern with Choice, is, in general, internally consistent: six of its eight smallest units (seven elements and one component) correlated with the index total minus the particular unit from .27 to .58. Elements 3c and 3d were not significantly related to the total score, however. Index IB was not correlated with each of the elements of IA, but the correlation of .23 (significant at the .01 level), between the two indices makes it clear that these relationships cannot be high, although probably high enough to show some communality.[16] Boys who were concerned with choice were somewhat more likely to make use of opportunities for occupational orientation. Dimension I therefore seems to have some cohesive meaning, but hardly to form a tight cluster.

Subsequent columns in Table 12 bring out the fact that five of the eight part scores of Index IA had statistically significant correlations with Index IIA: boys who were aware of the need to make choices, of the factors to consider in making a choice, and of the continued need for parental psychological support were likely to have information concerning the occupations they preferred. They were also likely to have planned for their education and occupation, as shown by the correlations with Index IIB. Some of the correlations with Index IIC were also significant. The majority

16 Index IB was not included among the variables in the matrices of intercorrelations, from which the other coefficients of correlation in Tables 12 through 17 were obtained. This index was still being scored when the other measures were ready to be intercorrelated. All correlations involving Index IB were obtained from a matrix in which total scores, but not part scores, of indices were included. Therefore, this index was correlated only with total scores of the other indices.

TABLE 12. CORRELATIONS OF MEASURES USED IN DIMENSION I WITH INDICES OF OTHER DIMENSIONS

| | IA | IA—1a Immediate | IA—1b Intermediate | IA—1c Ultimate | IA—2 Factors | IA—3a Parental | IA—3b Financial | IA—3c Military | IA—3d Special | IB Use of Resources |
|---|---|---|---|---|---|---|---|---|---|---|
| | Concern with Choice | IA—1 Need for Choice | | | | IA—3 Contingency | | | | |
| **Dimension I. Orientation to Vocational Choice** | | | | | | | | | | |
| IA. Concern with Choice | .. | .32 | .49 | .40 | .58 | .31 | .27 | .14 | .14 | .23 |
| IB. Use of Resources | .23 | .. | .. | .. | .. | .. | .. | .. | .. | .. |
| **Dimension II. Information and Planning** | | | | | | | | | | |
| IIA. Specificity of Information | .40 | .20 | .20 | .32 | .32 | .34 | .13 | .11 | .14 | .17 |
| IIB. Specificity of Planning | .48 | .31 | .38 | .22 | .26 | .15 | .27 | .18 | .19 | .07 |
| IIC. Extent of Planning Activity | .29 | .25 | .19 | .13 | .14 | .06 | .17 | .10 | .13 | .06 |
| **Dimension III. Consistency of Vocational Preferences** | | | | | | | | | | |
| IIIA. Consistency within Fields | -.04 | .01 | -.08 | -.05 | .10 | -.08 | -.03 | -.12 | .05 | -.20 |
| IIIB. Consistency within Levels | -.10 | .01 | -.17 | -.09 | -.03 | -.07 | -.03 | -.13 | .07 | -.19 |
| IIIC. Consistency within Families | -.13 | .04 | -.18 | -.09 | -.03 | -.11 | -.09 | -.17 | .03 | -.20 |
| **Dimension IV. Crystallization of Traits** | | | | | | | | | | |
| IVA. Patterning of Interests | .08 | .05 | .01 | -.01 | .06 | -.09 | .06 | .18 | .04 | -.01 |
| IVB. Interest Maturity | .06 | -.09 | .03 | .09 | .14 | -.12 | .11 | .08 | -.02 | -.10 |
| IVC. Liking for Work | .16 | -.10 | .01 | .20 | .16 | .04 | -.05 | .14 | .08 | .07 |
| IVD. Patterning of Work Values | .04 | .05 | .08 | .06 | .06 | -.04 | -.08 | -.12 | .08 | -.01 |
| IVE. Discussion of Rewards of Work | .16 | .09 | .03 | .14 | .15 | .05 | .00 | .28 | -.07 | -.05 |
| IVF. Acceptance of Responsibility | .56 | .31 | .34 | .33 | .29 | .34 | .33 | .16 | .30 | .24 |
| **Dimension V. Vocational Independence** | | | | | | | | | | |
| VA. Independence of Work Experience | .02 | .02 | -.10 | .07 | .02 | -.07 | .10 | .00 | .05 | .13 |
| **Dimension VI. Wisdom of Vocational Preferences** | | | | | | | | | | |
| VIA. Agreement: Ability and Preference | -.11 | -.12 | -.09 | .01 | .00 | -.16 | -.06 | -.10 | .01 | -.21 |
| VIB. Agreement: Interests and Preference | -.02 | -.10 | -.05 | -.06 | .14 | -.16 | -.02 | .08 | .01 | -.05 |
| VIC. Agreement: Interests and Fantasy Preferences | .00 | -.11 | -.03 | -.15 | .17 | -.14 | -.04 | .15 | .02 | -.22 |
| VID. Agreement: Level of Interests and Pref. | -.03 | .01 | .07 | .06 | -.08 | .10 | -.18 | -.04 | -.06 | .03 |
| VIE. Socioeconomic Accessibility | -.11 | -.02 | -.15 | .04 | -.04 | -.04 | -.21 | -.07 | -.03 | -.07 |

Note.—A correlation coefficient of .164 is significant at the .05 level, and of .230 at the .01 level, one-tailed test.

51

of the correlations between each part score of Index IA and its total score minus the particular part score were higher than the correlations between the part scores of IA and the total scores of IIA and IIB. Furthermore, all of the correlations between the part scores of IA and its total minus the part were higher than the correlations between the part scores of IA and the IIC total. The correlation between IA and IB was higher than the correlation between IB and either IIA or IIB. The present grouping of these measures thus appears to be appropriate.

The lack of significant relationships between the indices of Dimension I and those of Dimensions III, V, and VI casts doubt on the adequacy of the indices of Dimension I or those of Dimensions III, V, and VI, as measures of vocational maturity. On the one hand, the indices of Dimensions I, II, and one of those in IV (Index IVF) tended to show significant relationships with each other, and on the other hand the indices of Dimension I showed no relationship to the indices of Dimensions III, V, and VI.

The measures classified in Dimension I, and particularly the index Concern with Choice, were significantly related to one index of Dimension IV, Acceptance of Responsibility for Choice and Planning, but, in general, not to the others. It is not surprising to find that those boys who were best oriented to vocational choice were those who most fully accepted responsibility for making such choices and for making related plans. That there was no relationship between choice orientation and Patterning of Interests, Interest Maturity, Liking for Work, Patterning of Work Values, or Discussion of the Rewards of Work suggests that these indices of Dimension IV may belong in a different categorical system, along with Dimensions III, V, and VI. They may not be measures of vocational maturity, as defined here, at this grade level.

DIMENSION II.—Table 13 shows that Index IIA is internally consistent, with component-total correlations of .33 or above, all significant at better than the .01 level. Components 1, 2, 4, 5, and 6 of Index IIB also correlated satisfactorily with the index total score minus the score of the particular component. Components 7, 8, and 9 were less satisfactory, with only component 7 significant at even the .05 level. Index IIC has no part scores, only a total score, which was significantly related to Indices IIA and IIB, and

TABLE 13. CORRELATIONS OF THE MEASURES USED IN DIMENSION II WITH INDICES OF OTHER DIMENSIONS

Dimension II. Information and Planning

| | IIA. SPEC. OF INFO. | IIA—1 REQUIREMENTS | IIA—2 DUTIES | IIA—3 CONDITIONS | IIA—4 OPPORTUNITIES | IIB SPEC. OF PLANNING | IIB—1 H.S.: OBTAIN INFO. | IIB—2 H.S.: SPECIF. OF PLANS | IIB—3 H.S.: ALTERNAT. PLANS[a] | IIB—4 POST H.S.: OBTAIN INFO. | IIB—5 POST H.S.: SPECIF. OF PLANS | IIB—6 POST H.S.: ALTERNAT. PLANS | IIB—7 ENTRY PLANS | IIB—8 FACILITATE ENTRY | IIB—9 PLANNING FOR ADVANCEMENT | IIC EXTENT OF PLANNING ACTIVITY |
|---|---|---|---|---|---|---|---|---|---|---|---|---|---|---|---|---|
| **Dimension I. Orientation to Vocational Choice** | | | | | | | | | | | | | | | | |
| IA. Concern with Choice | .40 | .43 | .10 | .23 | .32 | .48 | .18 | .33 | | .34 | .38 | .27 | .11 | .27 | .22 | .29 |
| IB. Use of Resources | .17 | .. | .. | .. | .. | .06 | .. | .. | | .. | .. | .. | .. | .. | .. | .. |
| **Dimension II. Information and Planning** | | | | | | | | | | | | | | | | |
| IIA. Specificity of Information | : | .33 | .41 | .43 | .43 | .37 | .02 | .17 | | .19 | .28 | .15 | .34 | .18 | .47 | .29 |
| IIB. Specificity of Planning | .37 | .45 | .11 | .11 | .35 | .. | .46 | .43 | | .52 | .47 | .38 | .17 | .13 | .07 | .46 |
| IIC. Extent of Planning Activity | .29 | .41 | .08 | .15 | .14 | .46 | .34 | .25 | | .48 | .28 | .22 | .04 | .18 | .16 | .. |
| **Dimension III. Consistency of Vocational Preferences** | | | | | | | | | | | | | | | | |
| IIIA. Consistency within Fields | .08 | -.01 | .02 | .07 | .14 | -.19 | -.11 | -.13 | | -.31 | -.02 | -.11 | -.09 | .02 | .14 | -.13 |
| IIIB. Consistency within Levels | .04 | .08 | .05 | -.11 | .11 | .00 | -.04 | .00 | | -.09 | .01 | -.11 | .13 | .08 | .03 | -.03 |
| IIIC. Consistency within Families | .03 | .00 | .04 | -.09 | .14 | -.09 | -.01 | -.04 | | -.20 | -.02 | -.19 | .09 | .04 | .10 | -.12 |
| **Dimension IV. Crystallization of Traits** | | | | | | | | | | | | | | | | |
| IVA. Patterning of Interests | -.09 | .08 | -.10 | -.17 | -.05 | .05 | .02 | .10 | | .15 | -.10 | .01 | -.16 | .01 | -.01 | .05 |
| IVB. Interest Maturity | .14 | .19 | -.03 | .00 | .15 | .14 | .05 | .08 | | .20 | .08 | .06 | .17 | .12 | -.07 | .07 |
| IVC. Liking for Work | .03 | .06 | -.05 | .09 | .17 | -.09 | -.10 | -.04 | | -.21 | -.02 | -.12 | -.21 | -.07 | .03 | -.03 |
| IVD. Patterning of Work Values | .08 | .11 | -.01 | .05 | -.06 | -.03 | -.11 | -.10 | | -.13 | -.04 | -.04 | -.01 | -.05 | -.08 | .24 |
| IVE. Discussion of Rewards of Work | | .07 | -.07 | .09 | -.13 | .03 | -.05 | -.09 | | .03 | -.01 | .04 | -.01 | -.01 | .05 | .13 |
| IVF. Acceptance of Responsibility | .47 | .51 | .23 | .26 | .28 | .57 | .28 | .33 | | .40 | .44 | .27 | .29 | .25 | .15 | .51 |
| **Dimension V. Vocational Independence** | | | | | | | | | | | | | | | | |
| VA. Independence of Work Experience | .00 | .00 | -.04 | .08 | -.07 | .02 | -.07 | .07 | | .01 | -.05 | .04 | -.02 | .04 | .11 | .02 |
| **Dimension VI. Wisdom of Vocational Preferences** | | | | | | | | | | | | | | | | |
| VIA. Agreement: Ability and Preference | -.02 | -.05 | .05 | .05 | -.10 | -.01 | .04 | -.08 | | -.04 | .11 | -.03 | .11 | -.14 | .02 | .06 |
| VIB. Agreement: Interests and Preference | -.20 | -.10 | -.13 | -.19 | -.12 | -.19 | -.16 | -.09 | | -.07 | -.10 | -.08 | -.23 | -.03 | .00 | -.08 |
| VIC. Agreement: Interests and Fantasy Pref. | -.08 | -.12 | -.12 | -.01 | .02 | -.09 | -.21 | -.03 | | -.10 | -.13 | .15 | -.02 | .01 | -.07 | -.02 |
| VID. Agreement: Level of Interests and Pref. | -.04 | -.20 | .02 | .08 | -.02 | -.09 | -.03 | -.14 | | -.13 | -.11 | -.12 | -.03 | -.16 | -.05 | -.08 |
| VIE. Socioeconomic Accessibility | .00 | -.24 | .17 | -.06 | .14 | -.02 | -.23 | .00 | | -.10 | .04 | -.06 | .26 | -.06 | .14 | -.11 |

Note.—A correlation coefficient of .164 is significant at the .05 level, and of .230 at the .01 level, one-tailed test.
[a] No scores were available.

53

also to IA. The correlations between the total scores of Indices IIA and IIB, respectively, and the total score of IA were .40 and .48, significant at better than the .01 level. While three out of the four components of IIA had higher correlations with the IIB total than with the IA total, six out of eight components of IIB were more highly related to the IA total than to the IIA total. Boys who knew more about their preferred occupations, and those who had planned more, tended to be those who were better oriented to occupational choice, as we saw in examining the same data in another way in Table 12. There were no important tendencies for the indices of Dimension II to be related to those of Dimensions III, IV, V, or VI except in the case of Index IVF, Acceptance of Responsibility for Choice and Planning, which was substantially related to Indices IIA, IIB, and IIC.

DIMENSION III.—Table 14 reports the correlations between the consistency indices and between these indices and those of other dimensions. Consistency within Fields was somewhat related to Consistency within Levels of vocational preference ($r = .22$). This might give one some confidence in the adequacy of consistency of preferences as a trait, but the relationship was slight, and significant at only the .05 level. Since both field and level were included in the measure of Consistency within Families (family being defined as a combination of field and level) the correlations between these variables were naturally very high; the fact that level carried more weight than field in the family index ($r$'s of .81 and .62 respectively) was no doubt a function of the greater range of scores for the level index.

The general lack of relationship between the consistency indices and all other indices is noteworthy; all of the coefficients of correlation were low, and many were near zero or negative. Only 3 of 51 coefficients of correlation between the three consistency indices and total scores on the other indices were statistically significant in the hypothesized direction (Agreement between Level of Interests and Preferences as correlated with Consistency within Fields, and Agreement between Ability and Preference and Socioeconomic Accessibility as correlated with Consistency within Families). Consistency of vocational preferences, translated into behavioral refer-

TABLE 14. CORRELATIONS OF MEASURES USED IN DIMENSION III
WITH INDICES OF OTHER DIMENSIONS

|  | Dimension III Consistency of Vocational Preferences | | |
|---|---|---|---|
|  | IIIA | IIIB | IIIC |
| Dimension I. Orientation to Vocational Choice |  |  |  |
| IA. Concern with Choice | −.04 | −.10 | −.13 |
| IB. Use of Resources | −.20 | −.19 | −.20 |
| Dimension II. Information and Planning |  |  |  |
| IIA. Specificity of Information | .08 | .04 | .03 |
| IIB. Specificity of Planning | −.19 | .00 | −.09 |
| IIC. Extent of Planning Activity | −.13 | −.03 | −.12 |
| Dimension III. Consistency of Vocational Preferences |  |  |  |
| IIIA. Consistency within Fields | . . . | .22 | .62 |
| IIIB. Consistency within Levels | .22 | . . . | .81 |
| IIIC. Consistency within Families | .62 | .81 | . . . |
| Dimension IV. Crystallization of Traits |  |  |  |
| IVA. Patterning of Interests | −.14 | −.08 | −.18 |
| IVB. Interest Maturity | −.07 | −.13 | −.15 |
| IVC. Liking for Work | .08 | .05 | .10 |
| IVD. Patterning of Work Values | .00 | −.08 | −.11 |
| IVE. Discussion of Rewards of Work | −.01 | −.16 | −.15 |
| IVF. Acceptance of Responsibility | −.03 | .00 | −.05 |
| Dimension V. Vocational Independence |  |  |  |
| VA. Independence of Work Experience | −.09 | −.05 | −.04 |
| Dimension VI. Wisdom of Vocational Preferences |  |  |  |
| VIA. Agreement: Ability and Preference | .16 | .06 | .18 |
| VIB. Agreement: Interests and Preference | −.01 | −.12 | −.12 |
| VIC. Agreement: Interests and Fantasy Pref. | .10 | −.06 | −.01 |
| VID. Agreement: Level of Interests and Pref. | .26 | .04 | .14 |
| VIE. Socioeconomic Accessibility | .08 | .13 | .18 |

Note.—A correlation coefficient of .164 is significant at the .05 level, and of .230 at the .01 level, one-tailed test.

ents as in this study, thus appears to lack construct validity as a dimension of vocational maturity in the ninth grade.

DIMENSION IV.—Table 15 sets forth the relationships of the various proposed indices of Crystallization of Traits with each other and with the other indices of vocational maturity. Indices IVA through IVE had few significant intercorrelations: IVC and IVE, Liking for Work and Extent of Discussion of Rewards of Work, correlated .40 (they use much of the same interview material); IVB and IVE, Interest Maturity and Discussion of Rewards of Work,

# TABLE 15. Correlations of Measures Used in Dimension IV with Indices of Other Dimensions

|  | Dimension IV Crystallization of Traits | | | | | | | | |
|---|---|---|---|---|---|---|---|---|---|
|  | IVA PATTERNING OF INTERESTS | IVB INTEREST MATURITY | IVC LIKING FOR WORK | IVD PATTERNING OF WORK VALUES | IVE REWARDS OF WORK | IVF ACCEPTANCE OF RESPONSIBILITY | IVF-1, FOR CHOICE | IVF-2, FOR EDUCATIONAL PLANS | IVF-3, FOR OCCUPATIONAL PLANS |
| **Dimension I. Orientation to Vocational Choice** | | | | | | | | | |
| IA. Concern with Choice | .08 | .06 | .16 | .04 | .16 | .56 | .38 | .38 | .43 |
| IB. Use of Resources | -.01 | -.10 | .07 | -.01 | -.05 | .24 | ... | ... | ... |
| **Dimension II. Information and Planning** | | | | | | | | | |
| IIA. Specificity of Information | -.09 | .08 | .14 | .03 | .08 | .47 | .19 | .36 | .46 |
| IIB. Specificity of Planning | .05 | .14 | -.09 | -.03 | .03 | .57 | .38 | .42 | .40 |
| IIC. Extent of Planning Activity | .05 | .07 | -.03 | .24 | .13 | .51 | .40 | .35 | .33 |
| **Dimension III. Consistency of Vocational Preferences** | | | | | | | | | |
| IIIA. Consistency within Fields | -.15 | -.07 | .08 | .00 | -.01 | -.03 | .11 | -.15 | -.04 |
| IIIB. Consistency within Levels | -.08 | -.13 | .05 | -.08 | -.16 | .00 | -.02 | .00 | -.03 |
| IIIC. Consistency within Families | -.18 | -.15 | .10 | -.11 | -.15 | -.05 | .00 | -.11 | .00 |
| **Dimension IV. Crystallization of Traits** | | | | | | | | | |
| IVA. Patterning of Interests | ... | .24 | .08 | .04 | .04 | .01 | -.16 | .20 | .00 |
| IVB. Interest Maturity | .24 | ... | .15 | .09 | .24 | .10 | .06 | .10 | .05 |
| IVC. Liking for Work | .08 | .15 | ... | -.05 | .40 | .08 | .04 | .03 | .08 |
| IVD. Patterning of Work Values | -.04 | .09 | -.05 | ... | .11 | .05 | .11 | -.07 | .06 |
| IVE. Discussion of Rewards of Work | .04 | .24 | .40 | .11 | ... | .07 | .02 | .04 | .08 |
| IVF. Acceptance of Responsibility | .01 | .10 | .08 | .05 | .07 | ... | .17 | .43 | .36 |
| **Dimension V. Vocational Independence** | | | | | | | | | |
| VA. Independence of Work Experience | -.06 | -.06 | -.10 | -.10 | .06 | .17 | .05 | .09 | .21 |
| **Dimension VI. Wisdom of Vocational Preferences** | | | | | | | | | |
| VIA. Agreement: Ability and Preference | -.27 | -.09 | .00 | -.09 | .00 | .01 | .01 | .04 | -.06 |
| VIB. Agreement: Interests and Preference | .29 | .39 | -.02 | .02 | .00 | -.11 | -.12 | -.05 | -.06 |
| VIC. Agreement: Interests and Fantasy Pref. | .09 | .03 | .11 | -.15 | .09 | -.14 | -.13 | -.06 | -.09 |
| VID. Agreement: Level of Interests and Fantasy Pref. | -.27 | -.54 | .08 | -.10 | .02 | -.06 | .06 | -.14 | -.06 |
| VIE. Socioeconomic Accessibility | -.09 | -.13 | .18 | -.02 | .05 | -.07 | .16 | -.23 | -.11 |

Note.—A correlation coefficient of .164 is significant at the .05 level, and of .230 at the .01 level, one-tailed test.

56

correlated .24; and IVA and IVB, Patterning of Interests and Interest Maturity, correlated .24. Index IVF, Acceptance of Responsibility for Choice and Planning, which had part-total correlations of .17, .43, and .36, was unrelated to any other indices of Crystallization of Traits, but was related to indices in Dimensions I and II, as we have already shown.

Indices IVA and IVB, Patterning of Interests and Interest Maturity, were based solely on Strong's Blank, and Indices IVC and IVE were derived by the same analyst from interview material which overlapped considerably. Index IVF and its components, also interview-derived, used another type of content, and different components were scored by two different analysts working independently. It might be expected that some spurious clustering of these measures would be found as a result of similarity of source data and, in the case of Indices IVC and IVE, perhaps as an outcome of contamination. These few but systematic relationships are precisely the types which were found. Some of these measures do not seem to belong in the categorical system here being used; indeed, we have already seen, and it is again apparent in this table, that Index IVF is more closely related to some of the indices developed to measure other presumed dimensions of vocational maturity. The inference is that Indices IVA through IVE are not measuring vocational maturity, since they do not have a number of significant correlations with other presumed measures of vocational maturity.

DIMENSION V.—Table 16 reports the correlations of the components of Index VA, Independence of Work Experience, with the total index score minus the respective components, and with the indices of other presumed dimensions of vocational maturity. The highlighted block of coefficients makes it clear that the index is internally consistent: coefficients of correlation ranged from .32 to .68, all significant at better than the .01 level. But this index, the only one of our indices constructed to measure vocational independence in the ninth grade, was, in general, not related to the other presumed indices of vocational maturity. It was even unrelated to the other indices of Dimension IV, Crystallization of Traits, in which it was originally classified, except for a low but significant correlation between the Independence of Work Ex-

TABLE 16. CORRELATIONS OF THE MEASURES USED IN DIMENSION V
WITH INDICES OF OTHER DIMENSIONS

| | VA. IND. OF WORK EXPERIENCE | Dimension V Vocational Independence | | | | |
|---|---|---|---|---|---|---|
| | | VA-1 SOURCE OF WORK | VA-2 AUSPICES OF WORK | VA-3 SUPERVISION ON JOB | VA-4 RESPONSIBILITY ON JOB | VA-5 EXTENT OF PAID EXPERIENCE |
| **Dimension I. Orientation to Vocational Choice** | | | | | | |
| IA. Concern with Choice | .02 | .10 | -.11 | -.01 | .11 | -.03 |
| IB. Use of Resources | .13 | ... | ... | ... | ... | ... |
| **Dimension II. Information and Planning** | | | | | | |
| IIA. Specificity of Information | .00 | .01 | -.09 | -.03 | .10 | -.03 |
| IIB. Specificity of Planning | .02 | .13 | -.10 | .04 | .03 | -.02 |
| IIC. Extent of Planning Activity | .02 | .01 | -.17 | .08 | .14 | .01 |
| **Dimension III. Consistency of Vocational Preferences** | | | | | | |
| IIIA. Consistency within Fields | -.09 | -.21 | -.18 | -.04 | .04 | .03 |
| IIIB. Consistency within Levels | -.05 | -.01 | -.06 | .00 | .00 | -.12 |
| IIIC. Consistency within Families | -.04 | -.06 | -.07 | .01 | .03 | -.07 |
| **Dimension IV. Crystallization of Traits** | | | | | | |
| IVA. Patterning of Interests | -.06 | -.18 | -.01 | -.08 | .10 | -.08 |
| IVB. Interest Maturity | -.06 | -.16 | -.06 | .01 | .01 | -.01 |
| IVC. Liking for Work | -.10 | -.02 | -.06 | -.08 | -.06 | -.12 |
| IVD. Patterning of Work Values | -.10 | -.16 | .22 | .02 | .03 | -.03 |
| IVE. Discussion of Rewards of Work | .06 | .05 | -.06 | .07 | .06 | .08 |
| IVF. Acceptance of Responsibility | .17 | .17 | .04 | .15 | .20 | .05 |
| **Dimension V. Vocational Independence** | | | | | | |
| VA. Independence of Work Experience | ... | **.64** | **.60** | **.68** | **.58** | **.32** |
| **Dimension VI. Wisdom of Vocational Preferences** | | | | | | |
| VIA. Agreement: Ability and Preference | -.07 | -.06 | -.03 | -.01 | -.09 | -.06 |
| VIB. Agreement: Interests and Preference | .10 | -.08 | .11 | .13 | .16 | .04 |
| VIC. Agreement: Interests and Fantasy Pref. | -.11 | -.11 | -.08 | -.17 | -.05 | -.02 |
| VID. Agreement: Level of Interests and Pref. | .04 | .08 | .04 | .06 | -.03 | -.01 |
| VIE. Socioeconomic Accessibility | .01 | -.06 | -.06 | .06 | -.02 | .11 |

Note.—A correlation coefficient of .164 is significant at the .05 level, and of .230 at the .01 level, one-tailed test.

perience total score and the total score of Index IVF (Acceptance of Responsibility), and for three significant relationships out of a possible thirty between the five part scores of VA and the six index total scores of Dimension IV. Independence of Work Experience, as assessed in this study, therefore appears to be questionable as a measure of vocational maturity in the ninth grade, on the basis of significant correlations with variables to which, on *a priori* grounds, a relationship had been predicted.

TABLE 17. CORRELATIONS OF MEASURES USED IN DIMENSION VI
WITH INDICES OF OTHER DIMENSIONS

| | Dimension VI Wisdom of Preferences | | | | |
|---|---|---|---|---|---|
| | VIA | VIB | VIC | VID | VIE |
| Dimension I. Orientation to Vocational Choice | | | | | |
| IA. Concern with Choice | −.11 | −.02 | .00 | −.03 | −.11 |
| IB. Use of Resources | −.21 | −.05 | −.22 | .03 | −.07 |
| Dimension II. Information and Planning | | | | | |
| IIA. Specificity of Information | −.02 | −.20 | −.08 | −.04 | .00 |
| IIB. Specificity of Planning | −.01 | −.19 | −.09 | −.09 | −.02 |
| IIC. Extent of Planning Activity | .06 | −.08 | −.02 | −.08 | −.11 |
| Dimension III. Consistency of Vocational Preferences | | | | | |
| IIIA. Consistency within Fields | .16 | −.01 | .10 | .26 | .08 |
| IIIB. Consistency within Levels | .06 | −.12 | −.06 | .04 | .13 |
| IIIC. Consistency within Families | .18 | −.12 | −.01 | .14 | .18 |
| Dimension IV. Crystallization of Traits | | | | | |
| IVA. Patterning of Interests | −.27 | .29 | .09 | −.27 | −.09 |
| IVB. Interest Maturity | −.09 | .39 | .03 | −.54 | −.13 |
| IVC. Liking for Work | .00 | −.02 | .11 | .08 | .18 |
| IVD. Patterning of Work Values | −.09 | .02 | −.15 | −.10 | −.02 |
| IVE. Discussion of Rewards of Work | .00 | .00 | .09 | .02 | .05 |
| IVF. Acceptance of Responsibility | .01 | −.11 | −.14 | −.06 | −.07 |
| Dimension V. Vocational Independence | | | | | |
| VA. Independence of Work Experience | −.07 | .10 | −.11 | .04 | .01 |
| Dimension VI. Wisdom of Vocational Preferences | | | | | |
| VIA. Agreement: Ability and Preference | ... | −.06 | .16 | .00 | .27 |
| VIB. Agreement: Interests and Preference | −.06 | ... | .27 | −.32 | −.09 |
| VIC. Agreement: Interests and Fantasy Pref. | .16 | .27 | ... | −.06 | .03 |
| VID. Agreement: Level of Interests and Pref. | .00 | −.32 | −.06 | ... | .17 |
| VIE. Socioeconomic Accessibility | .27 | −.09 | .03 | .17 | ... |

Note.—A correlation coefficient of .164 is significant at the .05 level, and of .230 at the .01 level, one-tailed test.

DIMENSION VI.—Table 17 reports the correlations between the various indices of Wisdom of Vocational Preferences and between these indices and the other presumed indices of vocational maturity. While any one of these wisdom indices is, in and of itself, a very limited measure of wisdom, it might be argued with some cogency that these are constituents of a wise choice. For example, the wish to enter an occupation requiring a degree of intelligence similar to one's own is not the sum total of wisdom of choice (such things as having adequate financial resources, interests which will make the work congenial, and contacts which will help one get started are important, too); but one prerequisite of a wise vocational choice is awareness of the necessary intelligence. Taken as a group our indices of Wisdom of Vocational Preferences seem conceptually much more satisfactory than any one of them might alone.

The intercorrelations among these five indices were low, although three of the coefficients of correlation were statistically significant. Furthermore, few of the correlations between the Wisdom of Preferences indices and the other presumed indices of vocational maturity were significant; most were low and quite a few were negative. Thus, the measures of Wisdom of Preferences appear to lack construct validity at the ninth-grade level, according to our criterion.

### Conclusions: Dimensions and Indices

The data presented in Tables 12 through 17 enable us to draw conclusions concerning the adequacy of our proposed dimensions and indices of vocational maturity, judged from a construct validity standpoint. We found six indices which were internally consistent and positively interrelated, out of a total of twenty which were selected on *a priori* grounds, constructed, and tried out. These six intercorrelated indices seem to measure two dimensions of vocational maturity in the ninth grade: orientation to choice tasks, and use of resources. The orientation dimension contains five indices, the use dimension only one. These indices and the intercorrelations which appear to justify their clustering are shown in Table 18.

TABLE 18. Intercorrelations between Adequate and Marginal Measures of Vocational Maturity

|  | IA | IVF | IIA | IIB | IIC | IB |
|---|---|---|---|---|---|---|
| Dimension A. *Orientation to Choice Tasks* |  |  |  |  |  |  |
| Index IA   Concern with Choice | .. | .56 | .40 | .48 | .29 | .23 |
| Index IVF  Acceptance of Responsibility | .56 | .. | .47 | .57 | .51 | .24 |
| Index IIA  Specificity of Information | .40 | .47 | .. | .37 | .29 | .17 |
| Index IIB  Specificity of Planning | .48 | .57 | .37 | .. | .46 | .07 |
| Index IIC  Extent of Planning | .29 | .51 | .29 | .46 | .. | .06 |
| Dimension B. *Use of Resources* |  |  |  |  |  |  |
| Index IB   Use of Resources | .23 | .24 | .17 | .07 | .06 | .. |

The first dimension, consisting as it does of five indices, with intercorrelations ranging from .29 to .57, seems fairly well established and defined. The empirical data showed a definite clustering, and examination of the content reveals that this dimension deals with thinking about vocational choices, as evidenced by awareness of problems and factors of choice, feeling responsible for choosing and planning, and having both accumulated relevant information and made relevant plans.

The second dimension is less well established, for it is represented by only one index, and only three of five correlations with the indices of the first dimension were significant (two at the .01, one at the .05, level). The size of these coefficients suggests that this index does not belong to the same cluster as the others. Hence the conclusion that Use of Resources in Orientation, while it may be somewhat indicative of vocational maturity in grade nine, belongs in another dimension. Data presented in Chapter VI, as well as the material in this chapter, suggest that Use of Resources in Orientation is marginal as a measure of vocational maturity.

The other fourteen indices which were hypothesized as measures of vocational maturity in grade nine were found to fit into or yield virtually no clusters. They were, in general, unrelated to each other and to the six more promising indices. While it is true that the measures of consistency of vocational preferences were somewhat interrelated, they were virtually unrelated to other indices and the internal relationships may have been artifacts of the measurement method. The lack of relationships among these measures casts doubt on their construct validity, that is, on their conceptual adequacy as indices of vocational maturity in the ninth grade. This does not justify the conclusion that they would have no validity for predicting later vocational adjustment nor that they would not be good measures of vocational maturity at some other age level: consistency, independence, and wisdom as behaviorally defined here might prove to be good predictors of age of establishment in a stable career or very adequate measures of vocational maturity in the twelfth grade or at age twenty-two. Nor does our finding justify the conclusion that these are not good measures of something other than vocational maturity at the ninth-grade level: independence of work experience is an internally consistent index which may be a very adequate measure of just what its title suggests, the independence of a boy's work experience. What this kind of behavior is related to in the ninth grade remains to be ascertained.

## THE NATURE OF VOCATIONAL MATURITY
### IN GRADE NINE

Our findings concerning the nature of vocational maturity in the ninth-grade boys of the Career Pattern Study are summarized here in order to point up more clearly what does and what does not appear to constitute vocational maturity at this stage of development. The reader is reminded that we are defining vocational maturity in terms of the measures discussed in this chapter which have statistically significant positive correlations with each other. Those measures which do not have any appreciable number of significant positive correlations with the others are considered inadequate as measures of vocational maturity in grade nine.

### Indices Not Defining Vocational Maturity in Grade Nine

A number of attributes which were believed, either by the investigators or by other persons active in vocational guidance, to be aspects of vocational maturity in ninth-grade boys have been found unrelated to other interrelated characteristics which do appear to constitute vocational maturity. These apparently inadequate indices had been classified in the following dimensions: Consistency of Vocational Preferences, Crystallization of Traits (such as vocational interests and attitudes towards work), Vocational Independence, and Wisdom of Vocational Preferences (as judged by abilities, measured interests, and socioeconomic accessibility). Although these indices may be important in other respects, may prove to predict success, or may become significant at later stages of development, they are here seen as unrelated to vocational maturity in grade nine.

### Indices Defining Vocational Maturity in Grade Nine

Vocational maturity at this age level was found to consist of orientation to vocational choice tasks and, perhaps, use of resources in becoming oriented to occupations. Each of these is briefly described below.

ORIENTATION TO VOCATIONAL CHOICE TASKS includes these aspects: concern with or awareness of the need to make prevocational and vocational choices, both immediate, intermediate, and ultimate;

knowledge of the factors to consider in making a choice; awareness of the various kinds of contingencies which may affect one's
choices and one's career. It also consists of accepting responsibility
for making choices and for making plans, alone or, better still, with
the help of informed persons. It consists of having information
about the occupation of one's preference and of having plans for
training for and entering that occupation.

THE USE OF RESOURCES consists of consulting or talking with others
(parents, friends, or informed persons, e.g., counselors and persons
preparing for or working in the occupation under consideration)
about one's educational and occupational plans. It consists of observing the occupation in which one is interested, in real life or in
movies, for instance, and of participating in related activities, such
as school courses, clubs, and part-time jobs. It consists of reading
books and pamphlets about one's preferred occupation or about
other occupations in which one is interested. More broadly, it
consists of use by the individual of any resource to orient himself
to the world of work.

## Summary

Thus vocational maturity in the ninth-grade boys studied appears to consist of behavior which might be characterized as preparation for vocational choice, of orientation attitudes and activities.
It is behavior in which the subject looks ahead, considers what the
future may hold for him, and engages in thinking, planning, and
actions which may help him meet the future. The important
aspect is that the individual recognizes the eventual need for goals
and the desirability of developing them. According to our data,
vocational maturity in the ninth grade does not appear to involve
having consistent or realistic vocational preferences, having clear-
cut interests or work values, or having had independent work experience. It is not, at this stage, characterized by preferences which
are consistent with each other or with the realities of the self or
of the occupational world, or by any initial achievement of a place
for oneself in the working world. Vocational maturity in ninth-
grade boys is shown, not by where they have arrived vocationally,
but by how they are thinking about goals and what they are doing
about them.

# CHAPTER IV

# Factors in Vocational Maturity Measures

The examination of intercorrelations between the smallest units constituting our proposed indices of vocational maturity (in some instances components and in others elements) and the indices themselves, as reported in the preceding chapter, led to the conclusion that we had developed six adequate indices, five of which seem fairly well established and one of which appears marginal. The five fairly well-established indices are Concern with Choice, Acceptance of Responsibility for Choice and Planning, Specificity of Information about the Preferred Occupation, Specificity of Planning for the Preferred Occupation, and Extent of Planning Activity. The marginal index is Use of Resources in Orientation.

As a further check on the appropriateness of the grouping of elements or components into indices, a factor analysis was carried out. Such a procedure seemed additionally important in order to understand whether the factor structure of vocational maturity was unitary or multiple. The elements or components of the four most adequate indices of vocational maturity were included in the factor analysis,[1] as well as those of one index found inadequate, Independence of Work Experience, in which we were also inter-

---

[1] Three components of Index IIB, Specificity of Planning, were *not* used in the factor analysis: Alternative High School Plans (which had no scores), Planning to Facilitate Entry, and Planning for Advancement in the Occupation. The latter two

ested. The marginal index, Use of Resources in Orientation, was not included.

PROCEDURE

A centroid factor analysis was carried out,[2] and a total of nine factors was extracted. As the residuals began to increase instead of continuing to decrease after the extraction of the fourth factor, the procedure was reviewed.[3] Because of the presence of negative intercorrelations in the matrix, it was decided to carry out a principal axes factor analysis, using computer procedures.[4] The results of the two analyses agreed; since the principal axes method is more rigorous, it is reported here.

Table 19 gives the communality estimates for the twenty-seven variables (elements or components of the five indices) that were included in the factor analysis and the principal axes loadings for the five largest factors. The communalities were estimated by Burt's method (Cattell, 1952, p. 154). The four largest factors had sums of squares of loadings greater than 1.00 and that of the fifth approached 1.00. However, as the fifth factor accounted for only 3 per cent of the variance, the extraction of additional factors did not seem justified. These five factors were rotated according to the quartimax method (Neuhaus & Wrigley, 1954). Results of this rotation are shown in Table 20. (A four-factor rotation yielded similar results.)

It may be noted, by comparing Tables 19 and 20, that rotation

---

were omitted because they had low and non-significant correlations with the index total. The index Extent of Planning Activity, which had only a total score, was included in the factor analysis. On the basis of the coefficients of correlation reported in Chapter III, it was decided to group this measure with the remaining measures in Specificity of Planning for the Preferred Occupation, as an additional component. Extent of Planning Activity is therefore listed under Specificity of Planning in the present chapter.

[2] This analysis was planned and made for the first four factors by William Dubin, and was completed for five more factors by Leo Goldstein.

[3] We are indebted to Professors Herbert Solomon and Rosedith Sitgreaves for consultations on the statistical aspects of factor analysis in the work reported in the rest of this chapter.

[4] We are indebted to Professors Louis L. McQuitty and Charles F. Wrigley of the Michigan State University for providing the machine time and the technical assistance involved in the principal axes analysis.

TABLE 19. COMMUNALITY ESTIMATES AND PRINCIPAL AXES FACTOR
LOADINGS OF 27 VOCATIONAL MATURITY MEASURES

| Measures | Commu-nality Estimates | Factor Loadings | | | | |
|---|---|---|---|---|---|---|
| | | I | II | III | IV | V |
| *Concern with Choice: Awareness of—* | | | | | | |
| 1. Need for Immediate Choices | .53 | .43 | −.00 | .06 | .37 | .09 |
| 2. Need for Intermediate Choices | .55 | .55 | −.20 | .01 | −.30 | .32 |
| 3. Need for Ultimate Choices | .34 | .41 | .01 | −.30 | .01 | .07 |
| 4. Factors in Vocational Choice | .57 | .50 | −.05 | −.17 | −.18 | .44 |
| 5. Contingency Factors, Parental | .31 | .37 | −.11 | −.25 | −.08 | −.12 |
| 6. Contingency Factors, Financial | .33 | .37 | .08 | .17 | −.12 | .07 |
| 7. Contingency Factors, Military | .16 | .23 | −.03 | .09 | −.08 | .21 |
| 8. Contingency Factors, Special | .18 | .25 | .04 | −.06 | .08 | −.03 |
| *Acceptance of Responsibility* | | | | | | |
| 9. For Choice | .44 | .44 | −.03 | .01 | .30 | .18 |
| 10. For Educational Plans | .59 | .61 | .07 | .03 | −.07 | −.25 |
| 11. For Occupational Plans | .58 | .63 | .18 | −.11 | −.15 | −.26 |
| *Specificity of Information* | | | | | | |
| 12. Requirements | .59 | .65 | −.08 | .03 | −.23 | −.19 |
| 13. Duties | .31 | .24 | −.05 | −.44 | .01 | −.31 |
| 14. Conditions of Work | .37 | .31 | .06 | −.46 | .06 | −.12 |
| 15. Opportunities | .43 | .43 | −.12 | −.45 | .10 | .05 |
| *Specificity of Planning* | | | | | | |
| 16. High School: Obtain Information | .40 | .38 | −.09 | .38 | .23 | −.22 |
| 17. High School: Specificity of Plans | .53 | .46 | .02 | .24 | .49 | .10 |
| 18. Post-High-School: Obtain Info. | .54 | .56 | −.08 | .40 | −.08 | −.14 |
| 19. Post-High-School Plans | .55 | .57 | −.14 | .11 | −.12 | .20 |
| 20. Alternative Post-H.-School Plans | .41 | .41 | .00 | .16 | −.09 | .18 |
| 21. Entry Plans | .37 | .28 | −.04 | −.35 | .34 | .07 |
| 22. Extent of Planning Activity | .56 | .56 | −.04 | .27 | .08 | −.22 |
| *Independence of Work Experience* | | | | | | |
| 23. Source of Work | .61 | .17 | .74 | −.05 | .08 | .09 |
| 24. Auspices of Work | .51 | −.08 | .73 | −.07 | .08 | .10 |
| 25. Supervision on the Job | .56 | .10 | .77 | .06 | .01 | −.02 |
| 26. Responsibility on the Job | .56 | .20 | .66 | .05 | −.26 | −.05 |
| 27. Extent of Paid Experience | .26 | .00 | .38 | .03 | .01 | .05 |
| Sum of Squares of Loadings | | 4.64 | 2.40 | 1.42 | 1.01 | .88 |
| Percentage of Total Variance Accounted for by Each Factor | | 17.18 | 8.89 | 5.26 | 3.74 | 3.26 |
| Percentage of Total Variance Accounted for by All Five Factors:    38 | | | | | | |

changed the size of some of the factor loadings, but had little effect
on the factorial structure. The loadings of the first factor were
reduced somewhat, while the largest loadings of the other factors
were, in general, increased. Such changes are usual in rotation to
simple structure. Therefore, the results of the rotation were accepted and used as the statistical basis for consideration of the
psychological meaning of the variables measured.

TABLE 20. ROTATED FACTOR LOADINGS OF 27 VOCATIONAL
MATURITY MEASURES

| *Index* | *Factor* | | | | |
|---|---|---|---|---|---|
| | I | II | III | IV | V |
| *Concern with Choice: Awareness of—* | | | | | |
| 1. Need for Immediate Choices | .25 | .04 | .15 | .49 | .07 |
| 2. Need for Intermediate Choices | .39 | −.15 | .17 | −.01 | .57 |
| 3. Need for Ultimate Choices | .21 | .05 | .43 | .07 | .16 |
| 4. Factors in Vocational Choice | .21 | −.00 | .32 | .07 | .60 |
| 5. Contingency Factors, Parental | .30 | −.08 | .36 | −.06 | .03 |
| 6. Contingency Factors, Financial | .34 | .11 | −.04 | .06 | .24 |
| 7. Contingency Factors, Military | .14 | −.01 | −.00 | .07 | .29 |
| 8. Contingency Factors, Special | .17 | .06 | .16 | .12 | .02 |
| *Acceptance of Responsibility* | | | | | |
| 9. For Choice | .22 | .01 | .20 | .45 | .18 |
| 10. For Educational Plans | .63 | .12 | .18 | .05 | .01 |
| 11. For Occupational Plans | .62 | .23 | .30 | −.06 | .03 |
| *Specificity of Information* | | | | | |
| 12. Requirements | .68 | −.03 | .19 | −.06 | .14 |
| 13. Duties | .20 | −.03 | .50 | −.12 | −.22 |
| 14. Conditions of Work | .15 | .09 | .54 | −.01 | −.06 |
| 15. Opportunities | .18 | −.08 | .59 | .12 | .11 |
| *Specificity of Planning* | | | | | |
| 16. High School: Obtain Information | .47 | −.06 | −.17 | .35 | −.13 |
| 17. High School: Specificity of Plans | .29 | .06 | .01 | .65 | .05 |
| 18. Post-High-School: Obtain Info. | .66 | −.05 | −.17 | .15 | .12 |
| 19. Post-High-School Plans | .44 | −.10 | .11 | .15 | .42 |
| 20. Alternative Post-High-School Plans | .33 | .03 | −.01 | .13 | .34 |
| 21. Entry Plans | .03 | −.01 | .47 | .31 | −.01 |
| 22. Extent of Planning Activity | .62 | −.00 | .03 | .24 | −.03 |
| *Independence of Work Experience* | | | | | |
| 23. Source of Work | .03 | .75 | .08 | .11 | .07 |
| 24. Auspices of Work | −.19 | .73 | .01 | .04 | −.00 |
| 25. Supervision on the Job | .07 | .78 | −.05 | .02 | −.01 |
| 26. Responsibility on the Job | .23 | .67 | −.04 | −.19 | .11 |
| 27. Extent of Paid Experience | −.04 | .37 | −.04 | .02 | .03 |
| Sum of Squares of Loadings | 3.44 | 2.42 | 1.88 | 1.28 | 1.30 |
| Percentage of Total Variance Accounted for by Each Factor | 12.74 | 8.96 | 6.96 | 4.74 | 4.81 |
| Percent of Total Variance Accounted for by All Five Factors: 38 | | | | | |

## RESULTS

As Table 19 brings out, only 38 per cent of the variance was accounted for by the five extracted factors. Some consideration must therefore be given to possible reasons for the large amount of unexplained variance.

It may be that systematic variance amounted to little more than

38 per cent, the unexplained variance being largely error variance or a combination, in unknown proportions, of error variance and possible specific variance.

It is possible that the measures used in the factor analysis were of somewhat low reliability, which would make for error variance. It was seen in Chapter III that the indices (total scores) were sufficiently reliable when inter-judge agreement was the method of determining reliability. When odd-even reliabilities were computed for two of the indices, they were .57 for elements of one index and .88 for items of the other index (as corrected by the Spearman-Brown formula). Since the treatment of elements as items may lead to an underestimate of reliability, as discussed in Chapter III, these were deemed satisfactory index reliabilities. But in the factor analysis we were dealing, not with index (total) scores, but with element or component (part) scores. As these were based on considerably fewer items, they were quite probably less reliable, although their exact reliability is not known. Low reliability of the measures tends to lower the size of intercorrelations, resulting in lowered estimates of factor loadings. Thus, the relative unreliability of the part scores used in this study may have made the five extracted factors appear less important than they actually may be in describing vocational maturity.

On the other hand, we must also ask whether spurious clusters could have appeared in the factor analysis. All of the measures analyzed were derived from interviews. One might, therefore, wonder whether there could be some spurious similarities of scores arising from the bias of an interview analyst or from multiple use of the same interview excerpts. This would tend to result in high intercorrelations among, and similar factor structure in, the separate measures. Efforts were made to avoid this situation. The possibility of such an effect arising from scorer bias was minimized by scorer training, which resulted in an adequate level of inter-scorer agreement. Multiple use of a given type of interview excerpt for the several indices was minimized by a series of seminars and staff meetings in which sample content analyses, scoring manuals, and sample scored protocols were reviewed with this problem in mind.

*The Five Factors*

Table 20, reporting the rotated factor loadings of the twenty-seven elements or components, can be examined in order to determine the nature of each of the five factors. This is done in the paragraphs which follow.

FACTOR I. PLANNING ORIENTATION.—When the measures having factor loadings of .60 and above, .40 to .59, and .20 to .39 were grouped accordingly, the nature of Factor I appeared as follows:

| | |
|---|---|
| .60 or above | Acceptance of Responsibility for Educational Plans |
| | Acceptance of Responsibility for Occupational Plans |
| | Specificity of Information about Occupational Requirements |
| | Steps Taken to Obtain Information for Post-High-School Planning |
| | Specificity of Planning: Extent of Planning Activity |
| .40–.59 | Steps Taken to Obtain Information for High School Planning |
| | Specificity of Post-High-School Plans |
| .20–.39 | Awareness of the Need for Immediate Choices |
| | Awareness of the Need for Intermediate Choices |
| | Awareness of the Need for Ultimate Choices |
| | Awareness of Factors in Vocational Choice |
| | Awareness of Contingency Factors: Parental Psychological Support |
| | Awareness of Contingency Factors: Financial Means |
| | Acceptance of Responsibility for Choice |
| | Specificity of Information about Occupational Duties |
| | Specificity of High School Plans |
| | Specificity of Alternative Post-High-School Plans |

Factor I appears to be essentially a planning factor, as indicated by the first seven measures (all of those with loadings of .40 or above). Five of the measures with loadings or .20–.39 have to do with awareness of need for choices; two have to do with acceptance of responsibility for choice and for work; and two again have to do with planning. Since some awareness of need and some acceptance of responsibility seem essential to planning, the naming seems logical.

FACTOR II. INDEPENDENCE OF WORK EXPERIENCE.—Factor II emerged from this factor analysis, as did one of the indices from the inspectional cluster analysis of the matrix of intercorrelations reported in Chapter III, as a simple factor of independence of work experience. The five components (smallest units in this index) all had loadings of .37 or above, and four of them ranged from .67 to .78. The only element from any other index having an appreciable loading on this factor was that of Acceptance of Responsibility for Occupational Plans, and this was only .23. Thus the results of the factor analysis are consistent with the conclusion reached in Chapter III that Independence of Work Experience is distinct from the other interview-derived indices.

FACTOR III. THE LONG VIEW AHEAD.—Measures having heavy loadings on Factor III were as follows:

.40–.59    Awareness of Need for Ultimate Choices
Specificity of Information about Occupational Duties
Specificity of Information about Occupational Conditions
Specificity of Information about Occupational Opportunities
Specificity of Planning: Entry Plans

.20–.39    Awareness of Factors in Vocational Choice
Awareness of Contingency Factors: Parental Psychological Support
Acceptance of Responsibility for Choice
Acceptance of Responsibility for Occupational Plans

These measures appear to be characterized by the remoteness, from ninth-graders, of the situations or problems to which they refer, such as ultimate choices, what one does on the job, the conditions of work, entering the occupation, contingencies in respect to parental backing after high school, and responsibilitity for occupational rather than educational plans. In this context,

Awareness of Factors in Vocational Choice and Acceptance of Responsibility for Choice take on the coloring of the long view. Hence this factor may be termed one of looking ahead, and considering the problems which will arise in the more distant developmental tasks of young adulthood.

FACTOR IV. THE SHORT VIEW AHEAD.—Heavy loadings on Factor IV were shown by the following measures:

.60
or above  Specificity of High School Plans

.40–.59  Awareness of the Need for Immediate Choices
Acceptance of Responsibility for Choice

.20–.39  Steps Taken to Obtain Information for High School
Planning
Specificity of Planning: Entry Plans
Specificity of Planning: Extent of Planning Activity

These measures seem to have in common a reference to immediate issues: high school plans, immediate choices, information-getting for high school planning. In this context, acceptance of responsibility and planning activity can also have to do with the immediate, and entry into an occupation may well be thought of as the almost immediate goal of planning, while still in school, for a job to be obtained directly upon leaving school. Hence Factor IV may be characterized as one which involves a focus on the immediate future.

FACTOR V. THE INTERMEDIATE VIEW.—In Factor V the heavy loadings were found in the following measures:

.60
or above  Awareness of Factors in Vocational Choice

.40–.59  Awareness of the Need for Intermediate Choices
Specificity of Post-High-School Plans

.20–.39  Awareness of Contingency Factors: Financial Means
Awareness of Contingency Factors: Military Service
Specificity of Alternative Post-High-School Plans

One measure, Specificity of Information about Duties in the Preferred Occupation, has a negative loading (−.22) on this factor. Although the loading is not large, it does lend itself to the interpretation made of the elements which have positive loadings on this factor. The focus seems to be on the intermediate, on situations and problems which follow high school but which precede work, particularly on education, military service, and the contingencies which might make alternative plans necessary.

### The Indices and Their Factor Structure

We have examined the measures which have loadings on each factor in order to ascertain the nature of these factors and to name them. Now we turn to the obverse process, that of examining the factors which were most important in each of our measures. Table 21 shows the percentage of measures in each index having loadings of .20 or more on each rotated factor from Table 20. An examination of these tables throws light on the factorial structure of each of the indices.

TABLE 21. PERCENTAGE OF MEASURES IN A GIVEN INDEX HAVING
LOADINGS OF .20 OR MORE ON EACH ROTATED FACTOR

| Index | Factor | | | | |
|---|---|---|---|---|---|
| | I | II | III | IV | V |
| Concern with Choice | 75 | 0 | 37 | 12 | 50 |
| Acceptance of Responsibility for Choice and Planning | 100 | 33 | 67 | 33 | 0 |
| Specificity of Information about Preferred Occupation | 50 | 0 | 75 | 0 | 25[a] |
| Specificity of Planning for Preferred Occupation | 86 | 0 | 14 | 57 | 29 |
| Independence of Work Experience | 20 | 100 | 0 | 0 | 0 |

[a] The loading in this instance was negative.

CONCERN WITH CHOICE.—Factor I is the most important factor in the index Concern with Choice: 75 per cent of the measures of this index (six of eight) had loadings of .20 or more on this factor. Factor V is next most important, with loadings of .20 or more in half of the measures, followed by Factor III, with such loadings in slightly over one-third of the measures. Factors II and IV were of little importance in this index, although Factor IV had a loading of .49 in one measure, Awareness of the Need for Immediate

Choices. The Concern with Choice index is, then, a mixture of Planning, the Intermediate View (focusing on the intermediate future of late adolescence), and the Long View Ahead (focusing on the more distant future of young adulthood). Thus, this index appears to assess a concern with educational and occupational choice and planning for more than the immediate future.

ACCEPTANCE OF RESPONSIBILITY FOR CHOICE AND PLANNING.— Factor I had loadings of .20 or more in all three of the components of the Acceptance of Responsibility index. Factor III figures in two of the three components; Factor II plays a part in one; and Factor IV plays a part in a different one. Planning is thus the most important aspect of this index, although the Long View, the Short View, and Independence of Work Experience each contribute somewhat. Factor V, the Intermediate View, is not appreciably loaded in any of the parts of this index. As one might have expected, the Acceptance of Responsibility index appears to be largely a measure of Planning.

SPECIFICITY OF INFORMATION ABOUT THE PREFERRED OCCUPATION. —The index Specificity of Information about the Preferred Occupation is made up of four components, in three of which Factor III has loadings of .50 or more. Factor I had a loading of .68 in the component concerning Requirements and played some part in the Duties component (a loading of .20), while Factor V had a negative loading (–.22) in the latter. This index thus seems to be largely a function of the Long View Ahead and of Planning.

SPECIFICITY OF PLANNING FOR THE PREFERRED OCCUPATION.—The index Specificity of Planning for the Preferred Occupation is made up of seven elements, in 86 per cent of which Factor I had loadings or .20 or higher. Factor IV figured in more than half of the measures, with Factors V and III, respectively, playing a part in two and in one of the measures. This index thus appears to be one in which Planning, the Short View (focusing on immediate issues and possibilities such as high school plans), and to a lesser extent the Intermediate View (such as planning for post-high-school training) are the important factors.

INDEPENDENCE OF WORK EXPERIENCE.—The work experience index was loaded almost entirely on Factor II, with four of its five elements having loadings above .60 on this factor, and all of its elements having loadings greater than .20. Factor I contributed slightly to one of its elements. As discussed previously, the factorial composition of this index is rather distinct from that of the other indices.

## SUMMARY

In this chapter we have presented the results of a factor analysis of the part scores (elements or components) of the four most adequate indices of vocational maturity and of an additional index, Independence of Work Experience. The principal axes method was used. The factors extracted accounted for only 38 per cent of the variance. If it had been possible to correct the correlations for attenuation due to the presumed low reliability of the part scores, the percentage of variance accounted for would probably have been higher.

Five factors were extracted, the last of which accounted for only 3 per cent of the variance, and they were rotated by the quartimax method. The factor loadings of the various measures were examined, and the factors were identified by the following names: I. Planning Orientation; II. Independence of Work Experience; III. The Long View Ahead; IV. The Short View Ahead; V. The Intermediate View.

This chapter began with two questions, one concerning the adequacy of the grouping of the elements or components into indices, the other concerning the factorial structure of vocational maturity in the ninth grade. The factor analysis data show that the part scores were fairly well grouped into indices, although changes in combining could be made to reflect psychological structure somewhat more adequately. There would be no reduction in the number of measures in the process of recombining, and in improving the psychological structure of the measures the sociological (developmental task) structure would be impaired.

Independence of Work Experience was found to be virtually free of saturation by the factors which saturate the measures of vocational maturity deemed adequate at the ninth-grade level; it is explained largely by one factor, best called by the same name as the index. A factor which appears to involve a Planning Orientation is important to all four of the adequate indices of vocational maturity. Another factor, the Long View Ahead (the tendency to look ahead to the developmental tasks of young adulthood), is particularly important in the Specificity of Information and Acceptance of Responsibility indices. Still another factor, the Intermediate View (the tendency to look ahead to the intermediate tasks of late adolescence), makes a distinctive contribution to the index Concern with Choice. And a fourth factor, which appears to be the Short View (the tendency to focus on immediate developmental tasks more than on others), is of special importance in Specificity of Planning for the Preferred Occupation. Vocational maturity in the ninth grade thus appears to consist of one general factor, Planning Orientation, and three group factors which contribute differently to the four indices. These group factors reflect tendencies to focus on different time periods in the present and approaching life stages.

# CHAPTER V

# Correlates of Vocational Maturity

The major emphasis in this monograph is on testing the validity of the construct vocational maturity as it is operationally defined at the ninth-grade level by the measures used to assess the construct. Intercorrelations among these presumed measures of vocational maturity and findings from factor analysis of selected measures have been used to clarify which measures apparently indicate vocational maturity in our sample and which do not.

Further understanding of the construct validity of these measures of vocational maturity may be obtained by reviewing their correlations with some variables which do not seem to be measures of vocational maturity but which one might expect to be relevant to such measures. For convenience in distinguishing between presumed measures of vocational maturity and these other variables, the latter are referred to as *correlates*. In this chapter, the twenty-eight correlates selected for study are described.[1] Relationships between vocational maturity measures and correlates are discussed in Chapter VI.

The correlates, classified on a logical basis, are listed in Table 22. These twenty-eight variables were intercorrelated and the results are reported in Tables 23 through 30. Some of the correlates were

[1] Much of the material in this chapter is based upon work done by, or under the supervision of, William Dubin.

TABLE 22. Correlates of Vocational Maturity

*Presumed Predictor Variables*
  Intelligence
  Socioeconomic Status
    Parental Occupational Level [a]
    House Rating [a]
    Father's Educational Level [a]
    Mother's Educational Level [a]
    Cultural Stimulation
  Family Relationships
    Family Cohesiveness
    Father Identification
  Level of Aspiration
    Boy's Vocational Aspiration Level [a]
    Agreement between Levels of Vocational Aspiration and Expectation
    School Curriculum
    Presence of Parental Vocational Aspiration for Boy
    Parental Mobility
    Family Social Mobility
  Psychological Adjustment
    Thematic Aperception Test [a]
    Incomplete Sentences Blank [a]
*Criteria of Achievement in Various Areas*
  Peer Acceptance
  Participation in School Activities
  Participation in Out-of-School Activities
  Adolescent Independence
  School Achievement: Grades
  School Achievement vs. Underachievement
*Miscellaneous Variables*
  Age
  Birth Order [a]
  Urban vs. Rural Residence
  Religious Affiliation: Protestant
  Religious Affiliation: Catholic
  Intrinsic–Extrinsic Work Values [a]

[a] Signs of coefficients of correlation reported in this chapter and in Chapter VI that involved these variables were reversed when necessary.

treated as continuous measurements, while others were dichotomized. Pearson product-moment coefficients of correlation were
computed between the continuous measures. The coefficients of
correlation between dichotomized and continuous measures are
point-biserial $r$'s, and those between the dichotomized measures
are four-point coefficients.

High scores on most of the correlates represent a greater amount
of the trait or characteristic measured and low scores represent a
lesser amount. However, in some instances (shown in Table 22)

the opposite is true. For example, high ratings of parental occupational level indicate low socioeconomic status, and high scores on the two measures of adjustment indicate maladjustment. Signs were reversed when necessary in reporting coefficients of correlation, in order to report all relationships in a consistent manner.

Some scores were lacking on fifteen of the twenty-eight correlates. In these instances filler scores were used for statistical computation. Details are given in Appendix B.

## PRESUMED PREDICTOR VARIABLES

From various studies reported in the literature and from logical analysis of seemingly important influences on vocational behavior, certain correlates have been grouped as presumed predictors of vocational maturity. These were classified under the following headings: intelligence, socioeconomic status, family relationships, level of aspiration, and psychological adjustment.

### Intelligence

One would expect positive relationships between intelligence and behavior considered indicative of vocational maturity, because the more intelligent an individual is, the more capable one would expect him to be in dealing with developmental tasks in various areas of behavior, including the vocational. Findings in support of this expectation are seen in Terman's studies of the intellectually gifted: his subjects, all highly intelligent, have, in general, adjusted well in various areas of life—vocational, marital, etc. (Terman & Oden, 1947). Studies by Grace (1931), Sparling (1933), and Wrenn (1935) have demonstrated a positive relationship between intelligence and appropriate vocational goals.

The measure of intelligence used in our work at the ninth-grade level was the Otis Quick-Scoring Test of Mental Ability, Gamma, Form C. It was administered to entering ninth-graders by the staff of the high school in October, 1951. The mean Otis Gamma IQ of the core group was 102.47, with a standard deviation of 10.33. Otis Gamma IQ's represent the amount by which an obtained score exceeds or falls below the norm (defined in the test manual as the median score) for the individual's age added to or subtracted from 100. The Gamma IQ tends to be somewhat nearer 100 than do IQ's obtained by computing the ratio of mental age to chronological age.

### Socioeconomic Status

Various studies have demonstrated a relationship between socioeconomic status and vocational behavior. The work of Hollingshead (1949) showed the effects of socioeconomic differences, in the relatively static community of "Elmtown," upon the kinds of vocations young people entered. The American Council on Education survey of youth in Maryland during the depression (Bell, 1938) also demonstrated relationships between socioeconomic status and such matters as amount of schooling, ability to obtain employment, and type of employment obtained. Whether socioeconomic status is related to maturity of vocational behavior, and if so, in what ways it may be related to such behavior, is unknown. We hypothesized that the more favorable the socioeconomic status, the more mature the vocational behavior, on the assumption that more planful types of behavior are encouraged at the higher socioeconomic levels (see, for example, Ginzberg, 1948; Reynolds and Shister, 1949) and that planfulness is indicative of vocational maturity. Several different methods of assessing socioeconomic status were used in the Career Pattern Study. The intercorrelations among the measures are shown in Table 23; all relationships were statistically significant.

TABLE 23. INTERCORRELATIONS AMONG MEASURES OF
SOCIOECONOMIC STATUS

|  | Parental Occ. Level | House Rating | Father's Educ. Level | Mother's Educ. Level | Cult. Stimulation |
|---|---|---|---|---|---|
| Parental Occupational Level | .. | .32 | .45 | .48 | .41 |
| House Rating | | .. | .30 | .23 | .24 |
| Father's Educational Level | | | .. | .50 | .42 |
| Mother's Educational Level | | | | .. | .38 |
| Cultural Stimulation | | | | | .. |

Note.—A correlation coefficient of .164 is significant at the .05 level, and of .230 at the .01 level, one-tailed test.

PARENTAL OCCUPATIONAL LEVEL.—Parental occupational level was assessed by rating the occupational level of the principal breadwinner in the family, usually the father. A revision by Hamburger (1958) of the occupational rating scale in the Index of Status Characteristics (Warner, Meeker, & Eells, 1949) was employed.

The Warner Index of Status Characteristics combines ratings of occupation, source of income, type of house, and dwelling area into a weighted total, which is then converted into a rating of social class. In this procedure the occupational rating is weighted more heavily than the other variables. The Warner occupational rating scale is a modification of the Edwards occupational classification which was prepared for the United States Census; it takes account of gradations within occupational groups in skill and in prestige (Warner et al., 1949, p. 136), thus allowing for differences in level within an occupational group, as well as for differences between occupational groups.

The Hamburger revision uses ratings of occupations exclusively. It is similar to the original Warner occupational rating scale; the occupational categories are based on a modification of the Warner framework. In constructing the revision, consideration was given to the methods and findings of North and Hatt (National Opinion Research Center, 1947), Stubbins (1950), Roe (1956), Caplow (1954), and Thomas (1956). The Hamburger classification of occupations reflects consideration of prestige, income, amount of responsibility, levels of education and of skill, and behavior control. The social prestige of the occupation and its economic rewards were the factors given most consideration in establishing the revised classification.

The scale consists of seven levels, ranging from level one (including professions such as physician and lawyer; proprietors, managers, and officials of large businesses; and wealthy landowners) through level seven (including heavy manual labor of a non-regular kind; porters and messenger boys; migratory farm workers, and non-paying tenants on farms of relatively little economic value).

Two judges rated the parental occupations of boys in the study according to the manual for the Hamburger revision of the Warner Scale. Instances of disagreement in rating were discussed and 100 per cent agreement was reached. Ratings for the group were distributed as shown in Table 24. It is evident that the parental occupations of the Career Pattern Study core group tended to fall at

TABLE 24. DISTRIBUTION OF RATINGS OF
PARENTAL OCCUPATIONAL LEVEL

| Level | Frequency |
|---|---|
| 1 | 2 |
| 2 | 5 |
| 3 | 16 |
| 4 | 27 |
| 5 | 28 |
| 6 | 24 |
| 7 | 3 |

or below the middle level of the scale. The mean rating was 4.50, with a standard deviation of 1.30.

HOUSE RATING.—Ratings of the houses in which the subjects of the study lived were used as another method of assessing socio-economic status. The rating technique was adapted from the one used as part of the Warner Index of Status Characteristics, to which reference has been made in the preceding section. Houses were rated on a seven-point scale, ranging from ratings of one, for houses considered "excellent," through seven, for "very poor houses." Minor modifications had to be made in the criteria for assignment to categories developed by Warner and his associates (Warner et al., 1949, pp. 149–150), in order to make them appropriate to the Middletown situation.[2] Two judges independently rated forty-seven houses from the total ninth-grade group. Making the assumption of a continuous scale, a product-moment correlation between the two sets of ratings was computed, and a coefficient of .90 was obtained.

TABLE 25. DISTRIBUTION OF HOUSE RATINGS

| Rank | Frequency |
|---|---|
| 1 | 0 |
| 2 | 0 |
| 3 | 8 |
| 4 | 50 |
| 5 | 30 |
| 6 | 9 |
| 7 | 8 |

[2] In the Career Pattern Study ratings, less emphasis was given to amount of yard space than in the Warner criteria; front and side yards of any size are rare in Middletown, back yards are more frequent. The adaptation of Warner's procedure and the ratings were made by Charles F. Warnath and Charles S. Nicholas.

As indicated in Table 25, the distribution of ratings of house type was concentrated at points four and five on the scale (the "small house" categorizable as "average" or "fair"). This is consistent with the middle to lower-middle distribution of ratings on the occupational scale described in the preceding section. The mean house rating was 4.61, with a standard deviation of 1.01. The coefficient of correlation between occupational level and house ratings, .32, was not large, but was statistically significant at the .01 level.

FATHER'S EDUCATIONAL LEVEL AND MOTHER'S EDUCATIONAL LEVEL. —The level of education obtained by each of the parents was also classified on a seven-point scale, ranging from a rating of one (college plus professional school) through seven (less than grammar school graduation).[3]

The mean rating of the fathers' educational level was 5.42, which indicates that the average father had completed slightly more than eight grades of school. The standard deviation was 1.41. The mean rating of the mothers' educational level was 4.99, indicating some high school but less than high school graduation. The standard deviation was 1.36. The mothers had had slightly more education than the fathers.

CULTURAL STIMULATION.—This measure was obtained from a scale of the Biographical Inventory (one of the paper-and-pencil tests administered to the boys in the Career Pattern Study sample). The Biographical Inventory was developed specifically for the Career Pattern Study by Donald E. Super and others,[4] on the basis of previous research in the Air Force and a thesis by Craven (1958). The Biographical Inventory is a device to collect and to organize data about life experiences, for use in personality description or vocational prediction. The rationale for its use is based on the assump-

---

[3] The scale for classifying education was developed by Martha M. Heyde. For further information, see Heyde (1959).

[4] Junius A. Davis, Martin Hamburger, Charles F. Warnath, Martha B. Heyde, Lester Luntz, Raymond C. Hummel, and Helen P. Moser. Detailed information concerning the biographical inventory technique may be found in Super, D. E., & Luntz, L. Some uses of biographical inventories in describing adjustment and predicting success. Office for Social Science Programs, Air Force Personnel and Training Research Center, Technical Memorandum 57-1.

tion that factors in one's past or present life situation will affect present or future behavior.

The version of the Biographical Inventory used at the ninth-grade level by the Career Pattern Study is a multiple-choice test of sixty-five items about a variety of experiences which individuals may have had by early adolescence. There are from two through as many as twenty-five possible choices. Internally consistent scales were developed by item analysis procedures, using Flanagan's tables and rejecting items that correlated less than .35 with the total scores of their scales. The scales were found to be relatively independent of each other: with one exception the intercorrelations among the scales ranged from .00 through .33 in a study of the total ninth-grade group (Super & Luntz). Five scales were developed: Cultural Stimulation, Socioeconomic Status, Social Mobility, Family Cohesiveness, and Adolescent Independence. All scales except Socioeconomic Status were used as correlates; the latter was omitted because of its substantial correlation (.71) with Cultural Stimulation and because several other better established methods of evaluating socioeconomic status were used.

The Cultural Stimulation scale of the Biographical Inventory was significantly correlated with the other measures of socioeconomic status, as reported in Table 23. As its name implies, Cultural Stimulation inventoried a variety of cultural experiences (intellectual, artistic, literary, and scientific). Its relationship to such variables as parental occupational level and parental educational level suggests that, as one might reasonably expect, cultural experiences are more likely to be provided in homes where there is more opportunity to provide them.

*Family Relationships*

Two aspects of family relationships were measured as correlates and were classified as presumed predictor variables: family cohesiveness and father identification. Family cohesiveness was considered a predictor of vocational maturity on the assumption that a cohesive family offers a favorable environment for development in all areas, including the vocational. Father identification was considered a predictor of vocational maturity on the assumption that a boy in early adolescence who identifies with his father will find it easier to learn the male role and thus will have less difficulty with various vocational developmental tasks than the boy who does not identify with his father. The two measures had a rather low positive correlation of .25, significant at the .01 level.

FAMILY COHESIVENESS.—This correlate is one of the scales of the Biographical Inventory, which has been described. The Family Cohesiveness scale attempts to measure the extent to which the subject shares experiences with other family members, through play, work, planning together, and in other ways (Super & Luntz). Its correlations with the other Biographical Inventory scales used in our analysis were as follows: with Adolescent Independence, .25; with Cultural Stimulation, −.09; and with Social Mobility, .04.

FATHER IDENTIFICATION.—The Father Identification Test was administered in a group situation to the Career Pattern Study sample.[5] It consists of 165 scored items, from which five sub-scores and a total score were obtained. For the Career Pattern Study intercorrelational analysis, the total score was used. "Within the content of the ID [Father Identification] test, the son's perceptions of the presence or absense of conditions necessary for identification, the son's perceptions of his feelings for his father, and his attitudinal and behavioral similarity to his father, are all considered to be identification dimensions." (Henderson, 1958, p. 45)

The internal consistency of the Father Identification Test for the ninth-grade sample was .87 using the Kuder–Richardson method, or .91 as estimated with Spearman–Brown (Henderson, 1958, p. 51).

## Level of Aspiration

It seems reasonable to assume that the vocational level to which an individual aspires reflects his achievement drive. Furthermore, it may be proposed that an individual's achievement drive is related to his vocational maturity. Presumably, the greater the individual's need to achieve, the earlier he will begin to deal with the task of making vocational choices, if his achievement needs are channeled into vocational areas. This may result in unrealistic and

[5] This test was developed by Harold L. Henderson (1958).

inappropriate choices in some instances, but on the other hand it may tend to produce greater concern with choice and more frequent choice-oriented behaviors.

Having made these assumptions, various measures of level of aspiration were grouped together as presumed predictors of vocational maturity. It is probable that some of these measures reflect achievement drive rather directly (Boy's Vocational Aspiration Level, Agreement between Levels of Vocational Aspiration and Expectation); others reflect some of the sources of the drive, that is, the pressures upon the individual to achieve (Presence of Parental Vocational Aspiration for Boy, Parental Mobility, Social Mobility of the Family); at least one other (School Curriculum) is a composite.

Intercorrelations among the various measures of level of aspiration are given in Table 26. Only two of the fifteen coefficients were

TABLE 26. Intercorrelations among Measures of
Level of Aspiration

|  | Boy's Voc. Asp. Level | Agree.: Levels of Voc. Asp. and Expec. | School Curriculum | Pres. of Par. Voc. Asp. for Boy | Par. Mobility | Family Social Mobility |
|---|---|---|---|---|---|---|
| Boy's Vocational Aspiration Level | .. | .09 | .20 | .04 | −.10 | .10 |
| Agreement between Levels of Vocational Aspiration and Expectation |  | .. | −.04 | −.02 | −.04 | .05 |
| School Curriculum |  |  | .. | −.02 | .22 | −.01 |
| Presence of Parental Vocational Aspiration for Boy |  |  |  | .. | −.01 | .02 |
| Parental Mobility |  |  |  |  | .. | .04 |
| Family Social Mobility |  |  |  |  |  | .. |

Note.—A correlation coefficient of .164 is significant at the .05 level, and of .230 at the .01 level, one-tailed test.

statistically significant (at the .05 level): School Curriculum as correlated with Boy's Vocational Aspiration Level, and School Curriculum as correlated with Parental Mobility. The lack of relationship among the other variables throws doubt upon the assumption that they are measuring different aspects of the same underlying construct (achievement need or its manifestation in achievement drive). The idea that they are all predictors of vocational maturity therefore seems doubtful. Nevertheless, the six variables will be described, because their relationships to vocational maturity indices were investigated, and because an understanding of the variables used is, of course, necessary to an understanding of the findings.

BOY'S VOCATIONAL ASPIRATION LEVEL.—This measure was obtained by rating the boy's first vocational choice, as given in the fourth interview, which dealt with future plans. Level of choice was rated on the Hamburger revision of the Warner Scale. Interjudge reliability in rating level of vocational aspiration for the entire sample was very high: the product-moment correlation between the ratings assigned by two judges was .98.

The mean vocational aspiration level as rated on the seven-point scale was 3.02, with a standard deviation of 1.43. In contrast, the mean level of the parental occupations was 4.50 on the same scale. The boys tended, on the average, to aspire to occupations which were about one-and-one-half steps higher in occupational level than were the occupations of their fathers. Such a tendency is not surprising in our culture, where upward occupational mobility is encouraged and where a considerable amount of mobility is possible. Especially because the boys were, on the average, from middle-class and lower-middle-class homes, this trend was to have been expected. If they had been generally from homes at higher socioeconomic levels, it is probable that the average level of their aspirations and that of their parents' occupations would tend to coincide.

It is surprising that the level of the boys' vocational aspirations was not related to the mobility measures nor to whether the parents had aspirations for the boys. The lack of relationship may be due to inadequacies in the measures used. The significant relationship to school curriculum is understandable, because the higher the aspiration level, the more education will presumably be required to attain the goal.

AGREEMENT BETWEEN LEVELS OF VOCATIONAL ASPIRATION AND EXPECTATION.—Through a Life Planning Questionnaire,[6] information was obtained about the subjects' educational and vocational

---

[6] Developed by Martin Hamburger. For additional information about the questionnaire, see Hamburger (1958).

plans on both a presumed fantasy level (aspiration) and a realistic level (expectation). Ratings of level were made, using the Hamburger revision of the Warner Scale. In statistical treatment of the data, two categories were used: 1) a category, assigned a score of one, for cases where aspiration and expectation were at essentially the same level (plus or minus one step on the scale); and 2) a category, assigned a score of zero, for cases having a large discrepancy between levels of aspiration and expectation, and also for cases where no expected occupation was indicated. Most of the cases in the second category were of the latter kind; therefore, the dichotomy was largely those whose levels of vocational aspiration and expectation agreed versus those who made no statement of expected occupation.

There were 67 cases in the first category and 36 cases in the second category.[7] A majority of boys in the core group, then, tended to have little, if any, discrepancy between the levels of the occupations to which they aspired and those which they expected to enter. This does not necessarily mean that their choices were realistic, but rather that their levels of occupational aspiration and expectation tended to agree. As indicated in Table 26, this measure was not significantly related to any of the other presumed measures of level of aspiration.

School Curriculum.—Required courses at Middletown High School are given at both Regents and non-Regents levels, as described in Chapter II. Students who plan to attend college are more likely to be in the Regents-level sections of the courses. In preparing the variable School Curriculum for statistical analysis, all members of the core group who were in the non-Regents sections (N = 25) were put in one category (scored zero) and all those who were in the Regents sections (N = 80) were put in another category (scored one). The dichotomized variable was then correlated with other variables.

In spite of the large number in the Regents category as compared to the small number in the non-Regents category, this correlate had statistically significant, but low, relationships to two of the other presumed measures of level of aspiration (Boy's Vocational Aspiration Level and Parental Mobility). Apparently, the

[7] Two cases lacked data on this variable, as indicated in Appendix B.

higher the individual's own level of vocational aspiration and the more occupationally mobile the parents, the more frequently the individual was in the Regents sections of required courses, which demanded more effort.

PRESENCE OF PARENTAL VOCATIONAL ASPIRATION FOR BOY.—This variable was also treated as a dichotomy. Information concerning parental aspirations for their sons was obtained from the interviews with the parents.[8] These data were categorized as follows: 1) no specific vocational aspiration or no mention of such an aspiration for the son was scored zero; and 2) either a specific or a general vocational aspiration for the son was scored one. This is, then, essentially a measure of whether or not parents say they have aspirations for their children; it is not a measure of the level of such aspirations. It was not significantly related to other correlates classified as measures of level of aspiration.

PARENTAL MOBILITY.—When the parents were interviewed, they were asked about their own occupations and the occupations of their parents, in order to obtain information for evaluating the occupational mobility of the boys' families.[9] The levels of parental and grandparental occupations were rated according to the original Warner Scale, as slightly modified for Career Pattern Study work. Three categories were used for statistical analysis: 1) a category, assigned a score of zero, for downward mobile families, in which the parental occupational level was two or three steps below the grandparental occupational level on the Warner Scale; 2) a category, assigned a score of one, for relatively non-mobile families, in which the parental occupational level was equal to or was one step above or below the grandparental occupational level; and 3) a category, assigned a score of two, for upward mobile families, in which the parental occupational level was two or more steps above the grandparental occupational level. Best estimates were made in cases where the grandparental occupational level could not be clearly specified from the data.

A majority of the scores were in the second category, non-mobile,

[8] Charles S. Nicholas obtained the pertinent information by a content analysis of the parent interviews. See Nicholas (1958).
[9] These data were prepared by Mrs. Heyde.

scored one. In spite of the concentration of scores in one category, Parental Mobility had a small but significant correlation with School Curriculum. It was not related to the other variables in Table 26, however. The large number of indeterminate scores on the measure of Parental Mobility, as indicated in Appendix B, may explain the lack of significant results with this variable.

FAMILY SOCIAL MOBILITY.—A somewhat different measure of mobility was obtained from the Social Mobility scale of the Biographical Inventory. The Social Mobility scale of this test was designed to evaluate the mobility of the family, as inferred from the boys' perceptions of upward or downward movement in socioeconomic status. This scale correlated .00 with the Cultural Stimulation scale and .02 with the Socioeconomic Status scale of the Biographical Inventory, in a study of the entire ninth-grade sample (Super & Luntz). It correlated .05 with the Cultural Stimulation scale in the core group sample. Apparently, therefore, the Social Mobility scale is not measuring the same thing as the Cultural Stimulation and Socioeconomic Status scales. Social Mobility as assessed by the Biographical Inventory did not correlate significantly with any of the other presumed measures of level of aspiration, including Parental Mobility (see Table 26). Its failure to correlate with Parental Mobility may be due to the fact that the Biographical Inventory measure of Family Social Mobility was based on material reported by the boys, while the Parental Mobility measure was based on material reported by the parents, or it may be due to the number of indeterminate scores in the measure of parental mobility.

### Psychological Adjustment

The effects of personality traits and of psychological adjustment upon vocational choice and vocational adjustment have been the subject of much speculation and some research. Although some relationships have been found between personality traits and vocations entered, findings are not clear-cut and much work remains to be done in this broad area of investigation.[10]

No structured personality test was used with the Career Pattern

10 For discussions of the subject see Darley & Hagenah (1955), Roe (1956), Super (1949, 1957), Super & Bachrach (1957).

Study subjects at the ninth-grade level. Two different instruments were employed to assess psychological adjustment, the Thematic Apperception Test and the Incomplete Sentences Blank. Both of these measures were classified as presumed predictors of vocational maturity, on the assumption that individuals who are better adjusted are freer to deal with developmental tasks than are less well-adjusted individuals.

THEMATIC APPERCEPTION TEST (TAT).—The Thematic Apperception Test was individually administered to the subjects of the Career Pattern Study; fifteen cards of the TAT series were used.[11] Stories were tape-recorded, and scoring was done from typescripts of the protocols.

The method of scoring used in this study was not based on the need-press frame of reference usually employed. An attempt was made to devise a method which would yield one score indicative of general adjustment, based on all cards.[12] Dymond has developed a method of making composite ratings of TAT records for adjustment (Rogers & Dymond, 1954, Chapter 8), and use was made of her ideas, particularly her scaling of degree of adjustment, in the method used in the Career Pattern Study. Rotter's approach to assessing adjustment with the Incomplete Sentences Blank (Rotter & Rafferty, 1950), in which conflict responses are considered indicative of maladjustment and positive responses are considered indicative of adjustment, was also drawn upon in developing the Career Pattern Study method of scoring the TAT.

Inter-judge reliability in scoring the protocols according to the Career Pattern Study technique was determined by correlating the scores assigned by two judges, working independently, in twenty-five cases selected at random. The rank-order correlation was .77.

The TAT adjustment score had a low negative correlation with the Incomplete Sentences Blank (-.17). Examination of Table 28 shows that the TAT had statistically significant positive correlations with the following variables: Peer Acceptance (.32), Partici-

---

[11] The cards selected were 1, 2, 3BM, 4, 5, 6BM, 7BM, 8BM, 9BM, 10, 12BG, 13B, 14, 16, 17BM.

[12] The method was devised by Phoebe L. Overstreet. For details of the scoring procedure, see Appendix B.

pation in School Activities (.31), Participation in Out-of-School Activities (.21), and Cultural Stimulation (.19). Thus the TAT, as scored by the Career Pattern Study method, seems to assess aspects of adjustment relevant to peer relationships.

INCOMPLETE SENTENCES BLANK (ISB).—An adaptation of the Rotter Incomplete Sentences Blank closely resembling the original High School Form was administered to the Career Pattern Study subjects, in a group testing situation. Eleven boys in the core group did not take the test, and filler scores were used for them. Rotter's test has forty stems of sentences (incomplete sentences), which the subject is instructed to complete. In the Career Pattern Study adaptation, all of Rotter's stems were used, with a slight alteration in the phrasing of one of them, and seventeen additional stems were added. The additional stems were not used in the scoring for adjustment reported here.

Scoring criteria for high school boys were obtained from an unpublished manual prepared by Rotter (see Chapter II). Interjudge reliability in scoring has been high. In a study by Rotter, Rafferty, and Lotsof (1954) the correlation between scores assigned fifty high-school-male protocols by two judges was .96. An interjudge reliability coefficient of .96 was also found when two judges scored a sample of Career Pattern Study test protocols, and a coefficient of .99 was obtained by two other judges using a different group of Career Pattern Study protocols.

Rotter, Rafferty, and Lotsof (1954) assessed the internal consistency of the Incomplete Sentences Blank by determining odd-even reliability. The tests of fifty high school males and fifty high school females were studied. The corrected coefficients were .74 for males and .86 for females. However, as the authors noted, an odd-even coefficient may not accurately assess the internal consistency of the test. Different stems may evoke different areas of conflict, but odd and even items may not be equated in this respect. Therefore, in determining the split-half reliability of the ISB in the Career Pattern Study group, an attempt was made to set up equivalent halves of the test by matching stems for each half on the basis of subjective judgments of their response-evoking equivalence. For example, the stem "Boys" was assigned to one half and the stem "Other kids" to the other half, "Dating" to one half and "Dancing" to the other, and so on. Using the tests of fifty core group boys, a split-half coefficient of .80 was obtained, corrected to .89 by the Spearman–Brown formula.

Rotter found a cut-off score of 135 on his test to be useful in separating adjusted from maladjusted college students (Rotter & Rafferty, 1950, pp. 9–10). (As pointed out previously, high scores on the test are considered unfavorable.) Ten boys of the ninety-three in the Career Pattern Study core group who took the Incomplete Sentences Blank made scores of 135 or higher, which suggests that the distribution was restricted in terms of number of maladjusted individuals, as measured by this test. This is not surprising in a group of presumably normal young persons. Ten per cent of Rotter's adjusted college males made scores of 135 or above (Rotter & Rafferty, 1950, Table II, p. 9); 11 per cent of the Career Pattern Study group made such scores. However, 22 per cent of Rotter's normal high school boys had scores of 135 or above (Rotter, Rafferty, & Lotsof, 1954).

An examination of Tables 28 and 30 indicates that the ISB had generally low but significant positive correlations with Father Identification (.21), two measures of socioeconomic status (Parental Occupational Level, .26; and Father's Educational Level, .18), and urban rather than rural residence (.22). It had a low but significant negative correlation with age (–.20).

As pointed out in the preceding section, the correlation of the TAT and the ISB was low and negative, thereby not supporting the hypothesized positive relationship. Why the two projective tests were unrelated is not clear. Their lack of relationship may indicate that they measure different aspects of adjustment; each is related to a somewhat different cluster of variables in the matrix of intercorrelations. Another possible explanation of the lack of relationship between these two presumed measures of adjustment is that they assess feelings at different levels of the personality. Our data do not allow us to decide whether either of these explanations is correct, but the findings confirm the importance of using a variety of approaches to the evaluation of adjustment, when the aim is to get a rather complete description of the individuals being studied.

### CRITERIA OF ACHIEVEMENT IN VARIOUS AREAS

The correlates that have been described in the preceding sections of this chapter were classified as variables predictive of vocational maturity. Although cause and effect relationships cannot be demonstrated in an intercorrelational study of this kind, implicit in the classification of these variables as presumed predictors is the hypothesis that they are determinants of vocational maturity.

The correlates to be described in this section of the chapter are thought to be indicative of achievement in interpersonal relationships or in academic work. No assumption of a causal relationship to vocational maturity is made. However, if establishing effective peer relationships and handling school work efficiently are considered developmental tasks of adolescence, and if success with some developmental tasks is considered related to success with others, then it may be assumed that vocational maturity is related to achievement in other areas. A hypothetical construct of general maturity may be the mediating factor, or a hypothetical construct of effective functioning.

Intercorrelations among the achievement variables are given in Table 27. Nine of the fifteen coefficients of correlation were statistically significant at either the .05 or the .01 level.

### Peer Acceptance

One important aspect of functioning is the way an individual gets along with others. One method of assessing the quality of an individual's interpersonal relationships is to find out what others think of him. A generally accepted technique for this purpose is the Guess Who Test, in which peers show their reactions to each other by indicating persons whom they believe to fit various descriptions. Two items in the Guess Who Test used by the Career Pattern Study are used as examples. 1) "Here is a good sport; he enjoys things, win or lose." 2) "This is a 'wise guy'; he tries to get attention by annoying others." [13]

---

[13] The Career Pattern Study form of the Guess Who Test used at the ninth-grade level was prepared by Martin Hamburger and staff.

TABLE 27. INTERCORRELATIONS AMONG ACHIEVEMENT VARIABLES

|  | Peer Accept- ance | Partic.: School Activ. | Partic.: Out-of Sch. Act. | Adoles- cent Indepen. | School Achieve.: Grades | School Achieve. vs. Underach. |
|---|---|---|---|---|---|---|
| Peer Acceptance | .. | .57 | .22 | .10 | .23 | .19 |
| Participation in School Activities |  | .. | .38 | −.02 | .13 | .11 |
| Participation in Out- of-School Activities |  |  | .. | .18 | .26 | .07 |
| Adolescent Independence |  |  |  | .. | .21 | .03 |
| School Achievement: Grades |  |  |  |  | .. | .60 |
| School Achievement vs. Underachievement |  |  |  |  |  | .. |

Note.—A correlation coefficient of .164 is significant at the .05 level, and of .230 at the .01 level, one-tailed test.

The total score on the test, used as a measure of peer acceptance, is the algebraic sum of the positive and negative descriptions as-signed to an individual by his peers. There was a wide range of scores, from −14, representing a fairly large number of unfavorable ratings, to +49, representing a very high number of favorable ratings. The mean score of 2.83 indicates that the average rating tended to be on the positive side, but not far from zero, and the large standard deviation (9.77) is consistent with the wide range of scores. Within most of its range the distribution of scores was fairly symmetrical, but six scores were rather high, with three of these being very high.

Peer Acceptance had statistically significant correlations at either the .05 or .01 level (.19 through .57) with all except one of the other achievement variables (see Table 27). The boy who elicited favorable reactions from his peers also tended to participate in activities both in school and in the community, to make good grades, and to achieve rather than to underachieve in school work.

## Participation in School Activities

To obtain this measure, the subjects were rated for amount of involvement in extracurricular school activities.[14] Variety of ac-tivities and intensity of involvement were considered in assigning the ratings. Almost half of the core group (51 cases) did not partici-

[14] The measure was developed by George R. Hudson. For additional information, see Hudson (1953).

pate in any extracurricular activity. For 32 of the 54 boys who did participate, the amount of participation tended to be rather slight. This was at least partly due to the fact that the boys were freshmen in high school and therefore were probably not as participant in extracurricular activities as they might become later.

Participation in School Activities was significantly related to Peer Acceptance (.57) and to Participation in Out-of-School Activities (.38). It was not significantly related to Adolescent Independence or to either of the measures of school achievement. Evidently, those who tended to be active in sports or organizations within a school setting were also somewhat more likely to be active in out-of-school activities than were the others. The participants in school activities also tended to be more positively evaluated by their peers, as measured by the Guess Who Test. Perhaps they were better known by their peers because of their participation in activities, and they may have made favorable impressions on others because of whatever social tendencies influenced their participation.

## Participation in Out-of-School Activities

The amount of participation in out-of-school activities within the community was rated.[15] Activities included were those involving membership in institutions or institution-sponsored organizations, such as churches, the YMCA, Boy Scouts, 4-H Clubs. Informal neighborhood gangs or other informally organized groups were not included. The rating was based on the number of organizations to which an individual belonged and the extent of his participation in them. When possible, extent of participation was rated in terms of attendance, offices held, and rank achieved.

Only 13 of the 105 boys did not participate in out-of-school activities, as contrasted with 51 who did not participate in school activities. These findings indicate that on the whole the boys did engage in some organized activity. The greater amount of participation in out-of-school activities reinforces the view that the boys' newness in high school was a factor in their in-school participation.

An examination of Table 27 shows that Participation in Out-of-School Activities was significantly related to Peer Acceptance (.22),

[15] This measure was also developed by Hudson (1953).

Participation in School Activities (.38), Adolescent Independence (.18), and school grades (.26). Its correlation with Peer Acceptance is not as high as the correlation between Participation in School Activities and Peer Acceptance. This is understandable, because the boys who filled out the Guess Who Test were classmates in school, and, as pointed out in the preceding section, they were more likely to know those classmates who were active in school affairs. It is difficult to understand why Participation in Out-of-School Activities was significantly related to school grades, while Participation in School Activities was not. Perhaps the smaller number of boys active in school organizations, as compared to the number active in non-school organizations, attenuated the correlation of the former with grades.

### Adolescent Independence

Adolescent Independence, a scale of the Biographical Inventory, assesses independence of action as shown by the ability to make plans and decisions and to carry out activities without close parental supervision or control (Super & Luntz).

As shown in Table 27, Adolescent Independence was significantly but not highly correlated with Participation in Out-of-School Activities (.18) and with grades (.26). It was not significantly related to the other achievement variables.

### School Achievement: Grades

School achievement in terms of grades was measured by averaging grades made in the three subjects required of all ninth-graders (English, general science, and citizenship education).

The distribution of averages (on a 1–100 scale) ranged from 57 through 92, with a mean for the core group of 76.30, and a standard deviation of 6.44. A grade of 65 was required for passing, and an average of 85 was required for the Honor Roll.

As previously indicated, required courses were given in Regents and non-Regents sections. Grading standards for the Regents sections were higher and the course work was more difficult. For our statistical work, however, grades were included in one distribution regardless of whether they were based on Regents or non-

Regents standards, because obtained grades indicate the student's achievement in the level of work required of him.

School grades were significantly related to all of the other achievement measures in Table 27 except Participation in School Activities. Most of the coefficients of correlation were rather low, however. The highest relationship (.60) was between grades and the other measure of school achievement, as would be expected.

### School Achievement versus Underachievement [16]

Regression equations were computed on the basis of the correlation between school grades and IQ. (Separate regression equations were computed for the Regents and non-Regents groups.) A boy was considered an achiever (and given a score of one) if his obtained grade average was above his predicted grade average. He was considered an underachiever (and given a score of zero) if his obtained grade average was below his predicted average. The group had slightly more achievers (N = 54) than underachievers (N = 48).[17]

Achievement versus Underachievement in school was significantly related to two of the five other achievement variables, as shown in Table 27. It was rather highly correlated, as was pointed out in the preceding section, with grades in school. It had a small but significant relationship to Peer Acceptance (.19). It was not significantly related to participation in either school or out-of-school activities, or to Adolescent Independence.

### RELATIONSHIPS AMONG PREDICTOR AND ACHIEVEMENT VARIABLES

All of the coefficients of correlation among the measures classified as predictor or achievement variables are shown in Table 28. The coefficients of correlation within categories already presented in Tables 23, 26, and 27 are included, but Table 28 also includes correlations between variables in different categories. A one-

---

[16] This measure was developed by Alvin J. Bernstein. For further information about it, see Bernstein (1953).

[17] Data were available for 102 cases.

## TABLE 28. INTERCORRELATIONS AMONG PREDICTOR AND ACHIEVEMENT VARIABLES

| | Intelligence | Parental Occ. Level | House Rating | Father's Ed. Level | Mother's Ed. Level | Cult. Stimulation | Fam. Cohesiveness | Father Identification | Boy's Voc. Asp. Level | Agree.: Levels of Asp. and Exp. | Sch. Curriculum | Parental Voc. Asp. | Parental Mobility | Fam. Soc. Mobility | TAT | ISB | Peer Acceptance | Participation: Sch. Activities | Participation: Out-of-Sch. Activities | Adolescent Independence | School Achievement: Grades | School Achievement vs. Underachievement |
|---|---|---|---|---|---|---|---|---|---|---|---|---|---|---|---|---|---|---|---|---|---|---|
| Intelligence | : | .27 | .11 | .27 | .01 | .34 | .24 | .04 | .32 | .01 | .56 | .12 | -.01 | -.06 | -.12 | .08 | .04 | .06 | .24 | .28 | .49 | -.11 |
| Parental Occupational Level | | : | .32 | .45 | .48 | .41 | .18 | .27 | .21 | .20 | .25 | .20 | -.31 | .10 | .10 | .11 | .26 | .19 | .23 | .17 | .36 | .18 |
| House Rating | | | : | .30 | .23 | .24 | .05 | .15 | .04 | .04 | .11 | .10 | -.04 | .04 | .03 | .03 | .06 | .15 | .03 | .12 | .18 | .04 |
| Father's Educational Level | | | | : | .50 | .38 | .24 | .18 | .04 | .03 | .00 | .11 | -.04 | .00 | .01 | .03 | .06 | .18 | .08 | .08 | .14 | -.03 |
| Mother's Educational Level | | | | | : | .38 | .24 | .30 | .23 | .08 | .03 | .10 | -.08 | .10 | .04 | .01 | .02 | .18 | .05 | .19 | .22 | .17 |
| Cultural Stimulation | | | | | | : | .38 | .26 | .07 | .05 | .02 | -.02 | .08 | .08 | -.01 | .04 | .13 | .22 | .19 | .31 | .25 | .07 |
| Family Cohesiveness | | | | | | | : | .25 | .12 | .03 | -.06 | .06 | .04 | -.04 | .03 | .04 | .13 | .07 | .22 | .10 | .18 | .00 |
| Father Identification | | | | | | | | : | .23 | .05 | .10 | .10 | .06 | .03 | .10 | -.14 | .21 | .18 | .06 | .28 | .31 | .13 |
| Boy's Vocational Aspiration Level | | | | | | | | | : | .09 | .23 | .10 | .04 | .10 | .05 | -.07 | .05 | .18 | .29 | .16 | -.04 | .16 |
| Agreement: Levels of Vocational Aspiration & Expectation | | | | | | | | | | : | -.04 | -.02 | -.02 | -.04 | .05 | -.14 | -.03 | .15 | .08 | .21 | .01 | -.04 |
| School Curriculum | | | | | | | | | | | : | -.04 | -.01 | -.15 | .03 | -.11 | .05 | .04 | .08 | .02 | -.02 | -.14 |
| Presence of Parental Vocational Aspirations for Boy | | | | | | | | | | | | : | .04 | -.02 | -.18 | .00 | -.11 | .00 | .01 | -.19 | -.03 | -.05 |
| Parental Mobility | | | | | | | | | | | | | : | -.01 | .06 | .00 | -.15 | .01 | -.10 | .00 | .00 | .08 |
| Family Social Mobility | | | | | | | | | | | | | | : | .04 | -.10 | .07 | .05 | -.18 | .21 | .23 | .14 |
| Thematic Apperception Test | | | | | | | | | | | | | | | : | -.10 | -.02 | -.08 | -.01 | .00 | .16 | .09 |
| Incomplete Sentences Blank | | | | | | | | | | | | | | | | : | -.17 | .32 | .31 | -.05 | .26 | .11 |
| Peer Acceptance | | | | | | | | | | | | | | | | | : | -.15 | .00 | .02 | .21 | .11 |
| Participation in School Activities | | | | | | | | | | | | | | | | | | : | .57 | .10 | .23 | .11 |
| Participation in Out-of-School Activities | | | | | | | | | | | | | | | | | | | : | .18 | .26 | .07 |
| Adolescent Independence | | | | | | | | | | | | | | | | | | | | : | .21 | .03 |
| School Achievement: Grades | | | | | | | | | | | | | | | | | | | | | : | .60 |
| School Achievement vs. Underachievement | | | | | | | | | | | | | | | | | | | | | | : |

Note.—A correlation coefficient of .164 is significant at the .05 level, and of .230 at the .01 level, one-tailed test.

tailed test of significance was used, on the assumption that the predictor and achievement variables should be positively related to each other. Detailed discusion of the between-category relationships is beyond the scope of this monograph, but it is interesting to note two variables, socioeconomic status as assessed by parental occupational level and participation in out-of-school activities, which had the greatest number of statistically significant relationships with other variables. However, the coefficients of correlation in the table are not all independent of each other.

## MISCELLANEOUS VARIABLES

The remaining six variables are described in this section of the chapter, but their interrelationships are not discussed, because they do not constitute a meaningful grouping. They were grouped together because they did not seem to fit into any of the other categories used in this chapter to classify the correlates, not because it was felt that they logically belonged together. Intercorrelations among these miscellaneous variables are shown in Table 29, and intercorrelations between these variables and others classified as predictors or as criteria of achievement are given in Table 30.

TABLE 29. INTERCORRELATIONS AMONG MISCELLANEOUS VARIABLES

|  | *Age* | *Birth Order* | *Urban– Rural* | *Protes- tant* | *Cath- olic* | *Intr.–Extr. Values* |
|---|---|---|---|---|---|---|
| Age | .. | −.06 | .01 | −.22 | .21 | .09 |
| Birth Order |  | .. | .00 | −.10 | −.01 | .07 |
| Urban–Rural |  |  | .. | .04 | .01 | .13 |
| Protestant |  |  |  | .. | −.87 | −.19 |
| Catholic |  |  |  |  | .. | .12 |
| Intrinsic–Extrinsic Work Values |  |  |  |  |  | .. |

Note.—A correlation coefficient of .195 is significant at the .05 level, and of .254 at the .01 level, two-tailed test.

### Age

The average age of the boys in the core group was 14 years, 4 months, with a standard deviation of 10.28 months. (Further information is given in Chapter II, Table 10.)

TABLE 30. CORRELATIONS BETWEEN MISCELLANEOUS VARIABLES
AND PREDICTOR AND ACHIEVEMENT VARIABLES

| Predictor and Achievement Variables | Age | Birth Order | Urban– Rural | Protes- tant | Cath- olic | Intr.- Extr. |
|---|---|---|---|---|---|---|
| Intelligence | −.61 | .16 | −.03 | .02 | −.10 | .03 |
| Parental Occupational Level | −.17 | .16 | .08 | .00 | −.10 | .07 |
| House Rating | −.10 | .05 | .08 | .13 | −.18 | −.04 |
| Father's Educational Level | −.27 | .13 | .13 | .16 | −.22 | .07 |
| Mother's Educational Level | −.08 | .15 | .11 | .08 | −.09 | .08 |
| Cultural Stimulation | −.25 | .13 | .12 | −.01 | −.05 | .12 |
| Family Cohesiveness | −.26 | .05 | −.02 | .04 | −.04 | .16 |
| Father Identification | −.18 | .12 | −.04 | −.04 | .04 | .03 |
| Boy's Vocational Aspiration Level | −.21 | .01 | .14 | −.27 | .24 | .00 |
| Agreement between Levels of Vocation Aspiration and Expectation | −.04 | −.15 | −.11 | .07 | −.09 | .05 |
| School Curriculum | −.38 | .21 | −.01 | .05 | −.03 | −.02 |
| Presence of Parental Vocational Aspiration for Boy | .04 | .06 | −.02 | −.20 | .13 | −.09 |
| Parental Mobility | −.02 | .21 | −.22 | −.08 | .11 | −.01 |
| Family Social Mobility | .01 | .11 | .17 | −.04 | .07 | .04 |
| Thematic Apperception Test | .10 | .03 | .14 | −.08 | .02 | −.08 |
| Incomplete Sentences Blank | −.20 | .02 | .22 | .01 | −.07 | −.08 |
| Peer Acceptance | .08 | .04 | .07 | −.12 | .06 | .07 |
| Participation: School Activities | .12 | .00 | .18 | −.23 | .09 | .06 |
| Participation: Out-of-School Activities | −.11 | .03 | .34 | .02 | −.04 | .05 |
| Adolescent Independence | −.23 | .17 | −.01 | .23 | −.24 | .21 |
| School Achievement: Grades | −.29 | .16 | .05 | −.11 | −.01 | .14 |
| School Achievement vs. Underachievement | .10 | .07 | .10 | −.13 | .04 | .10 |

Note.—A correlation coefficient of .195 is significant at the .05 level, and of .254 at the .01 level, two-tailed test.

Although it was hypothesized that age would be positively related to vocational maturity over a period of time, one would not expect to find this relationship with a group of boys of varying ages who were in the same grade in school. Some selection had inevitably occurred, so that the older boys tended to be less intelligent than the younger ones within the same class. The correlation between age and IQ for the Career Pattern Study core group was −.61, which is a substantial negative correlation. Less intelligent individuals are presumably less able to deal with various developmental tasks; on the other hand, the older, less intelligent boys would have had more time for attempting to deal with developmental tasks than younger but more intelligent boys.

## Birth Order

Birth order was one of the variables selected for study, because studies of natural scientists have found that they tend to be only children or eldest sons (Roe, 1953; Super & Bachrach, 1957). If position in the family is a factor in selecting natural science as an occupational field, it might also be a factor in other occupational choices.

Two categories were used for this variable: one category, assigned a score of zero, for boys who were first-born children or only children; another category, assigned a score of one, for boys who were not first-born children and who were not only children. The subjects were fairly evenly distributed in these categories; 49 had a score of zero and 56 had a score of one.

## Urban versus Rural Residence

Because Middletown High School served the neighboring rural community, as well as residents of the city, it had a substantial number of students from non-urban areas. The relation of urban or rural residence to our vocational maturity measures was therefore investigated. This variable was treated as a dichotomy: those with urban residences were scored one, and those with non-urban residences (either village or farm) were scored zero. Somewhat less than one-third of the core group (N=30) were in the non-urban category.

## Religious Affiliation

Studies of scientists in the United States have suggested that there may be relationships between the kind of religion in the family background (Protestant, Catholic, or Jewish) and the achievement of scientific eminence (Super & Bachrach, 1957). Religious affiliation was included as a correlate in the Career Pattern Study to explore its relationship to measures of vocational maturity.

To facilitate statistical treatment of the data, membership in either of the two religions of the majority of the Career Pattern Study core group was scored twice. In the first case, a score of one was given to Protestants, and members of the other religions (Catholic or Jewish) were given a score of zero. Similarly, on a separate scoring, a score of one was given to Catholics, and members of the other religions (Protestant or Jewish) were given a score of zero. The core group was 56 per cent Protestant (N=59) and 37 per cent Catholic (N=39).

### Intrinsic–Extrinsic Work Values

The score for this correlate was obtained by content analysis of the fourth interview in the series of interviews with the boys.[18] Statements pertaining to work values (rewards derived from work) were scaled according to the amount of emphasis on intrinsic rewards of work or extrinsic rewards. Low scores indicated intrinsic values (emphasis on rewards from factors inherent in the work, such as enjoyment of the work activity), and high scores indicated extrinsic values (emphasis on rewards from factors external to the work tasks, such as monetary rewards). A five-point scale was used.

Inter-judge reliability of the scales was determined by correlating the scoring of two judges for twenty cases selected at random. The rank-order correlation was .87 (Yoganarasimhiah, 1957).

### SUMMARY

In this chapter, variables termed correlates of vocational maturity have been described. These variables were not considered to be measures of vocational maturity, but were thought to be relevant to such measures. Twenty-eight correlates were studied, classified on an *a priori* basis as presumed predictor variables (measures of intelligence, socioeconomic status, family relationships, level of aspiration, and psychological adjustment), criteria of achievement in various areas (peer acceptance, participation in school activities, participation in out-of-school activities, adolescent independence, and measures of school achievement), and miscellaneous variables (age, birth order, urban versus rural residence, religious affiliation, and intrinsic–extrinsic work values).

---

[18] The scoring procedure was developed, and the data analyzed, by Malavalli Yoganarasimhiah. For further information see Yoganarasimhiah (1957), and Appendix B.

Statistically significant relationships were found among the five measures of socioeconomic status. The two measures of family relationships were also significantly related to each other, although the correlation coefficient was rather small. The measures of level of aspiration were, in general, unrelated, as were the two measures of psychological adjustment. Slightly over half of the coefficients of correlation among the six achievement variables were statistically significant, but were, in general, rather low. As would be expected, few significant relationships were found among the miscellaneous variables.

# CHAPTER VI

# Variables Associated with Vocational Maturity

This chapter presents the relationships between the five indices of vocational maturity that were deemed adequate and various biosocial characteristics, environmental conditions and circumstances, personal characteristics directly bearing on vocations, personality characteristics, and achievement in various areas of adolescent activity.[1, 2, 3] Relationships between the sum of several vocational

---

[1] As indicated in Chapter IV, Index IIB, Specificity of Planning for the Preferred Occupation, was changed after the correlations among vocational maturity measures discussed in Chapter III had been obtained. Three of its original components (Alternative High School Plans, Planning to Facilitate Entry, and Planning for Advancement in the Occupation) were dropped, and the adequate index, Extent of Planning Activity, was grouped with it as a new component. In computing the coefficients of correlation between total scores on indices of vocational maturity and correlates, total scores on the revised Index IIB were used. With the elimination of Extent of Planning Activity as a separate index, the number of adequate indices was reduced from six to five.

[2] The classification of correlates used in this chapter differs somewhat from that in Chapter V, which was concerned exclusively with correlates. Index–correlate relationships are explored in the present chapter, and the correlates have been reclassified. We are particularly indebted to Charles N. Morris for major contributions to the development of this classification.

[3] A positive relationship between each correlate and index was hypothesized. Accordingly, a one-tailed test of significance was used with the coefficients of correlation reported in this chapter.

104

maturity index scores, termed the *VM Index Total,* and the other variables are also reported.[4]

The indices of vocational maturity have been discussed in Chapter III; the other variables which might be causes, concomitants, or consequences of vocational maturity, called correlates in this monograph, have been described in Chapter V.

## BIOSOCIAL CHARACTERISTICS

Two biosocial characteristics were studied in relation to measures of vocational maturity: age and intelligence. It should be pointed out, however, that in the case of age the distribution was such as to severely limit the conclusions which may be drawn from these data. Since the subjects were all ninth-graders, the age range was limited. At the same time, the older boys tended to be the less intelligent boys, who had repeated some of their schooling, while the younger boys were the brighter ones, who had been accelerated. Under the circumstances, relationships involving the age variable are likely to be different from those found in a sample which included all grades. For example, one would expect both age and intelligence to be positively related to vocational maturity in a causal manner. But since in any given grade, age and intelligence tend to be negatively related, it is unlikely that they will each be positively related to a third variable.

TABLE 31. Correlations between Vocational Maturity Indices and Biosocial Characteristics

| Indices | Age | IQ |
|---|---|---|
| VM Index Total | −.15 | .29 |
| Concern with Choice | −.10 | .16 |
| Acceptance of Responsibility for Choice and Planning | −.14 | .25 |
| Specificity of Information | −.08 | .12 |
| Specificity of Planning | −.17 | .37 |
| Use of Resources | −.05 | −.12 |

Note.—A correlation coefficient of .164 is significant at the .05 level, and of .230 at the .01 level, one-tailed test.

4 The total scores on the four indices that were considered most adequate on the basis of their intercorrelations (Concern with Choice, Acceptance of Responsibility for Choice and Planning, Specificity of Information, and Specificity of Planning) were converted to $z$ scores, and the $z$ scores were added, to obtain the VM Index Total.

As shown in Table 31, none of the vocational maturity measures was significantly related to age. It appears that the older
ninth-graders in this study were no more mature vocationally than
the younger boys in the same grade. Merely being older did not
cause them to be more concerned about the vocational choices
they needed to make, or would soon need to make, nor did it
cause them to take more responsibility for making choices and
plans, to acquire more information about their preferred occupations, or to make more use of resources for becoming vocationally
oriented. Since intelligence tended to be positively correlated
with vocational maturity, it may well be that the handicap of
being less able more than offset the advantage of being older.

As mentioned above and as shown in the last column in Table
31, vocational maturity was related to intelligence. The VM Index
Total and IQ had a rather low positive correlation, significant at
the .01 level. The more intelligent boys did have a slight tendency to think more about the choices they needed to make, they
tended to accept more responsibility for choice and planning, and
while they did not know more about their preferred occupations
(perhaps because the brighter boys were younger), and had not
made better use of orientation resources, they had done more
planning. The failure of intelligence to be related to information
and use of resources, even when age was negatively related to
intelligence, is difficult to understand. Nevertheless, it is clear
that vocational maturity as here defined tended to be related to
intelligence within this limited age range.

## ENVIRONMENTAL VARIABLES

Three types of environmental variables were studied in relation
to vocational maturity: measures of socioeconomic status, status
in the family, and the pressures arising from aspirations characterizing the boys' environment. These relationships are shown in
Table 32.

### Socioeconomic Status

As shown in Table 32, there were four significant correlations, in a
total of twenty, between the five separate vocational maturity

TABLE 32. Correlations between Vocational Maturity Indices
and Environmental Variables

| Indices | Socioeconomic Status | | | | Family Status | | Mobility | | | | | | | |
|---|---|---|---|---|---|---|---|---|---|---|---|---|---|---|
| | PAR. OCC. LEV. | H'SE RATING | FATHER ED. LEV. | MOTHER ED. LEV. | FAMILY COHESIVE. | BIRTH ORDER | PAR. VOC. ASP. FOR BOY | SCH. CURRIC. | PAR. MOBILITY | SOC. MOBILITY | CULTURAL STIM. | URBAN-RURAL | PROTESTANT | CATHOLIC |
| VM Index Total | .27 | >.01 | .09 | .02 | .18 | .12 | −.03 | .29 | .13 | −.03 | .32 | −.23 | −.18 | .02 |
| Concern with Choice | .20 | −.01 | .19 | .10 | .09 | .20 | −.07 | .24 | .11 | −.05 | .33 | −.09 | −.10 | −.01 |
| Accept. of Responsib. | .16 | −.09 | .00 | −.06 | .21 | .12 | .09 | .14 | .03 | .03 | .24 | −.23 | −.16 | .00 |
| Spec. of Info. | .22 | .01 | .00 | .04 | .14 | .06 | −.15 | .26 | .20 | .00 | .24 | −.23 | −.13 | −.02 |
| Spec. of Planning | .26 | .05 | .10 | .00 | .16 | −.02 | .01 | .25 | .07 | −.06 | .21 | −.18 | −.18 | .09 |
| Use of Resources | −.08 | −.18 | −.11 | −.10 | −.04 | .13 | −.03 | .06 | .04 | .15 | −.09 | −.13 | −.08 | .01 |

Note.—A correlation coefficient of .164 is significant at the .05 level, and of .230 at the .01 level, one-tailed test.

indices and various measures of socioeconomic status. These measures of socioeconomic status were correlated among themselves, as we saw in Chapter V. But it is noteworthy that the best-established measure of socioeconomic status (Parental Occupational Level) was significantly related to three of the four indices of Orientation to Vocational Choice and its relationship to the remaining index of this dimension approached significance.[5] Type of dwelling and parental educational levels were, in general, unrelated to vocational maturity in ninth-grade boys, with the exception of the low but statistically significant correlation between Father's Educational Level and Concern with Choice. The use of resources index was not related to any of the measures of socioeconomic status.

## Status in Family

The second type of environmental variable studied in relation to vocational maturity was status in the family. The Family Cohesiveness measure reflects the extent to which the family shares activities and interests, as perceived by the boy himself; the meas-

[5] In Chapter III, the indices of vocational maturity that were deemed most adequate were classified in a dimension termed Orientation to Choice, and the index deemed marginally adequate was classified in a dimension termed Use of Resources. See Table 18.

ure of birth order, as described in Chapter V, groups first and only children in one category, younger children in a second category. The results suggest that in families which tended to share interests and activities, there was also a slight tendency for the boys to accept responsibility for making vocationally related choices and plans, even though they were no more concerned with the need to make choices nor were they better informed about their occupational preferences than boys from less cohesive homes. The correlation between Family Cohesiveness and Specificity of Planning approached significance at the .05 level. There was no relationship between Family Cohesiveness and Use of Resources in Orientation. Birth Order was related to Concern with Choice only, indicating a slight tendency for first or only children to have been more concerned with making pre-vocational and vocational choices than other children.

*Mobility*

The aspirations and values characterizing the boy's environment, which might exert mobility pressures on him, were measured in several ways: 1) by whether or not a boy's parents expressed vocational aspirations for him; 2) by the school curriculum in which the boy was enrolled; 3) by assessment of parental mobility, social mobility of the family, and cultural stimulation; 4) by urban-rural residence; and 5) by religion. The presumed role of parental ambition needs no explanation. The rationale for using curriculum in this way was based on the hypothesis that the Regents-level courses may tend to reinforce academic values and objectives. Parental mobility as shown in educational and occupational histories, family social mobility as assessed by the Biographical Inventory, and richness of the cultural environment as shown by home factors and urban residence were also viewed as indicators of pressure to achieve. Being a Protestant rather than a Roman Catholic was viewed in the same way, because of the role of the Protestant ethic in modern enterprise, and because of studies which have, until very recently, shown more upward mobility among Protestants than among Roman Catholics.

No significant relationships were found between vocational maturity and Presence of Parental Vocational Aspirations for the

Boy. Apparently, whatever pressures these parents put, or failed to put, on their ninth-grade sons to work toward specific occupational goals were not associated with orientation to vocational choice or use of resources. The measures Parental Mobility and Family Social Mobility were also unrelated to the five indices of vocational maturity, except for a low but significant positive relationship between mobility in the parental occupational history and the possession of information about his preferred occupation on the part of the son. Perhaps parents who have moved around in the world of work are better equipped to familiarize their children with that world.

Religious affiliation was unrelated to the indices of vocational maturity. School curriculum and cultural stimulation in the home were, however, rather consistently related to vocational maturity. The boys who were in Regents sections of required courses tended, significantly although not to a high degree, to be more oriented to choice than other boys; they were more concerned with choice, better informed, and more planful. The same was true of boys from homes which provided more stimuli to intellectual and general cultural growth, and these boys also tended to be more accepting of responsibility for making choices and plans. The expected positive relationships between urban residence and the measures of vocational maturity were not found. Instead, all correlations were negative; that is maturity tended to be associated with rural residence, perhaps because the rural boys often wanted to become farmers and thus were more highly oriented toward choice at the ninth-grade level.

### The Relation of Vocational Maturity and Environmental Variables

Environmental variables appear to be related to vocational maturity, for various measures of orientation to vocational choice were significantly, although not closely, correlated with parental occupational level, status in the family, and mobility as reflected particularly in the school curriculum and cultural stimulation in the home. On the other hand, the index concerning use of resources in occupational orientation was unrelated to any of the variables reflecting the nature and quality of the environment.

It should, of course, be emphasized that none of the coefficients of correlation in Table 32 were high enough to make possible predictions concerning individuals. The relationships were low, with the significant correlations tending to be in the .20–.30 range. They aid in identifying the variety of possible determinants and outcomes of vocational maturity, helping thus to clarify our understanding of what vocational maturity is. Their value should lie in the suggestions they yield for curriculum-planning and orientation-planning rather than for individual appraisal in vocational counseling.

## VOCATIONAL CHARACTERISTICS

Characteristics of the individual which have to do clearly and directly with occupations, referred to as vocational characteristics, include measures of vocational aspiration level, of agreement between levels of aspiration and expectation, and of emphasis on intrinsic rather than extrinsic work values. These have all been described in Chapter V. Relationships between each of these variables and indices of vocational maturity are shown in Table 33.

TABLE 33. CORRELATIONS BETWEEN VOCATIONAL MATURITY INDICES
AND VOCATIONAL CHARACTERISTICS

| Indices | Boy's Vocational Aspiration Level | Agreement: Aspiration–Expectation | Intrinsic–Extrinsic Work Values |
|---|---|---|---|
| VM Index Total | .32 | .34 | .11 |
| Concern with Choice | .22 | .20 | .08 |
| Acceptance of Responsibility for Choice and Planning | .27 | .34 | .14 |
| Specificity of Information | .20 | .27 | .11 |
| Specificity of Planning | .34 | .26 | −.02 |
| Use of Resources | .00 | .06 | .11 |

Note.—A correlation coefficient of .164 is significant at the .05 level, and of .230 at the .01 level, one-tailed test.

It is noteworthy that the four orientation to choice indices were significantly related both to the level of the vocational preferences and to the agreement in levels of preferred and expected occupations. The boys who paid more attention to vocational choice in the ninth grade tended to be those who aspired to occupations at a higher level and those who stated expectations which agreed with their aspirations. On the other hand, the use made of orientation resources was not related to these variables. None of the vocational maturity indices, nor the VM Index Total, was related to the stressing of intrinsic work values, that is, to the relative emphasis put upon satisfactions derived from the nature of the work rather than from by-products of the work such as earnings, associations, and free time.

### PERSONALITY CHARACTERISTICS

Aspects of personality were assessed by three measures. Two of these measures were concerned with adjustment, one of them derived from fifteen cards of Murray's Thematic Apperception Test, the other from Rotter's Incomplete Sentences Blank, as described in Chapter V. The other was the score on Henderson's Test of Father Identification. Results are shown in Table 34.

TABLE 34. CORRELATIONS BETWEEN VOCATIONAL MATURITY INDICES AND PERSONALITY CHARACTERISTICS

| Indices | Adjustment | | Father |
| | TAT | ISB | Identification |
|---|---|---|---|
| VM Index Total | .01 | −.03 | .12 |
| Concern with Choice | .04 | .07 | .06 |
| Acceptance of Responsibility for Choice and Planning | .00 | −.05 | .12 |
| Specificity of Information | .06 | −.16 | .03 |
| Specificity of Planning | −.06 | .04 | .19 |
| Use of Resources | −.01 | .05 | −.07 |

Note.—A correlation coefficient of .164 is significant at the .05 level, and of .230 at the .01 level, one-tailed test.

As defined here, vocational maturity was not related to personal adjustment in the ninth grade; correlations between all the vocational maturity indices and the two adjustment measures were not significant and were, in general, near zero. The only statistically significant coefficient of correlation in Table 34 was that between Specificity of Planning and Father Identification. It may be a chance relationship; on the other hand, it may imply that vocational planning and father identification were slightly related.

ACHIEVEMENT IN VARIOUS AREAS OF ADOLESCENT ACTIVITY

The individual's immediate success in dealing with two developmental tasks of early adolescence—achievement in school and in interpersonal relationships—was assessed in several ways. School achievement was measured by grades, and by the relationship of actual grades to grades expected on the basis of intelligence. Achievement in interpersonal relationships was assessed by measures of participation in school activities and in out-of-school activities, by a sociometric measure of peer acceptance, and by a Biographical Inventory measure of general adolescent independence or emancipation from the family. (All of these measures are described in more detail in Chapter V.) Coefficients of correlation between these variables and vocational maturity indices are shown in Table 35.

TABLE 35. CORRELATIONS BETWEEN VOCATIONAL MATURITY INDICES
AND ACHIEVEMENT IN VARIOUS AREAS

| Indices | School Achievement | | Interpersonal Relationships | | | |
|---|---|---|---|---|---|---|
| | GRADES | ACHIEVE.–UNDERACHIEVE. | PARTIC.: SCHOOL ACTIV. | PARTIC.: OUT-OF-SCHOOL ACTIV. | PEER ACCEPTANCE | ADOLESC. INDEPEND. |
| VM Index Total | .38 | .26 | .28 | .22 | .12 | .24 |
| Concern with Choice | .30 | .28 | .16 | .25 | .03 | .15 |
| Acceptance of Responsibility for Choice and Planning | .40 | .28 | .24 | .21 | .07 | .21 |
| Specificity of Information | .08 | .08 | .26 | .10 | .14 | .23 |
| Specificity of Planning | .38 | .14 | .21 | .15 | .14 | .14 |
| Use of Resources | -.02 | .23 | -.08 | -.02 | -.21 | .08 |

Note.—A correlation coefficient of .164 is significant at the .05 level, and of .230 at the .01 level, one-tailed test.

Grades and School Achievement vs. Underachievement were related to most indices of vocational maturity. Concern with Choice and Acceptance of Responsibility were significantly correlated with the two school achievement measures; Specificity of Planning was related to grades; and Use of Resources was related to achievement rather than underachievement. Specificity of Information about the Preferred Occupation was, however, related to neither achievement measure. The correlations between three of the orientation to choice indices and grades are particularly noteworthy, for they ranged from .30 to .40, despite lower correlations with IQ (.16, .25, .37). With intelligence (which correlated .49 with grades) held constant, the coefficients were not greatly changed: the resulting first-order partial correlations between grades and Concern with Choice, Acceptance of Responsibility for Choice and Planning, and Specificity of Planning, respectively, were .26, .33, and .25. The correlation of the VM Index Total with grades was .38, or .29 with intelligence partialed out. The measures of vocational maturity having to do with choice or planning were thus rather consistently related to academic achievement in the ninth grade.

Participation in activities tended to be correlated with vocational maturity as judged by choice-orientation indices. Acceptance of Responsibility for Choice and Planning, Specificity of Information, and Specificity of Planning were all significantly related to Participation in School Activities, and the Concern with Choice relationship approached significance. Concern with Choice and Acceptance of Responsibility for Choice and Planning were also significantly related to Participation in Out-of-School Activities. On the other hand, Use of Resources was unrelated to the two measures of participation in activities. Since participation in activities is itself a type of use of resources, this failure to find a relationship is noteworthy. Perhaps it results from the fact that our measures of participation emphasize social groups, whereas the Use of Resources for Orientation index, as defined here, is largely an individual and vocational matter.

Peer acceptance was not significantly related to any of the measures of vocational maturity in Table 35. Adolescent Independence had rather low but significant correlations with three of the measures (Acceptance of Responsibility for Choice and Planning, Specificity of Information about the Preferred Occupation, and the VM Index Total).

Achievement in various areas of activity thus appeared to be related, on the whole, to vocational maturity in the ninth grade. Boys who were most concerned with choice, who accepted responsibility for choice and planning, who were informed about and planned for their preferred occupations, and, in the case of one relationship, who used resources for orientation, these boys tended to be those who were most successful in handling developmental tasks such as school studies, participating in various types of activities in and out of school, and achieving a degree of independence from their families.

## SUMMARY

In concluding this chapter, it seems important to synthesize our findings in order to see which characteristics were associated with vocational maturity in the ninth-grade boys we studied. It may be equally important, also, to review the attributes which were not associated with our measures of vocational maturity. The following variables had statistically significant positive coefficients of correlation with the VM Index Total (the sum of the four orientation-to-choice indices):

Intelligence
Parental Occupational Level
Family Cohesiveness
School Curriculum
Cultural Stimulation
Boy's Vocational Aspiration Level
Agreement: Levels of Aspiration and Expectation
School Achievement: Grades
Achievement–Underachievement
Participation in School Activities
Participation in Out-of-School Activities
Adolescent Independence

The following variables were not significantly related to the VM Index Total:

> Age (within one school grade)
> House Rating
> Father's Educational Level
> Mother's Educational Level
> Birth Order
> Presence of Parental Vocational Aspiration for Boy
> Parental Mobility
> Social Mobility
> Urban rather than Rural Residence
> Protestant
> Catholic
> Intrinsic vs. Extrinsic Work Values
> Adjustment (as assessed by TAT and ISB)
> Father Identification
> Peer Acceptance

The Use of Resources index, which was not included in the VM Index Total, was significantly correlated with only one of the twenty-eight variables (achievement–underachievement).

Since the statistically significant coefficients of correlation were modest in size, it is obvious that there were many ninth-grade boys who possessed one or more of these characteristics but were not vocationally mature, and also that many boys who were oriented to vocational choice lacked some of these characteristics.

# CHAPTER VII

# The Vocational Maturity of
## Ninth-Grade Boys

What do the vocational maturity indices that have been discussed in this monograph indicate about vocational behavior? What did these ninth-grade boys do in dealing with vocational developmental tasks? The vocational behavior of the ninth-grade boys in the Career Pattern Study core group is described in this chapter by showing the frequency with which different scores on several of the vocational maturity measures were obtained. It is not our intention, however, to present norms of vocational behavior in the ninth grade.

Obviously, findings of this study, as of other research studies, are at least in part a result of the particular methods used and the subjects observed. Now that we are about to describe the behavior of our subjects as assessed by our measuring devices, it is appropriate to restate some points made in earlier chapters concerning our methods and our subjects.

### METHODOLOGICAL CONSIDERATIONS

The indices of vocational maturity used at the ninth-grade level were quantified on an *a priori* basis. Scoring weights for the various measures were based on judgments about behaviors assumed to

116

be indicative of different degrees of vocational maturity. The accuracy of the quantification and the appropriateness of the behavioral dimensions studied has not as yet been validated as indicators of vocational maturity by relating the scores obtained by the subjects in the ninth grade to their subsequent vocational behavior.

The vocational behavior of ninth-grade boys is described, not the vocational behavior of a strictly defined age group, since age varied within the group studied. While the average age of the core group was slightly over fourteen years, there was a range in age from twelve years, nine months to seventeen years, six months. However, the standard deviation was less than one year (10.28 months). Within the core group, 53 of the boys were fourteen-year-olds; 33 boys were younger than fourteen, and 19 were older. Only 5 boys were twelve-year-olds and only 4 were sixteen or older.

Preparing to make vocational choices was assumed to be the major vocational developmental task of the early exploratory life stage (the expected life stage of ninth-graders). The indices of vocational maturity were intended to show how these ninth-grade boys dealt with this vocational developmental task: the indices were attempts to measure various aspects of behavior that seemed relevant to the process of preparing to make vocational choices.

Distributions of scores on some of the measures used to assess vocational maturity were found to be skewed. Various explanations of the departure from normality displayed by such distributions may be suggested, but we cannot state with any certainty which, if any, of these explanations is correct. It is, of course, quite possible that different distributions were skewed for different reasons, so that one explanation may apply in one instance and another in a different instance.

An obtained distribution may be non-normal because the distribution of the behavior in the population from which the sample is drawn is non-normal. Although distributions of various measures, such as height, weight, and intelligence, do tend to be normal if an adequate sampling is obtained, all distributions are not necessarily normal. Some vocational behaviors may be distributed non-normally if they are measured at a particular point in time—for example, either early or late in the period of development of the behavior. This may explain the skewed distributions of some of the vocational maturity scores. By the ninth-grade level some behaviors may not yet be well established, while others may already have become so.

On the other hand, skewness of some of the distributions of vocational maturity scores may be due to inadequacies of measurement or sampling. The measures of vocational behavior may have been to some extent inadequate: the scales may have been inaccurate, with unequal spacing between steps, so that the actual occurrence of the behavior was not accurately reflected by the scales. Or the sample of boys from whom the data were obtained may not have been representative of the population in which the behavior occurs. While the behavior being studied may be normally distributed in the population, its distribution in a particular sample of the population may not necessarily be normal.

## DISTRIBUTIONS OF VARIOUS VOCATIONAL MATURITY SCORES

In the following pages, the vocational behavior of the Career Pattern Study core group as assessed by various measures of vocational maturity is described and discussed. Part scores or total scores on most of the indices that appeared to be adequate and on some of the indices that did not appear adequate are presented, as illustrative of the findings.

### Concern with Choice

In Chapter III it was concluded that certain indices were better than others as indicators of vocational maturity at the ninth-grade level with our sample. One of the best measures was Concern with Choice (Sturm, 1958; Dubrow, 1959; see also Appendix A). It is not surprising that Concern with Choice should be a useful index of vocational maturity, because choices with vocational implications are required at high school entrance.

As illustrated in Figures 2 and 3, the boys showed a good deal of concern with immediate and intermediate choices.[1] One of the components of the index Concern with Choice assessed behavior

---

[1] Unless otherwise indicated, the data in this chapter are presented in raw score, not in standard score, form.

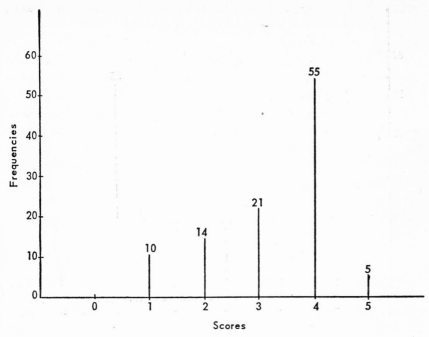

*Figure 2.*   Distribution of Raw Scores: Awareness of the Need for Immediate Choices

presumed to be indicative of awareness of the need for choice. On the *a priori* assumption that awareness would vary depending on the degree of immediacy of the choice, three different elements of this component were scaled separately: 1) Awareness of the Need for Immediate Choices (concerning high school curricula and courses); 2) Awareness of the Need for Intermediate Choices (such as choice of college, technical institute, apprenticeship); and 3) Awareness of the Need for Ultimate Choices.

None of the ninth-grade boys in the Career Pattern Study core group failed to mention concern with immediate choices, and more than half of them (N = 55) were scored four, the fifth step of the six-step scale ("Mentions relationships of immediate to intermediate and/or ultimate choice"). Only one boy in the group failed to mention concern with intermediate choices, and the same number (55) scored four, the fifth step of the scale for intermediate choices ("Mentions relationship of intermediate to ultimate choice"), as

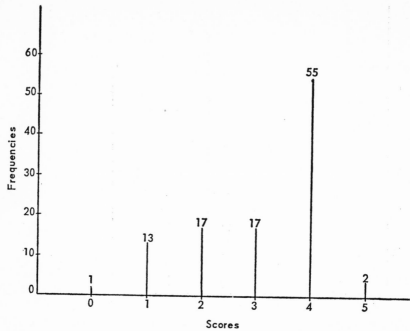

*Figure 3.* Distribution of Raw Scores: Awareness of the Need for Intermediate Choices

had scored at the corresponding step of the scale for immediate choices. These ninth-graders, then, seemed to be aware of the need for the choices that were confronting them or would be confronting them in the not too distant future.

Because Awareness of the Need for Ultimate Choices was scaled somewhat differently from the other two elements of this component, direct comparisons could not be made of the boys' vocational behavior as exemplified by this scale and behavior indicated on the two other scales. It may be seen from an examination of Figure 4 that the scores on the Ultimate Choice scale tended to concentrate at one, the second step of this four-step scale ("Mentions further choices to be made," such as means of entry or specialty in the field), with 55 boys scoring at this step. All boys mentioned some ultimate choice, but 20 of them merely mentioned a choice without elaborating it and thus received a zero score on this scale.

A second component of the index Concern with Choice explored the factors considered by the subject in making vocational

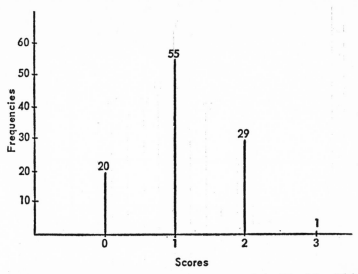

*Figure 4.* Distribution of Raw Scores: Awareness of the Need for Ultimate Choices

choices. The distribution of raw scores on this component, termed Awareness of Factors in Vocational Choice, is graphically illustrated in Figure 5. A score of one was given for each separate statement by the individual about factors to be considered in vocational choice (such as mental ability, special aptitudes, interests, amount of education, earnings, and physical conditions of work). The number of statements ranged from one through twenty; 15 boys made ten statements each. The distribution of scores on this component tended to approximate a symmetrical, bell-shaped curve, in contrast to the rather skewed distributions found with some of the other measures of vocational maturity. This may indicate that awareness of factors to be considered in making vocational choices is a kind of vocational behavior that is normally distributed at this grade level. On the other hand, the rather symmetrical distribution may reflect the greater opportunity for range of scores on this measure than on the four-step or six-step scales.

## Use of Resources in Orientation

One of the measures of vocational maturity used at the ninth-grade level, Use of Resources in Orientation, attempted to assess the use

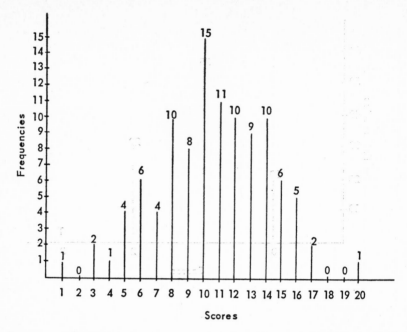

*Figure 5.* Distribution of Raw Scores: Awareness of Factors in Vocational Choice

made of resources by the boys in learning about the world of work. Scoring was done from typescripts of interview protocols, and consisted of the total number of resources the subject mentioned having used in orienting himself to the world of work. Any source of information which had been used was scorable, if the boy himself made a connection between the information obtained and occupational orientation. The distribution of scores on this measure is shown in Figure 6.[2] Eight boys gave no indication of having used such resources, while one boy reported using twelve sources of information.

## Specificity of Information about the Preferred Occupation

It was assumed that having information about the preferred occupation would characterize the vocationally mature boy who was dealing with the task of preparing to make vocational choices.

[2] The distribution includes 101 scores, not 105, because four cases lacked data on Index IB.

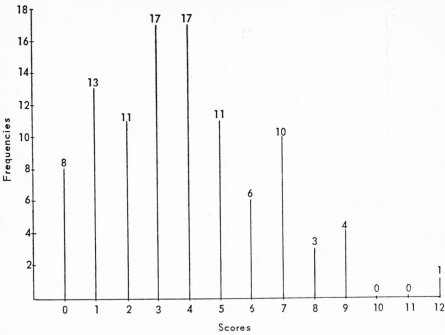

*Figure 6.* Distribution of Raw Scores: Use of Resources in Orientation

Therefore, measures of Specificity of Information about the Preferred Occupation were used as an index of vocational maturity (Nolte, 1956; see Appendix A). The components of this index concerned specificity of 1) information about the requirements of the preferred occupation (such as high school background, training and/or education, economic requirements, psychological and physical requirements), 2) information about its duties (what is done, why, how well it must be done), 3) information about the conditions of work (monetary rewards, hours, security, physical and psychosocial conditions), and 4) information about opportunities in the preferred occupation (such as entry, supply and demand, advancement, and transfer).

Distributions of the raw scores on these components and of the total scores are presented graphically in Figures 7 through 11. It is apparent from an examination of these figures that they display two somewhat different kinds of distribution. The distribution of scores for Specificity of Information about Requirements of the

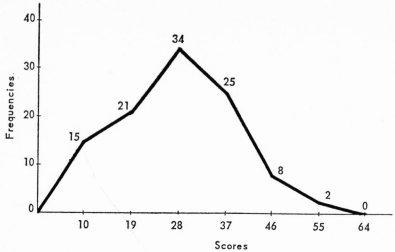

*Figure 7.* Distribution of Raw Scores: Specificity of Information about Requirements of the Preferred Occupation

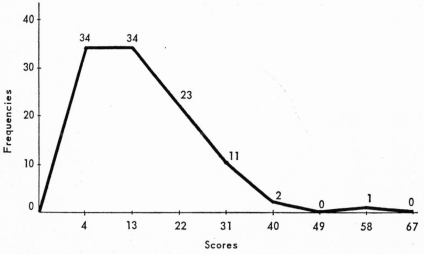

*Figure 8.* Distribution of Raw Scores: Specificity of Information about Duties of the Preferred Occupation

Preferred Occupation tends to be symmetrical, as does, to a lesser degree, the distribution of total scores. On the other hand, the distributions of scores for Specificity of Information about Duties, Conditions, and Opportunities in the Preferred Occupation are all positively skewed.

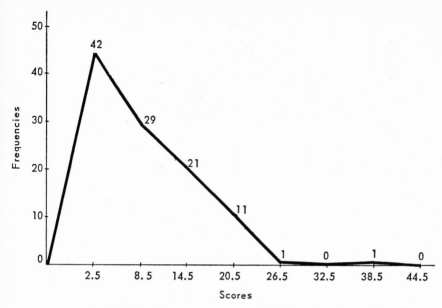

*Figure 9.* Distribution of Raw Scores: Specificity of Information about Conditions of Work in the Preferred Occupation

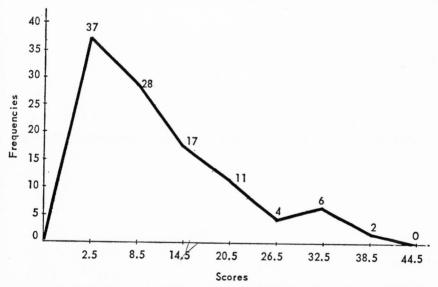

*Figure 10.* Distribution of Raw Scores: Specificity of Information about Opportunities in the Preferred Occupation

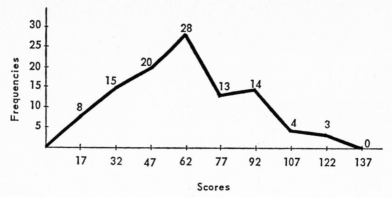

*Figure 11.*    Distribution of Raw Scores: Specificity of Information about the Preferred Occupation (Total)

The ninth-grade boys in the Career Pattern Study core group made higher scores on the measure of information about requirements of their preferred occupations than they did on the measures of information about duties, conditions of work, and opportunities.[3] This finding implies that the boys had greater opportunity to learn about the requirements of their preferred occupations than about some other aspects of them, or that they tended first to learn about requirements and later to learn about other aspects, such as conditions of work.

It is realistic to give consideration fairly early to the matter of qualifying for entry into a desired occupation, in order to make appropriate preliminary educational plans. For example, the ninth-grader at Middletown High School had to choose between a Regents or a non-Regents curriculum. If his preferred occupation was one that would require college graduation, then the appropriate early educational choice for him was the Regents curriculum. It is, therefore, not surprising that these ninth-grade boys tended to know more about occupational requirements than about duties, conditions of work, or opportunities.

One wonders, however, whether the knowledge these boys had

[3] Comparisons of the raw score distributions of the components of this index may properly be made because the components were weighted to yield the same possible total number of points. However, such comparisons are based upon the assumptions that the scales have true zero points and equal steps. If these assumptions are incorrect, the conclusions drawn from comparing the scales may also be incorrect.

about their preferred occupations was sufficient for the prevocational decisions they would need to make. Although most of this group were still at a rather early stage of the choice-making process, should they have known more about duties, conditions of work, and opportunities than they seemed to? Or would further information about such matters have been superfluous at a time in the choice-making process when orientation to a broad area might perhaps have been more appropriate than orientation to specific details of occupations?

*Specificity of Planning for the Preferred Occupation*

Another aspect of vocational behavior assessed by data from the interviews with the Career Pattern Study ninth-graders was their planning for their preferred occupations (Wolk, 1958; see Appendix A). Results obtained with four of the components of this index of vocational maturity are graphically presented in Figures 12 through 15. The index had nine components relevant to various

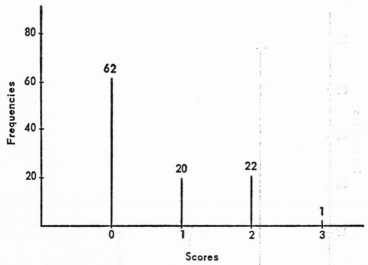

*Figure 12.* Distribution of Raw Scores: Steps Taken to Obtain Information for High School Planning

aspects of planning. The components were arranged in chronological sequence from high school planning through planning for occupational advancement.

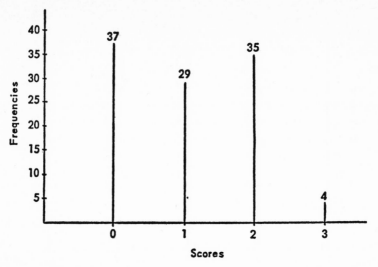

*Figure 13.* Distribution of Raw Scores: Specificity of High School Plans

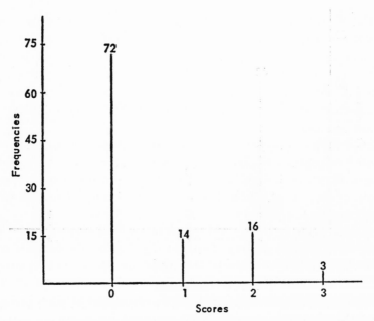

*Figure 14.* Distribution of Raw Scores: Steps Taken to Obtain Information for Post-High-School Planning

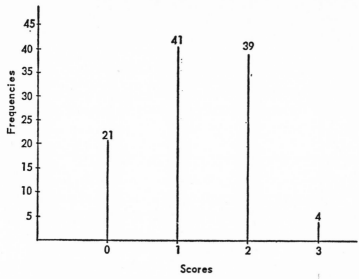

*Figure 15.* Distribution of Raw Scores: Post-High-School Plans

Of the 105 ninth-graders, 62 made no mention of Steps Taken to Obtain Information for High School Planning (the first component of this index; see Figure 12). Of course, it is possible that some of these boys had taken steps to obtain such information, but did not report this in their interviews. Scores on the second component of the index (Specificity of High School Plans) are shown in Figure 13. Thirty-seven boys either made no mention of high school plans for their preferred occupations or mentioned inappropriate plans (as shown by a zero score on the scale). However, 68 of the boys showed knowledge of the relationship of some of their high school courses to their occupational plans (as indicated by scores of one through three on the same scale).

Steps Taken to Obtain Information for Post-High-School Planning were evaluated by the fourth component of the index, shown in Figure 14. There was a large number of zero scores and a small number of scores of one through three on this scale. Seventy-two of the group of 105 did not mention discussion of such plans or exploration of resources; only 33 reported discussion, or exploration of resources, in order to obtain information for post-high-school planning. However, most of the group reported post-high-school plans, shown by the number scoring above zero on component five (Post-High-School Plans; see Figure 15).

## Acceptance of Responsibility for Choice

Just as it is reasonable to assume that an individual must be aware of the need for making choices in order to prepare to make vocational choices, so it is reasonable to assume that acceptance of responsibility for making choices is indicative of mature behavior in dealing with the task of making vocational choices. Accordingly, a measure of the degree to which the Career Pattern Study ninth-grade boys accepted responsibility for choice was used as an indicator of vocational maturity. Figure 16 presents the distribution of scores on one of the components of the index Acceptance of Responsibility for Choice and Planning (see Appendix A).

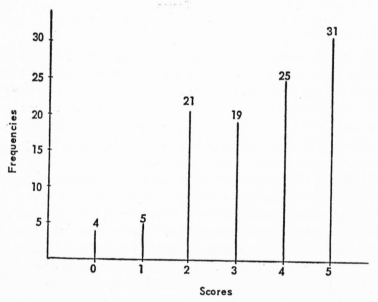

Figure 16. Distribution of Raw Scores: Acceptance of Responsibility for Choice

It is evident from an examination of Figure 16 that these ninth-graders tended, on the whole, to accept responsibility for making choices. The distribution is negatively skewed, with the greatest frequencies at the two highest steps of the six-step scale. Only four boys rejected responsibility for choice (scored zero), and only five made no mention of acceptance or rejection (scored one). Twenty-one boys mentioned responsibility for choice, but expected others to carry the responsibility (scored two); this kind of behavior is exemplified by an interview response such as, "I could take the Ag. course—that's what my Dad advises." Acceptance of the responsibility for choice (scored three), was mentioned by 19 boys: for example, "I'll have to decide for myself. Nobody else'll do it for you!" Twenty-five boys scored four, the step described as mentioning acceptance of responsibility for choice with attitude that this is good; 31 scored five, the step described as mentioning acceptance of responsibility for choice and desire for help in exercising it. For example, a boy stating, "I'm going to talk it over with my counselor before I decide—if it still looks good I'll take Ag." would be given a score of five.

## Interest Maturity

The Interest Maturity scale of the Strong Vocational Interest Blank was tried as one method of assessing the vocational maturity of the Career Pattern Study ninth-grade boys. The scoring of the scale is based on contrasting the interests of 15-year-old boys and of men aged twenty-three to twenty-seven (called a 25-year-old group for convenience of designation) (Strong, 1943, Chapter 12 and p. 715). The Career Pattern Study used a modification of the Strong Blank with simplified directions and an easier vocabulary, to make the reading level more appropriate for 14-year-olds.[4]

The rationale for the use of the Interest Maturity scale was that the more mature boys would tend to have interests more like 25-year-olds than like 15-year-olds and therefore would score higher on the scale than would less mature boys. However, we saw in Chapter III that the intercorrelations among the various indices of vocational maturity did not support the assumption that Interest Maturity is a measure of vocational maturity at the ninth-grade level. The explanation may lie in the finding reported by Strong (1943, p. 285):

[4] Developed by Donald E. Super and Martin Hamburger, with the permission of Edward K. Strong, Jr.

Statistically IM is the quantitative measurement of the differences in interests of 15- and 25-year-old men—the degree to which one has the interests of the latter in contrast to the former. Our data indicate, however, that IM is not closely associated with age, since the correlation between the two is only about .50. Our data indicate, moreover, that it is associated with occupational interests, negatively with scientific and linguistic interests, and positively with office-worker-accountant interests and with interest in people (Groups V and IX).

The distribution of Interest Maturity standard scores of the Career Pattern Study core group is given in Figure 17. It is inter-

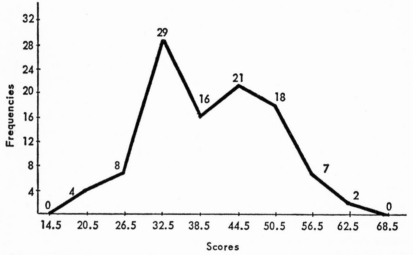

*Figure 17.*  Distribution of Standard Scores: Strong Interest Maturity Scale

esting to note the similarity of the Career Pattern Study boys to Strong's group, indicated by the fact that a standard score of 40.5 on the Interest Maturity scale was at the fifty-first percentile of the Middletown group (average age slightly over 14 years), while standard scores of 39.2 and 40.3 were at the fifty-first and fifty-fifth percentiles, respectively, of Strong's 15-year-old group (Strong, 1943, Table 68, p. 263).

### Agreement between Ability and Preference

Using the rationale that boys whose vocational preferences are appropriate for their abilities are more mature vocationally than boys whose preferences are not appropriate for their abilities, a measure of agreement between intellectual ability and preference was used as one index of vocational maturity (see Appendix A). This index was treated as a dichotomy; boys were categorized according to whether they did or did not have sufficient general intelligence for the occupation of their first preference. Arbitrary cut-off scores were used to delimit the categories.

There was more disagreement between abilities and preferences (N = 59) than agreement (N = 46). From this point of view, over half of the group seemed to have made unwise choices. Of course, the expressed preferences of at least some of the boys may not have represented firm vocational decisions, in the sense of subsequent serious attempts to prepare for or enter the occupations preferred in the ninth grade. Other studies, such as that by Schmidt and Rothney (1955), have shown that choices made early in the high school period do not tend to be permanent. It is, of course, not necessarily desirable that early choices remain stable.

Inappropriateness of early preferences (in terms of agreement with ability) may turn out to be an important factor in contributing to changes in expressed preferences at later grade or age levels. If an individual cannot succeed in the training prerequisite to a particular occupation, or if he finds that he cannot do the work required by the occupation, then, sooner or later, failure experiences may force him to change his vocational goals. This can be a rather painful way of making vocational decisions. On the other hand, a shift from less realistic to more realistic choices may occur as a part of the developmental process, before failure experiences have begun to accumulate. The ninth-grade data do not, of course, indicate what will happen in the vocational planning of the boys with unwise choices. Follow-up information will tell us more about what actually occurs.

One wonders why this wisdom-of-preference type of measure did not turn out to be an adequate index of vocational maturity at the ninth grade, using as a criterion of adequacy statistically significant correlations with other indices. None of the intercorrelations with the adequate vocational maturity indices, as discussed in Chapter III, was significant. Agreement between ability and preference was not significantly related to measures of concern with choice, use of resources, specificity of occupational information, specificity of planning, and acceptance of responsibility for choice and planning. In other words, boys who seemed most oriented to the task of preparing to make occupational choices were no more likely to make wise choices than boys who were less oriented to this task. Why?

Perhaps because concern with choice and having information about the occupation of one's preference is not sufficient for making appropriate choices without realistic self-understanding. The idea seems reasonable that one must know and accept one's own assets and limitations before being able to make wise vocational choices, choices which reflect an integration of self factors and occupational requirements. Lack of agreement between abilities and preferences may be caused by overestimation of one's abilities. If college students tend to overestimate their abilities, as indicated by Torrance's study (1954), for example, it is not surprising that this may happen among ninth-graders.

It may be that development in the ninth grade is not sufficiently advanced for a majority of boys to have the knowledge of their own capacities that will enable them to make wise choices. That this self-knowledge may be possible at this level, however, is shown by the finding that 44 per cent of the 105 boys in the Career Pattern Study core group had made wise choices, in the sense that their intelligence and preferences tended to agree.

### Agreement between Measured Interests and Preference

Another of the indices of vocational maturity devised to assess wisdom of vocational preferences was Agreement between Measured Interests and Preference. This is a measure of the amount of agreement between expressed vocational preferences and interests as measured by the CPS adaptation of the Strong Vocational Interest Blank (for details, see Appendix A).

Twenty-seven of the boys had no interest pattern in the Strong group to which their expressed preference corresponded, and 16 had only tertiary interest patterns in the Strong groupings appropriate to their expressed preferences. Twenty-two of the boys had secondary interest patternings, and 31 had primary interest patternings, in the Strong groupings that corresponded to their expressed preferences.[6] Thus, 45 per cent of the group had little or no agreement between their expressed vocational preferences and their measured interests, while 55 per cent of the group had come to substantial agreement between preferences and interests. Slightly over half of the group, then, had appropriate vocational preferences as defined by agreement between preferences and interests.

As pointed out earlier, this index was not found to be adequate as a measure of vocational maturity in grade nine, because it did not correlate significantly with any of the other presumed indices of vocational maturity. A boy could score high on the Concern with Choice index, or on any of the other vocational maturity indices that were deemed adequate, and yet make any score from high to low on the index Agreement between Measured Interests and Preference.

Again the question arises: Why? It is unlikely that defensiveness, unwillingness, or inability to accept unpleasant facts about oneself can explain the failure of this index to correlate significantly with other indices (although defensiveness may explain the failure of Agreement between Ability and Preference to correlate significantly with other indices). Whether the lack of significant relationships of this with other indices was due to some artifact of the method of measurement, to a developmental trend that is different for this index than for those deemed adequate, to its being an independent trait, or to some other reason is not known.

*Vocational Maturity Index Total*

As described in Chapter VI, the total scores of the vocational maturity indices that were considered the most adequate were added to obtain a Vocational Maturity Index Total. The indices included in the VM Index Total were Concern with Choice, Acceptance of Responsibility for Choice and Planning, Specificity of Information, and Specificity of Planning.

The distribution of the VM Index Total scores is shown in

---

[6] Scores are reported for 96 boys, not for all 105, because the remaining nine cases did not take the Strong test or expressed preferences that could not be classified in any of Strong's groupings.

Figure 18. The curve has a fairly symmetrical shape, in contrast to the rather skewed distributions of some of the vocational maturity index part scores or total scores. Obviously, a wider variety of vocational behaviors is represented by the VM Index Total scores than by any of the separate indices, and this may be the reason for the rather symmetrical distribution.

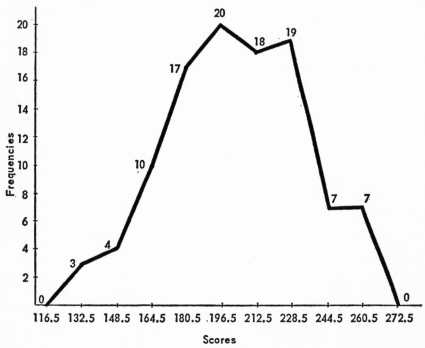

*Figure 18.* Distribution of Sums of Standard Scores: Vocational Maturity Index Total

## VOCATIONAL MATURITY PROFILES

Profiles of scores on the various vocational maturity indices may be used to illustrate variations in different areas of vocational behavior. Accordingly, profiles of the vocational maturity scores made by three ninth-grade boys are shown in Figures 19, 20, and 21. The boys were selected on the basis of their scores on the VM Index Total: one had the highest VM Index Total score in the core group; one's score was near the median; and another's score was among the lowest in the group.

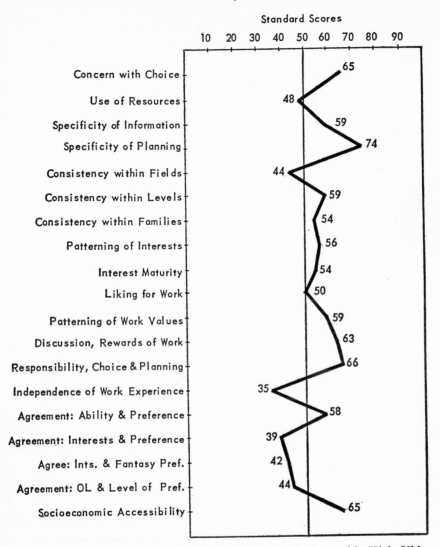

Standard Scores

*Figure 19.* Vocational Maturity Profile, Ninth-Grade Boy with High VM Index Total

Boy A, with a high VM Index Total, was of superior intelligence and was making very satisfactory grades in school. His psychological adjustment, as evaluated by the Incomplete Sentences Blank, was quite good. Although he had a preferred occupation, he was uncertain whether he really would enter it and he seemed actively involved in the choice-making process. During the course of his

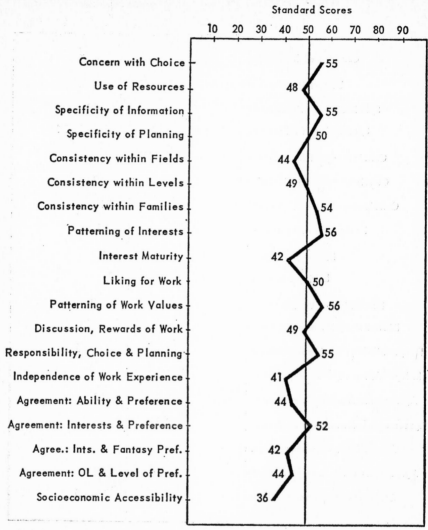

*Figure 20.* Vocational Maturity Profile, Ninth-Grade Boy with Average VM
Index Total

four interviews with a Career Pattern Study staff member, he
seemed to be shifting the focus of his preferences. His generally
high orientation to choice is seen in his standard scores on the
indices of Concern with Choice, Specificity of Information, Specificity of Planning, and Acceptance of Responsibility for Choice and

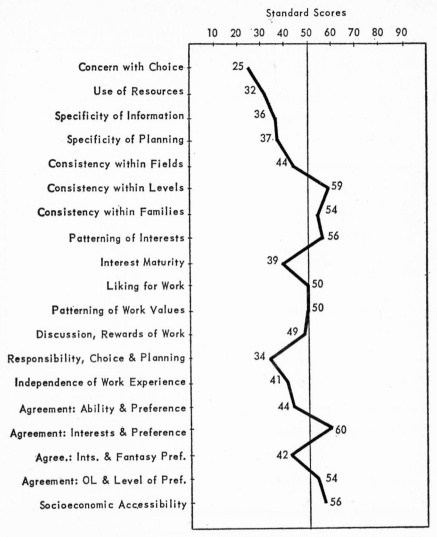

Standard Scores

*Figure 21.*  Vocational Maturity Profile, Ninth-Grade Boy with Low VM Index Total

Planning. Although his vocational preference was in line with his intelligence, there was less agreement between his interests and his preference. The gradual shifting in vocational choice that seemed to be coming about during his first year in high school might well reflect this fact.

Boy B, with an average VM Index Total, had scores within the average range on many of the vocational maturity indices. His intelligence was high average, and his adjustment, as assessed by the Incomplete Sentences Blank, seemed adequate. His academic achievement was below his potential, but he was passing his courses. He had a vocational preference and was making plans to implement it, but the wisdom of his preference seemed somewhat questionable. One had the impression that he was, to some extent, over-aspiring vocationally.

Boy C, with a rather low VM Index Total, had a preponderance of vocational maturity scores below 50. Less intelligent than either of the other two boys, his academic achievement was adequate. Adjustment was good, according to the Incomplete Sentences Blank. He had very little to say about his vocational plans and gave a general impression of immaturity in his discussion of plans. Although his measured interests agreed with his preference, his intelligence did not. His short-range vocational plans seemed more appropriate for him than the long-range plans he mentioned.

## SUMMARY

In this chapter, distributions of part scores or total scores made by 105 ninth-grade boys on various measures of vocational maturity were presented and discussed. Attention was given to the question why vocational maturity indices designed to measure wisdom of vocational preferences were not significantly related to the vocational maturity indices considered adequate as measures of vocational maturity in the ninth grade, and some tentative answers were suggested. However, some questions remain unanswered.

The distribution of VM Index Total scores was also shown Vocational maturity profiles of three boys with high, average, and low scores, respectively, on this measure were presented and briefly discussed.

# CHAPTER VIII

# Summary

In the first chapter of the monograph, we asked questions about the readiness of ninth-grade boys to make the kinds of prevocational and vocational choices which society, through the present organization of schools and curricula, expects them to make.

The conceptual framework of this study is developmental. Generalizations concerning the development of vocational behavior were stated in postulate form in Chapter I. Vocational choice is seen as a process, extending over a period of time. It is a sequence of lesser decisions, some of them decisions as to the level toward which to strive, some of them decisions as to the field in which to work, which bring about a progressive reduction of the number of alternatives open to the chooser. The vocational behavior of the individual is a function of his personal resources and of the demands which society makes upon him. Vocational behaviors and vocational developmental tasks can be classified according to life stages, each life stage confronting the individual with some new developmental tasks peculiar to that stage.

In Chapter I, also, a distinction was made between vocational maturity and vocational adjustment. Two definitions of vocational maturity were proposed; the one used in this monograph defined vocational maturity as the maturity of an individual's vocationally related behavior in his actual life stage (whether or not it is the life stage expected for him) as shown by his behavior in dealing with vocational developmental tasks as compared with the behavior of others dealing with the same developmental tasks. Vocational adjustment is judged by the extent to which vocational behavior results in the accomplishment of a developmental task with long-term satisfaction to the individual in meeting socialized objectives.

## SUBJECTS

The subjects of this phase of the Career Pattern Study were 142 boys who, together with a similar group of girls, constituted the ninth-grade class of Middletown High School, Middletown, New York, in 1951–52. Middletown is a small manufacturing and market city, with a population of some 22,500, about sixty-five miles northwest of New York City, and in the heart of a rich dairy valley. It may be fairly characterized as a "middle town," as shown by a variety of statistical information reported in Chapter II.

Most of the data on the subjects of this monograph were obtained from a core group of 105 boys (those for whom a maximum amount of needed data were available), who were similar in important respects to the total class from which they were drawn. Boys in the core group were also rather similar in the same respects to boys in the ninth-grade class of the preceding year.

## INDICES OF VOCATIONAL MATURITY

The rationale for constructing indices of vocational maturity was derived from developmental psychology, and in particular from the principles of differentiation, realism, and independence. A list of behaviors and characteristics which might constitute maturity of vocational behavior was derived from these principles, from the literature, and from counseling experience. A list of possible dimensions and indices of vocational maturity in the ninth grade resulted.

### Measurement Methods and Results

Methods of measuring these behaviors or characteristics were next explored. In some instances, existing instruments lent themselves to this purpose with little or no modification: for example, Strong's Vocational Interest Blank yields a measure of interest maturity based on the differences between 15-year-olds and 25-year-olds. In other instances no ready-made measures existed, and it was necessary to rely on content analysis of existing material, in order to assess these behaviors. As each boy had taken an extensive battery of tests and inventories, and had had a series of four tape-recorded interviews, considerable material was available from which such indices could be derived.

The Career Pattern Study staff and seminars conceptualized, outlined, tried out, and revised the various indices of vocational maturity. After scoring manuals had been developed which satisfied the staff, studies of inter-judge agreement in scoring each of the interview-derived indices were conducted. These reliability coefficients, as reported in Chapter III, show the reliability of judges, but not the reliability of the data obtained by the interviews; the inter-judge reliability correlations (rho) ranged from .78 to .96. In two instances, internal consistency studies were made. It was concluded that the various indices were sufficiently reliable for research purposes.

The appropriateness of the grouping of parts of interview-derived measures into indices, and of the grouping of indices into dimensions, was examined by intercorrelating the various measures. Twenty indices (and their part scores), classified into six dimensions, were studied. Six of the indices, later reduced to five, had a sufficient number of statistically significant positive intercorrelations to be considered adequate as measures of vocational maturity at the ninth-grade level. The following indices were deemed adequate:

> Concern with Choice
> Acceptance of Responsibility for Choice and Planning
> Specificity of Information about the Preferred Occupation
> Specificity of Planning for the Preferred Occupation
> Extent of Planning Activity
> Use of Resources in Orientation

All of these measures were based on material from interviews.

Extent of Planning Activity was later combined with Specificity of Planning for the Preferred Occupation, thus reducing the number of adequate indices to five. Use of Resources in Orientation was considered only marginally adequate, because its correlations with the other adequate indices were lower than their correlations with each other.

The remaining fourteen indices, some interview-derived and some based on standard measures, did not have a sufficient number of significant positive correlations with each other or with the indices listed above to be considered adequate. Although they may be adequate measures of vocational maturity at other stages of development, they did not appear to be measuring this construct in the ninth grade. The inadequate indices, and the dimensions in which they were classified, follow.

Consistency of Vocational Preferences
    Consistency of Vocational Preferences within Fields
    Consistency of Vocational Preferences within Levels
    Consistency of Vocational Preferences within Families

Crystallization of Traits
    Degree of Patterning of Measured Interests
    Interest Maturity
    Liking for Work
    Degree of Patterning of Work Values
    Extent of Discussion about Rewards of Work

Vocational Independence
    Independence of Work Experience

Wisdom of Vocational Preferences
    Agreement between Ability and Preference
    Agreement between Measured Interests and Preference
    Agreement between Measured Interests and Fantasy Preference
    Agreement between Occupational Level of Measured Interests
       and Level of Preference
    Socioeconomic Accessibility of Preference

On the basis of the intercorrelations among indices, it was concluded that vocational maturity in the ninth grade consists of a dimension termed Orientation to Vocational Choice Tasks, made up of four indices (Concern with Choice, Acceptance of Responsibility for Choice and Planning, Specificity of Information about the Preferred Occupation, and Specificity of Planning for the Preferred Occupation), and perhaps also of a less well-established dimension termed Use of Resources, made up of one marginally adequate index (Use of Resources in Orientation).

*Factor Analysis*

The elements and components of several interview-derived indices of vocational maturity were subjected to a principal axes factor analysis (reported in Chapter IV), in order to ascertain the best grouping of the sub-tests and to throw light on the factorial structure of the indices. A total of twenty-seven variables constituted the matrix which was analyzed, all of these from the indices of Concern with Choice, Acceptance of Responsibility, Specificity of Information, Specificity of Planning (to which the former index Extent of Planning Activity was added), and Independence of Work Experience.

Five factors were extracted, accounting for 38 per cent of the variance. No more factors were extracted, however, because the fifth accounted for only three per cent of the variance and additional factors would not be very meaningful. The relatively small proportion of variance accounted for was attributed to the relative unreliability of the sub-tests (elements or components), which were shorter than the indices, a characteristic which would lower the obtained intercorrelations. These factors were rotated, following the quartimax method, to obtain simple structure.

The factor loadings of the various measures were examined to ascertain the nature of the factors. Four of the five factors appeared largely, and with various loadings, in the indices which had been shown to be adequate measures of vocational maturity in the ninth grade, and one of the five factors appeared almost exclusively in the inadequate index, Independence of Work Experience. The following four factors, therefore, seem to comprise vocational maturity in the ninth grade, as measured in our study:

Planning Orientation (a general factor)
The Long View Ahead          The Short View Ahead
The Intermediate View

A better combination of the elements and components of our measures than that currently represented by the indices therefore appears possible, at least for the psychological understanding of the behavior. However, there may still be some special value in the more situational, developmental-task-oriented classification which, based on logic and the inspection of correlations, led to the index grouping.

When the factorial structure of the indices was examined, Concern with Choice was found to be largely a Planning Orientation to Life, or Planfulness, the general factor in all four adequate indices of vocational maturity. Acceptance of Responsibility for Choice and Planning was made up largely of Planfulness and of The Long View Ahead; Specificity of Information about the Preferred Occupation consisted of Planfulness and The Long View Ahead, in a somewhat different combination; and Specificity of Planning for the Preferred Occupation was made up of Planfulness and The Short View Ahead.

## Conclusion

Vocational maturity in the ninth grade, as assessed by our measures, was defined by the findings as behavior in preparation for vocational choice, as planning and looking ahead. The lack of significant intercorrelation among the Consistency, Crystallization, Independence of Work Experience, and Wisdom indices led to the conclusion that, in grade nine, vocational maturity is not characterizable as goal-attainment, as the having of consistent, realistic, preferences, nor as having begun to make a place for oneself in the world of work.

### CORRELATES OF VOCATIONAL MATURITY

Twenty-eight variables were selected for study as possible correlates, that is, causes, consequences, or concomitants, of vocational maturity (in a cross-sectional analysis, such as that reported in this monograph, no evidence is available as to which of these three a correlate actually is). Some of these were presumed to be predictor variables: among them were intelligence, socioeconomic status, family relationships, level of aspiration, and psychological adjustment. Others were classified as criteria of achievement in various areas, such as peer acceptance, participation in school activities, adolescent independence, and grades. A third category, difficult to classify, was simply labeled miscellaneous. It included age, birth order, urban versus rural residence, and so forth. The correlates might also be classified as biosocial, environmental, vocational, personality, and achievement characteristics. These measures, and their intercorrelations, were discussed in some detail in Chapter V.

### INDEX–CORRELATE RELATIONSHIPS

The correlations of these twenty-eight variables with the four most adequate indices, with the total of these four indices, and with a fifth, marginal index of vocational maturity were reported and discussed in Chapter VI. The coefficients of correlation tended not to be high, the highest being an $r$ of .40 between Acceptance of Responsibility and school achievement in terms of grades.

The following descriptive statements summarize the significant index-correlate relationships. Vocational maturity in the ninth-grade boys studied was associated with 1) living in an intellectually and culturally stimulating environment, 2) having the mental ability essential to respond to that environment, 3) responding to these stimuli by aspiring to occupations at higher rather than lower socio-economic levels, and 4) achieving in one's activities. The following more concrete description of these generalizations will clarify their meaning in this study.

*Living in a stimulating environment* consisted of coming from a moderately high socioeconomic level, having experiences both in and out of the home which were culturally enriching, and taking Regents rather than non-Regents courses. These may not, of course, have a causal relationship to vocational maturity; some or all may be concomitants or outcomes of maturity. In any case, they tended to be associated.

*Having the mental ability to respond to stimulation* provided by the environment consisted, in this study, of making a higher rather than a lower score on a test of intelligence. It is essentially ability to reason, particularly with verbal symbols.

*Responding to achievement stimuli* consisted of aspiring to occupations at higher rather than lower socioeconomic levels, thus seeking to engage in activities which often require the use of higher levels of ability.

*Achieving* consisted of getting good grades, participating in and being elected to offices in school activities and clubs, belonging to out-of-school organizations, such as the Boy Scouts and 4-H Club, and doing things which involved a degree of independence from the home and family, such as going on overnight trips and buying one's own clothes.

Although these characteristics may manifest themselves also in other ways, these were the ways in which the procedures and data of this study permitted them to appear. Furthermore, since the co-efficients of correlation were all low or moderate in size, many vocationally mature boys must, in individual cases, have lacked any given characteristic which was found to be associated with vocational maturity.

Variables which did not prove to be related to vocational maturity in the ninth grade were also considered. Vocational maturity in ninth-grade boys appeared not to be related to age within the grade group, to birth order, to religious affiliation, to family aspirations, to acceptance by peers, or to personal adjustment.

### THE VOCATIONAL MATURITY OF NINTH-GRADE BOYS

In Chapter VII the distributions of scores on various indices were examined, in order to develop a normative picture (but not norms) of vocational behavior at this stage of development.

Concern with vocational choice, as evidenced by awareness of the need for prevocational and vocational choices and by related behaviors, was found to be rather general at this level, although the tendency was to focus on the more immediate choices.

The specificity of information which these boys had about their preferred occupations was rather substantial in so far as occupational requirements were concerned, and this may be sufficient for ninth-graders, who need to make decisions largely of direction rather than of actual entry. But knowledge of duties, conditions of work, and other important characteristics of the occupation was found to be limited.

The specificity of planning was also low; more than half of the ninth-graders had apparently done little about getting information on which to base high school plans. About one-third of the boys made no mention of appropriate high school plans related to their preferred occupations, and post-high-school planning was not very different. Acceptance of responsibility for choice was, on the other hand, fairly widespread in the group.

When these four indices were combined to yield a total score for vocational maturity, the distribution was symmetrical. Whether the mean is normal, high, or low for boys at this grade level cannot of course be ascertained without data from other groups.

In addition to the indices that were considered most adequate, the distributions of scores on some of the other indices were examined.

The distribution of scores on the Interest Maturity Scale of the Strong Vocational Interest Blank was fairly symmetrical, and the median of the Career Pattern Study group was near that of 15-year-olds reported by Strong. Although this scale seemed not to be a measure of vocational maturity as we have defined it, being unrelated to our cluster of indices, it is noteworthy that the boys in the Career Pattern Study scored at the expected place on this scale.

The intelligence of almost one-half of these ninth-grade boys was appropriate for the occupations to which they aspired, but slightly more than half of them wished to enter occupations that seemed inappropriate in terms of the intelligence required. The findings concerning measured interests and vocational preferences were similar to those for abilities and preferences. Almost half of the boys had vocational preferences which did not agree with their interests as measured by Strong's Vocational Interest Blank.

The lack of relationship between wisdom of choice and vocational maturity as measured in this study was considered, and it was pointed out that being concerned with the choice problem and having information might not be sufficient for the making of wise choices, without self-understanding and self-acceptance. Apparently the typical ninth-grade boy has not yet reached a stage at which wisdom of vocational preference can be expected, according to the measures of wisdom used in this study.

# CHAPTER IX

# Implications for Education
## and Guidance

What are the implications of the findings of our research, presented in preceding chapters and summarized in Chapter VIII, for education and for guidance? What can the educational administrator, the curriculum planner, the classroom teacher, the school counselor, and the practicing psychologist learn from this study that will help him in his work with junior and senior high school students or with subject matter?

The first part of this chapter deals briefly with implications for the curriculum, instruction, and orientation. The second part focuses on guidance through appraisal and counseling.

### CURRICULUM, INSTRUCTION, AND ORIENTATION

It was shown, in Chapters III and IV, that vocational maturity in ninth-grade boys, as evaluated by intercorrelations among measures, is primarily orientation to the need to make educational and vocational choices, including acceptance of responsibility for choosing and planning, and a planning and information-getting approach to the orientation and choice process: it is, essentially, planfulness.

It was also shown that consistency of vocational preferences, the
150

wisdom of these preferences, the independence of work experience, and the crystallization of traits bearing on vocational choice, did not intercorrelate appreciably with other measures. These were therefore judged not to constitute vocational maturity in the ninth grade. In the subsequent development and experiences of these boys, these variables may prove to be indicative of vocational maturity—for example, they may be highly predictive of early establishment in an occupation—but they are not, while these boys are still in ninth grade, related to other desirable vocational characteristics.

In view of these findings, curriculum approaches which foster planfulness would appear to be most appropriate. The schools have, for many years, attempted to prepare pupils for the making of curricular, i.e., prevocational, choices in grades eight and nine. The junior high school came into existence partly to serve as a "vestibule school," in which boys and girls could explore a variety of subjects as a basis for choosing between the varied curricula of the high school. In New York State, the ninth-grade course in social studies includes a unit on occupations and on self-analysis: students typically study the occupational structure, take interest and aptitude tests, and make a study of specific occupations. Much of the counseling which is carried on in eighth and ninth grades is designed to bring about wise prevocational choices.

In Middletown, for example, every eighth-grade boy and girl in the junior high school fills out a form for the junior and senior high school counselors. The parents do the same. This form calls for statements of educational and vocational objectives: it asks how much education, and what type of education, the pupil is likely to seek, and in what kind of institution he is likely to seek it; it asks what occupation he is considering entering, and what occupation the parents would like him to enter. The junior high school counselor gives the pupil intelligence and achievement tests, and interviews him concerning ninth-grade and later plans. When the pupils enter the ninth grade at the senior high school, the counselor has the forms they filled out late in the eighth grade, and their cumulative records from the junior high school; Regents (state examination) and non-Regents (local standards) programs are planned partly on the basis of data thus made available. These are choices of *level,* determined largely by academic ability and motivation. Choices of mathematics and language, of commercial and industrial arts, or of agriculture courses are also made. These last are choices of *field* or *direction,* a more complex type of choice than that of level, and more clearly prevocational in nature. While the pupil is pursuing his ninth-grade work, he takes an interest inventory and some aptitude tests, and further interviewing is done as additional choices of level and especially of field are made for tenth-grade courses in the light of achievement to date and of aspirations for the future. In the occupations unit of his ninth-grade social studies course, he studies occupations in Middletown and in the United States, and considers the importance, in relation to occupational success and satisfaction, of the kinds of traits that are measured by the tests taken in that course and in the junior high school.

While it is true, as shown in other studies, that mental ability can be sufficiently well appraised by this time to provide a good basis for estimating the *amount* and *level* of education which is likely to be appropriate for an individual, the data of this study suggest that a substantial number of boys are not yet ready, in the ninth grade, to decide on direction of endeavor, or, specifically, on a future occupation. This early adolescent stage is one, not of making and implementing a vocational choice, but rather of developing planfulness, of preparing to make a series of educational and occupational decisions.

The objective of education in the ninth grade should be, then, in so far as careers are concerned, to help the student become ready to make a series of choices. The finding of a normal distribution of awareness of factors to be considered in making a choice shows that many needed help in this respect, for the ideal distribution would presumably show the great majority of boys at the upper end of the scale, well aware of what to consider in choosing an occupation or a career. Most ninth-grade boys in this study were aware of the immediate choices which they were being required to make (the guidance program itself uses procedures and devices which seem to have been sufficient to cause this), and many of these boys were aware of intermediate choices, but there was minimal awareness of the more remote choices to be made after leaving school. Although it is logical to expect less understanding of the remote than of the immediate choices, what seems remote to a ninth-grader is not actually remote: it is "later than they think."

An understanding at least of the life stage immediately ahead of one, and some orientation to the characteristics of later stages, seems essential to planful and sound, rather than accidental and haphazard, vocational development. One method of fostering such understanding would be through discussion of developmental tasks typically faced in adolescence and of various ways to cope with these tasks. This type of discussion, based partly on cases, could make clear the sequential nature of vocational choice and bring out the progressive elimination of some types of choices as experience helps the individual find that certain activities hold little appeal or promise of success for him. It might help students to see the gradual narrowing-down of goals as some spheres of activity repeatedly yield less and others greater success and satisfaction. At the same time, the role of various personal and social factors in determining how adolescents deal with the various developmental tasks can be made clearer through the sharing of experiences and the study of the experiences of others.

Our findings suggest that the typical ninth-grader tends to accept responsibility for making his own choices and for making his own plans. But lack of relationships between consistency of vocational preferences, wisdom of preferences, and other measures, together with the number of boys whose choices are unwise, judging by their aptitudes, interests, or socioeconomic resources, suggests that the typical ninth-grader does not understand himself and his potentialities as well as he should in order to choose between levels, and still less among fields of endeavor as reflected in the curricular alternatives open to him. At this stage of development when adolescents are beginning to be called upon to make a series of prevocational and vocational choices, they need experiences which help them to develop better self-understanding and self-acceptance.

Furthermore, many boys do not make good use of the resources that are available to aid them in their orientation to careers. They tend to know something about the *requirements* of the occupation to which they aspire, but little about the *duties, conditions* of work, and *opportunities* in the preferred occupations. The typical ninth-grade boy, therefore, needs to be given a broader perspective on the world of work. Since his preferences may not remain stable, helping him to get a better understanding of the currently preferred field is not sufficient; he needs to know about other types of occupations which may in due course appeal to him more, and particularly to develop a perspective on the world of work which will enable him to orient himself more quickly to unfamiliar occupations. He needs to know what to look for, where to find out about it, and how to develop an understanding of an occupation. He needs a general framework of occupational information, plus knowledge of how to fill in the details of any part of that framework.

Since vocational maturity as assessed in our study was associated with living in a culturally stimulating environment and with achievement in a variety of scholastic, extracurricular, and out-of-school activities, it is clearly one function of education to do what it can to provide such an environment and to encourage students to take advantage of the activities which it offers. The school may well ask what it is doing to help seventh-, eighth-, and ninth-grade students to broaden their horizons, to explore potentially challenging but unfamiliar fields, and to experience the satisfactions that come with achievement, recognition, and mastery.

### APPRAISAL AND COUNSELING

The counselor working with ninth-grade boys uses a variety of tools and methods in seeking an understanding of his students. In particular, he relies on tests of intelligence and of achievement in order to get insights into potential for education, into the level and quality of attainment which may be expected of a student. He often uses interest inventories in order to ascertain, as objectively as possible, the nature of the pupil's interests. He obtains information about the education, occupation, and aspirations of the parents in order to make judgments concerning the material and psychological support upon which the boy can count in planning and obtaining an education. And, by means of questionnaires and interviews, he seeks to get from the student himself some indications of his values, motivation, and aspirations.

The results of this study of ninth-grade boys suggest, as have others before it, that taking the student's vocational aspirations at face value is often a mistake, that seeking to help him formulate a specific occupational objective at the ninth-grade level may be a strategic error. Vocational preferences are unstable at this stage, and often unwise when judged by intellectual and other requirements. In particular, consistency of vocational preferences and wisdom of these preferences (as judged by intelligence, interests, and socioeconomic status) are unrelated to each other and to other variables which, according to our criteria, do seem to constitute vocational maturity. However, these vocational preferences may be significant for exploratory purposes, for they can provide a starting point for orientation activities. In the ninth grade, vocational preferences are not necessarily objectives, but they may be steppingstones in the path ahead.

The counselor would do well, in appraising the vocational development and evaluating the vocational prospects of a ninth-grade boy, to supplement ability and interest measures with assessments of vocational maturity, with data which enable him to estimate the student's orientation to vocational choice, his awareness of the need to make decisions, and his planfulness.

This project has, as yet, made available no economical methods of doing this, for our indices of vocational maturity have been derived from interviews which were designed to provide data for a variety of purposes, and the method of deriving them involves a time-consuming process of interview analysis. In its more recent work, the Career Pattern Study staff is devoting some time to devising questionnaire methods of appraising vocational maturity. Practical methods may eventually result from these efforts, but in the meantime the counselor and teacher must rely on information and insights obtained in interviews and on homemade questionnaires. Orientation to vocational choice and planfulness can be judged by the kinds of questions a pupil asks about high school courses and curricula, by the extent to which he sees relationships between these and post-high-school education and occupation, by the nature and variety of the factors which he takes into account in considering choices, by his awareness of the contingencies which may affect the attainment of his ambitions, by how much information he has about training and work in his preferred field, and by the amount and kind of planning which he has done for high school and later educational and work experiences.

The ninth-grader who knows something of the educational choices he will be called upon to make, who is aware of the implications of these choices for later educational and occupational choices, who knows what factors he should be considering in making these choices, who is aware of possible contingencies, who has been asking questions of his peers and of his elders and has been using other resources for improving his orientation to the world of work, and who relates this information to himself is vocationally mature for a ninth-grader. Working with a boy who is vocationally mature is essentially the familiar process of vocational counseling. It involves helping him to assemble, review, and assimilate relevant information about himself and about his situation, which will enable him to draw immediately called-for conclusions as to the implications of these choices for future decisions.

The ninth-grade boy who knows little about the choices which he will be called upon to make, who is unaware of the implications of these choices for later educational and occupational choices, who does not know what factors he should take into account in making choices, and who is unaware of contingencies is vocationally immature. These boys, and they are numerous, are not ready for vocational or educational counseling of the directional decision-making type, involving the choice of one curriculum or occupation rather than another. Their preferences are too unstable, their sense of urgency is too weak, their background of information is too limited, their readiness to make choices has not been developed. They need more orientation to the life stage at which they find themselves and to the vocational developmental tasks which they are about to encounter. Orientation to and readiness for choice needs to be created, although it must be recognized that little is known about how it develops or may be cultivated. After it has begun to develop, vocational counseling of the decision-making type may become appropriate, particularly if the decisions are viewed as exploratory, one-step-at-a-time choices.

Working with a vocationally immature boy involves getting

clues as to how he may be helped to improve his orientation, and then helping him to find, use, and evaluate the experiences which may do this. It is not so much counseling concerning choice, as counseling to develop readiness for choice, to develop planfulness. It involves helping him to understand the personal, social, and other factors which have a bearing on the making of educational and vocational decisions, and how they may operate in his own vocational development. It involves helping him to realize the nature of the resources which he can use to improve his own occupational orientation (for example, occupationally related school subjects, books, friends), and to develop some skill in using them. And it involves assisting him in acquiring a better understanding of the occupational field which interests him most, even while he comes to understand that this may not be his long-term aspiration (for example, in learning about engineering he follows some procedures which will help him, later, to learn more about market research or accounting as an occupation).

In either case, working with the vocationally mature or with the vocationally immature, the counselor needs to keep in mind the developmental nature of vocational choice, and the dynamic nature of the individual who does the choosing and who is developing not only in vocational but also in other areas. Specific vocational preferences may give the counselor clues concerning exploratory activities to be tried, but preferences expressed at the ninth-grade level should not be viewed as definite vocational objectives. While the counselor does well to keep possible intermediate and ultimate goals in mind, he must remember that these goals are still tentative and that educational and other life experiences may be used to try them out. Therefore vocational objectives should be kept as general as possible early in the student's experience, letting the more specific objectives emerge from the more general, on the basis of further experience. For example, it may be enough, when in the ninth grade, for the bright student who is thinking about a possible career in engineering to decide to prepare for college, exploring scientific and technical subjects while in high school. He may study algebra in the ninth grade instead of general mathematics, but also, since he may eventually choose another field, he may elect a foreign language for his fifth subject and thus keep doors open to all high level fields. Limiting and postponing specificity of choices will keep most doors open as long as possible, allowing additional exploration; it will not close doors and preclude possibly desirable and different later choices by a premature commitment to an objective incompatible with such choices. The task of the vocational conselor in the ninth grade is essentially a matter of furthering vocational development rather than of fostering specific vocational choices.

## SUMMARY

This chapter has pointed out that the vocational maturity of ninth-grade boys is such that to require the making of a specific vocational choice at that stage of development is often premature. Education in the ninth grade should be so organized as to make available experiences which foster a planful approach to developmental tasks, to arouse an awareness of the need to make pre-occupational and occupational choices, and to orient adolescents to the kinds and sequences of choices which they will be called upon to make and to the factors which they should consider in making these choices. It should not require the making of definitive, directional, educational and occupational choices in this grade. Guidance in the ninth grade should appraise the student's planfulness, readiness to make vocational choices, concern with the need to choose, and awareness of the factors to be considered in choice. It should help students learn to find and use experiences which foster this readiness, and to make required preliminary choices in ways which keep as many doors open as possible for as long a time as possible. It should proceed on a tentative, step-by-step, developmental basis.

APPENDIX A

Scoring Manuals for
Indices of Vocational Maturity

INDEX IA. CONCERN WITH CHOICE [1]

*General Directions*

*Concern with Choice* consists of three components, *Awareness of the Need for Choice*, *Awareness of the Factors in Vocational Choice*, and *Awareness of Contingency Factors* (events which might upset plans). The purpose of this index is to assess the individual's orientation to the vocational developmental tasks of early adolescence, including the anticipation of the tasks with which he will soon be confronted. These components were formulated on the basis of a review of relevant concepts in the literature and of staff and seminar discussion; their assessability in the interviews was tested by the culling of relevant excerpts from sample interviews.

The interview analyst should read the interview for the boy whose vocational maturity is being appraised, excerpting relevant statements and classifying them according to the scales in this manual.

*Scoring.* Component 1 consists of three elements, Component 3 of four elements; each of these elements is rated on a scale which ranges from 0 to 3 or 5. For example, Element *a* of Component 1 ranges from 0 to 5, the lowest point on the scale being "No mention of concern with immediate choices," the

[1] M. Dubrow. Factors related to the vocational readiness of adolescent boys. Unpublished doctoral dissertation, Teachers Coll., Columbia Univer., 1959. Pp. 18–26 and pp. 66–76. For a slightly modified version, see also: J. Sturm. Awareness of need to choose an occupation in relation to home and economic independence factors. Unpublished doctoral dissertation, Teachers Coll., Columbia Univer., 1958.

highest being "Mentions steps for the implementation of immediate choices": the scaling is based on jury decisions as to the degree of concern manifested by statements excerpted from interviews and used as samples. The final rating for each element consists of the highest rating assigned to any excerpt falling in that category, converted to a normalized T-score. The T-scores for the elements are summed to give a component score.

Component 2 differs from the others in this index in that it consists of 21 items, each of which is given a rating of 0 or 1, depending on whether or not the boy mentions it as a factor to consider in making a choice; the score of this component is the sum of these items. It is converted, like the sums of the other components, into a T-score, and the sums of the components scores become the index score.

## COMPONENT 1. AWARENESS OF THE NEED FOR CHOICE

*Element a. Immediate choices* (high school curricula and courses)
0—No mention of concern.
1—Mentions a need to choose, or one or more available alternatives.
"I don't know yet what courses I'll take next term."
"I may take Shop or Ag."
2—Mentions a choice or steps to aid in making a choice.
"I plan to take all the Math I can."
"I'm going to talk to somebody who took it last year to find out what it's like."
3—Mentions reason(s) for a choice.
"I plan to take all the Math I can because I like to work with numbers."
"I'm good at it."
4—Mentions relationships of immediate to intermediate and/or ultimate choice.
"I plan to take all the Math I can, because it will help me get into engineering school."
"An engineer has to know a lot about Math."
5—Mentions steps for the implementation of immediate choice.
"I have talked with my Math teacher and counselor about it, and they think I can swing it."

*Element b. Intermediate choices* (college, technical institute, apprenticeships, learner's job)
0—No mention of concern.
1—Mentions the need to choose, or one or more available alternatives.
"I don't know whether I'll go to a two-year or a four-year college."
"When I finish high school, I'll decide about college."
2—Mentions a choice or steps to aid in making a choice.
"I want to go to an engineering college."
"When I turn sixteen, I'd like to quit school and get some sort of a farm job."
3—Mentions reason(s) for a choice.
"I'll probably go to engineering school, because I've always liked

Math and drawing" *or* "because my parents expect me to go."
"I'd like to get a farm job, because I like to be outdoors."
4—Mentions relationship of intermediate to ultimate choice.
"You have to have a college degree to be an engineer."
"You need at least two years of college to work in engineering."
"I want to get a job on a farm because one day I hope to have a farm of my own."
5—Mentions steps for the implementation of choice.
"I've talked with my counselor about M.I.T. and R.P.I. and I've studied their catalogs."
*Element c. Ultimate choices*
0—Mere mention of choice without elaboration.[2]
"I want to be an engineer."
1—Mentions further choices to be made (means of entry, specialty in field).
"After I finish my Electrical Engineering course, I can go into Electronics or the light and power field."
"I may have to start in as a Junior Engineer or Draftsman."
2—Mentions specific details of above choices.
"If I go into the light and power field, I could specialize in illumination, manufacturing of equipment, or public utilities."
"In electronics I might specialize in radio and TV or go into industrial work."
"Most big companies start new engineering grads as Junior Engineers or Draftsmen. They may shift you from one department to another."
3—Mentions outcomes of choices of alternatives within the occupation.
"Electronics is an up and coming field, with lots of possibilities."
"Public Utilities offers steady work and security. It may be harder to get into than Electronics."

COMPONENT 2. AWARENESS OF FACTORS IN VOCATIONAL CHOICE

A score of 1 is given for each of the statements by the boy which shows that he considers that it expresses a factor to be considered in vocational choice. (It will be noted that many of the statements listed under the items of Component 2 are complex and so may qualify for classification under more than one item. Thus it is often only one part of a statement that causes it to be listed with a given item.)
(1) *Mental ability: academic standing*
"I guess if I can get to the Agricultural College, that is, if I get good marks, I want to try to have a little farm of my own, if I can get it."
"I have to have at least a 90 average to get a scholarship at N.Y.U., so I can study to become a lawyer."
"I want to be a mechanic, so I've got to get good marks in shop or they won't take me on the job."

---

[2] If the boy indicates his ultimate choice, i.e., his vocational preference, and offers no additional information relevant to any of the other items, he receives a zero score.

(2) *Special aptitudes and abilities*

"I feel that mechanical ability would be helpful in forest ranging. It would be helpful in location of farms and stuff like that."

"I plan to follow the business course throughout high school, because I want to be a banker when I get out."

"I want to take as much Math as I can, because I'll have to keep books on the farm."

(3) *Interests*

"I'd like to do what my brother is—salesman. I like to sell like that. I'd like to sell different things like parts of cars, jig saws, and stuff."

"I want a job that's interesting. Other people work just because they have to. Some people work because they like to be around children. Other people, like the mayor, work just for having the honor of it."

"I'm interested in banking or being a secretary because I just thought of something that I don't have to use too much energy in and that seemed to be most interesting."

(4) *Values*

"I want to get money out of working. That's what everybody wants."

"My father feels that a man should have a job where he can have some opportunity for his own initiative."

"As a missionary, you're working for the good of other people, not working for your own good."

(5) *Personality characteristics*

"I would like to work on my own. I don't think I could stand having the boss tell me to do things over and over again."

"To be a farmer you have to be the kind of guy who helps others in exchanging jobs and work."

"I hope that by the time I'm a senior I'll have made up my mind about if I have any qualities for the priesthood or not. It's hard to look at yourself and know what qualities you have."

(6) *Physical and health requirements*

"To be a mechanic I'd have to do heavy work, and I'm not certain that I have the physical build for it."

"I might not be able to get in the Air Force. I have weak eyes."

"I want to be a banker because I have had nephritis for a few years, and I have to have an easy job physically, but I'd rather drive a bulldozer."

(7) *Sacrifices*

"I'll have to go to night school and work at the same time, so it will mean that I'll have to give up a number of free-time activities."

"To be a priest, you would have to give up the idea of having children—the sexual stuff."

"I don't want to leave Middletown, but if I can't get a job here, I'd have to go some place else."

(8) *Amount of schooling; general education; training*

"To be a forest ranger, you have to take high school for four years and then wait three years. Then after that you go through a naturalist school for two years."

"After high school to be a secretary you have to go to business school for a couple of years.

"You have to have a high school education to be a salesman."

(9) *Cost of training and/or of getting started*

"No, it ain't too hard to get started on a farm, but you gotta have all the kinds of new machinery and all like that, which is pretty high."

"I'd like to get two years technical training in mechanics or forest ranging after high school. I figure that maybe I can work on the outside and go to night school, and I can earn my way through school that way."

"When I first go into the seminary, it'll cost about $500 a year. And, then, when you get into the third and fourth year of college, you have to have $2000 to $3000 a year."

(10) *Availability of necessary educational and training facilities*

"I can get to an agricultural college up-state, if I get good marks."

"I can get a pretty good pre-law course at N.Y.U."

"I could get training as a mechanic in a repair garage, where I would be grinding cylinders, fixing motors, different parts and stuff like that."

(11) *Earnings*

"I'd like to sell because it really brings in the money."

"Getting ahead means making money, and on the farm I'd like to earn about $1000 a month and have about $500 clear."

"I'd like to work in a factory where there are good wages."

(12) *Other benefits: retirement, leave provisions, etc.*

"I'd like to have a job close enough so I could spend weekends with my family. I'd like to get some time off, not just work all the time."

"I couldn't stick to an office job with just one week's vacation a year."

"If I owned a mink ranch, I could take a trip to France."

(13) *Physical conditions*

"I want to be a forest ranger because I want to work outdoors."

"The thing wrong with a factory job is that you're all cooped up. I'd like to work outside."

"As a missionary, I might have to go when it was muddy and see someone who was sick in my parish."

(14) *Hours*

"I like selling because it offers more money, easier work, and better hours."

"When you work on the farm, you have to get up early and do the chores and work through until everything is bedded down."

"I don't like the State Hospital job because the hours are so irregular."

(15) *Regularity of employment, security, etc.*

"I want a job with good pay, a job with a future you can depend on."

"I want to be a farmer because the money is good and you never get laid off. Every day you have a job. The guy in the factory works along and business gets slack and he has to stop work for a while, but the farmer never stops."

"I'd like to have a job where I could retire at 60 and have a nice little pension coming in."

(16) *Psychical conditions: variety, routine, challenge, work under pressure*
"If I work in a store, it's gotta be a clean place; it's gotta have a good management; it can't be a cheap store, it's gotta be reliable."

"I'd rather do routine clerical work than work which involves working with people. But I wouldn't mind supervising people."

"I was just thinking of something where I'd be doing different things all of the time. Secretary seems to be the most interesting."

(17) *Social conditions: congeniality of fellow workers, etc.*
"I wouldn't mind routine clerical work, if I had good people to work with."

"I'd like to be a person who is pleasant to work with and have friends on the job."

"I'd want somebody good to work with who wouldn't slow you down too much and have a good boss."

(18) *Location*
"The main reason I'd like to join the Air Force is to get out of Middletown."

"If I become a missionary, I'll have to leave Middletown and probably go to some place like China."

"As a forest ranger, I'd be in one of the national or state parks."

(19) *Advancement*
"I think that the most important aspect of a good job is having a good future."

"I'd like to have a job where I could better myself and get ahead."

"I can't see any future in Middletown. It's too old-fashioned, has too many businesses, and is overcrowded."

(20) *Supply and demand*
"I'd sooner sell than drive a truck, but the place is lousy with salesmen."

"I don't think there'll be many opportunities in banking when I get out of high school in Middletown."

"If the prices are high for farm goods when I graduate from high school, I'll remain on the farm and make some money."

(21) *Familial attitudes and wishes*
"Dad doesn't have any definite feelings about my job choice, but he mentioned that it would be good to have a farmer in the family."

"My father feels that I would have to get a job in a big garage to be successful."

"My parents think that I should decide for myself what type of work I want to do."

COMPONENT 3. AWARENESS OF CONTINGENCY FACTORS

*Element a. Continued parental psychological support*
0—Does not mention, or says he does not know, parents' attitudes toward his plans.

1—Knows whether they approve of his plans, or implies that having their approval is important.

"My father thinks this is the right thing for me."

"My mother doesn't like the idea of my becoming a flyer."

"That is something I will have to talk to my folks about."

2—Is aware that his parents may change their views and that this would alter his plans.

"Of course, if my grades don't improve, they might say it costs money to go to college and it's taking a chance."

"Perhaps if I show them that pamphlet I saw at the school, they will change their minds."

3—Incorporates the possibility that his parents may change their views (or refuse to change their views) regarding his plans.

"If they won't let me be a flyer, I could always be a ground mechanic."

"If they change their minds about letting me go to college, I'd take a job some place and do it part-time."

"I'm going to work real hard and if I get good grades perhaps they'll say it's OK for me to go to college."

*Element b. Continued financial means*

0—No mention of financial considerations.

1—Mentions financial considerations (cost of training, capital required to get started, etc.), or, if no special expense is involved, shows that he is aware of this.

"I don't know if my folks will be able to send me to college."

"They train you, so your training doesn't cost you anything."

2—Mentions unforeseen financial factors which might affect his plans.

"As things are now, my folks wouldn't have any trouble sending me to college, but you never can tell."

"If I keep up my grades, I might be able to get a scholarship, but I might not do so well later on."

3—Has alternative plans in case present plans fall through.

"If my folks should decide they can't make it, I guess I'd just have to work my way through college."

"If I can't get the kind of job I want here in Middletown, I'd have to go some place where there is a 'Y.' Otherwise, I wouldn't be able to come out on my pay."

*Element c. Military service* (including war)

0—No mention of military service.

1—Recognition of the possibility of military service.

"Of course, I might get drafted."

2—Indicates how military service would interfere with his plans.

"I might be able to finish college."

"If I get drafted, I might get out of the habit of studying and decide not to go to college."

3—Incorporates the possibility into his plans.

"If I'm drafted before I start my apprenticeship, I may be able to get my training in the army."

"Even if I didn't finish college before I got drafted, the Government would help me afterwards."

*Element d. Special factors* (business cycles, labor market, technological change; changed family situation; hazards; competition—despite one's ability to meet requirements, there exists the possibility of being refused entrance to occupation or training, or advancement to a higher position—the possibility may be recognized in someone else's job)

    0—No mention of special contingency factors.

    1—Shows awareness of any one or more of above factors.

> "Jobs may be scarce by the time I leave school."
>
> "There are a lot of boys who'd like to be pilots."
>
> "My uncle was a salesman, but he gave it up. There are too many salesmen on the road these days."

    2—Indicates how any one or more of above special contingency factors could interfere with his plans.

> "By the time I'm ready for a job, there won't be a housing shortage and it won't be easy to get work as a carpenter."
>
> "I could have a pretty good average and still not get into medical school."
>
> "If my folks got sick, I guess I couldn't leave town to try for a better job."
>
> "I'd like to get a job as a clerk and then work my way up to office manager. Of course, there'll be other people with the same idea and your chances might not be too good."

    3—Makes provision for any one or more of above special contingency factors in his plans.

> "I'd study typing and office work so if I got hurt as a lineman, I'd try for an inside job with the power company."
>
> "Maybe I should learn cabinet-making too; that way I'd be safe if there was a slow-down in the building line."
>
> "If they'll only take experienced people, I could move where there are more opportunities, so as to get the experience; then I could come back."
>
> "If I can't get in as an apprentice, I'd try to find someone who'd take me on as a helper."

## INDEX IB. USE OF RESOURCES IN ORIENTATION [3]

The scores for this index are derived from the interview protocols. The basic criterion for a scorable response is the boy's verbalization of a connection, meaningful to himself, between a resource which he has used in his environment and the application of this resource in orienting himself to the world of work. The resources used are not limited to the formal organizations which usually provide occupational information such as guidance counselors, employment agencies, etc., but can be any source which the boy has used to obtain information. Also, "orienting himself to the world of work" is not to be

[3] Manual prepared by William McC. Eastman, with some suggestions from Phoebe L. Overstreet, based on earlier work by Robert L. Jacobson and Helen P. Moser.

construed as meaning only implementation of a definite vocational choice, although this is one orientation. Besides this specific choice, other orientations, such as elimination of a previous possibility of employment, gaining additional information about a previous choice, orientation to a broad occupational field, e.g., "business" or factory work which S is considering or has considered, and opening up new choice areas are also scorable. All scorable responses are assigned a weight of 1, with no regard to source or content. This equivalence of source and content may seem to violate some of the principles of vocational maturity, but since there is no way of ascertaining what are "good" or "bad" sources of information in terms of their relative impact on the boy's vocational development, the assumption of equivalence seems a valid one.

In addition to the basic criterion of "ability to see a connection," the following rules should be used in scoring a response:

A. The two parts of the response, the resource and the connection, should appear in the same interview. This will avoid "long-shot" inferences by the scorer.

B. A statement in direct response to a question by the interviewer is scorable only when the boy makes the connection. If the interviewer makes the connection for him, the response is not scorable. For example, the following interchange:

S. "I'm taking shop math this year, as my fifth course."
I. "For any particular reason?"
S. "Yes, I'm planning to go into manufacturing and it will help me there."

This is scorable, since the boy (S) has made the connection himself, and the resource is one which he has taken the initiative (see "C" below) in using, the fifth course being an elective. Contrast the following example:

S. "I'm taking shop math this year, as a fifth subject."
I. "Do you think it will help you in your work?"
S. "Yes, it will, because I'm going into manufacturing."

This response is not scorable, since the interviewer has furnished the connection to the boy. (Examples are by Eastman, not from interview protocols.)

C. Since all of the boys are equally exposed to resources within the school, only those resources which indicate that the boy has taken the initiative in exploring a school resource will be scored. This is intended to eliminate the stereotyped responses in answer to some of the standard questions, such as the response "I'll get a better job" to the interviewer's question "What do you get out of going to school?"

D. A response which is duplicated will be scored only once. Duplication of a response is defined as the repetition of an identical response. However, when the boy mentions more than one resource for the same orientation or two orientations for the same resource, two scores will be entered.

E. In general, the scorer should attempt to be as conservative as possible in scoring, and seek to avoid "forcing" connections which are not clearly made by the boy.

F. The scorer should not allow his own judgments as to the suitability of the resource or orientation to enter the scoring. Although the reasoning employed by the boy may seem unrealistic to the scorer, it presumably has meaning to the boy, and as such should be scored.

G. If the boy gives a response indicating that he possesses occupational information without indicating the source of this information, the response will not be scored. Obviously he has made use of a resource to gain this information, but since the resource has not been indicated, the scorer cannot be sure that the resource used is not the same as one already scored. If a score were given for the information without knowledge of the resource, duplication of resources might result.

The following procedure for scoring should be used:

1. The scorer should read the interviews *seriatim,* excerpting all scorable responses on a sheet of paper with the case number, interview number and page number of the response.

2. After reading all the interviews, the scorer should again check the responses which he has listed as scorable, using the identifying number to locate them, to make sure that the response is scorable.

3. The number of scorable responses should then be added to give the total score, which should be entered on the individual scoring sheet. (It should be noted that interviewer differences in pursuing this topic could result in apparent subject differences. Interviewer differences with this index were not studied; studies of the interviewer effects on other indices and measures, e.g., Dubrow, Heyde, indicate that these effects were generally negligible.)

## INDEX IIA. SPECIFICITY OF INFORMATION ABOUT THE PREFERRED OCCUPATION [4]

*Outline of Components*

COMPONENT 1. REQUIREMENTS: a. High School Background; b. Training and/or Education; c. Economic Requirements; d. Psychological Requirements; e. Physical Requirements.

COMPONENT 2. DUTIES: a. What is done; b. Why it is done; c. How well it must be done.

COMPONENT 3. CONDITIONS OF WORK: a. Monetary Rewards; b. Hours; c. Security; d. Physical Conditions; e. Psychosocial Conditions.

COMPONENT 4. OPPORTUNITIES: a. Entry; b. Supply and Demand; c. Advancement and Transfer.

[4] H. W. Nolte. The relationship of information regarding preferred occupations to intelligence, experience and other factors. Unpublished doctoral dissertation, Teachers Coll., Columbia Univer., 1956. Pp. 100–114. See also pp. 22–40.

*Scoring System*

Each of the four interviews should be carefully read and scored according to the manual. Particular attention should be paid to the fourth interview for it usually contains most of the scorable material. The parent interview will not be used for scoring.

Scores of 0, 1, or 2 will be assigned as follows:

0—A score of 0 will be assigned when the subject has made no mention of the item, element or component under consideration, or when the statement is too general or too vague to be scorable.

1—A score of 1 is assigned whenever the subject demonstrates an awareness of information about the item. General, broad statements that are not detailed or specific but indicate or imply some correct knowledge of the aspect of vocational information in question will be given a score of 1. The listing of only one aspect of an item will usually earn a score of 1.

2—A score of 2 is assigned whenever the subject demonstrates a specific awareness of information about the item. Relatively full explanations that are quite specific and/or detailed and that indicate broad, accurate knowledge of the item in question will be given a score of 2. Here the subject has explained his statement more fully and has specified just what is desired, required, performed and/or for what reason. With some items the subject may also receive a score of 2 by listing two or more requirements, duties, or advantages involved in a job without giving further information, but the statements must be specific. The items where this scoring criterion is applicable are indicated by parenthetical statements in the manual. For an example see item 1c (3).

Borderline: In some cases the scorer may be undecided about whether to assign a score of 0 or 1, or a score of 1 or 2. If the information was produced by the subject spontaneously he will be given the benefit of the doubt and receive the higher score. But he should be given the lower score if his statement consisted of a minimal response to a direct question, or if the interviewer seemed to suggest the response to the subject. This method will apply only when the scorer has not been able to use the examples in the manual to reach a decision.

Miscellaneous: No credit or penalty will be given for statements containing misinformation.

The maximum score per item is 2. If two statements apply to an item only the higher score will be recorded. If two one-point scores apply to an item the score given on the item would still be only one point. After weighting the component scores, fractions should be rounded off to the nearest whole number.

A statement should be scored only if it is in direct reference to a preference or in the context of a discussion about that preference. If the boy is merely repeating his mother's opinion or talking about what he would like, or if it is not clear what he is talking about, a score of zero is given.

Score cannot be given unless a boy actually says something indicating his knowledge on a point, even though you know he must have that knowledge.

Exceptions to the above rules are indicated in the manual.

Prorating: As many items as possible were selected that applied to all vocational preferences. But some important aspects of information, such as those items dealing with economic requirements, work hazards, and union membership, do not apply to all preferences. It would penalize those boys with this information about their preferences if this information was not scored.

When an item does not apply to a person's preference he would be penalized unless the scores were prorated. For example, a boy who wants to become an officer in the army would be penalized on item 3c (3) because there are no military unions or professional groups. Since this item is not applicable to this preference, a prorated score should be given to make the item fair.

If an item clearly does not apply to a preference, a score will be assigned by prorating from the other elements of the component. Taking item 3c (3) and the military preference as an example again, suppose the subject earned a total of fourteen credits (raw score) on Component 3. Since he earned an average of one point on each pertinent item, prorating would give him one point for the item that was not pertinent. His total raw score would then be fifteen. The subject's average score per suitable item was computed and added for each unsuitable item in the component.

Weighting: By definition, all of the components have equal weight. Yet Components 1 and 3 have fifteen while Components 2 and 4 have only nine items.

A person earning the top score on every item in Component 1 or 3 would have a raw score of 15 (items) multiplied by 2 (top score on the individual items) or 30 points. A person earning the top score on every item in Component 2 or 4 would have a raw score of 9 (items) multiplied by 2 (top score on the individual item) or 18 points. In order to keep the weight of each component equal, the raw score of Components 1 and 3 should be multiplied by 3, and the raw score of Components 2 and 4 should be multiplied by 5. Thus the top weighted score for each component would be 90 points ($15 \times 2 \times 3 = 90$, and $9 \times 2 \times 5 = 90$). The top possible weighted score for the whole scale would be 90 multiplied by 4 or 360 points.

*Scoring Manual*

COMPONENT 1. REQUIREMENTS

a. *High School Background*

(1) Knows what educational level is required for entrance into the vocation, training, or college program.

0—"I'll go into the Navy after I finish high school."

"I don't think that I will go beyond the Junior year."

1—"I don't have to finish school to get that job."

"I'd have to finish school to get that job."

"I'll have to go to college." (It can be safely assumed that a person saying this knows he will have to finish high school.)

2—"I'll have to graduate from high school and go on to college."

"You only need a tenth-grade education for that job."

"I need a Regents diploma for that job."

"My uncle told me he would give me a job whenever I decided to quit school."

(2) Knows the academic standing required for entrance into the vocation, training, or college program.

0—"I hope I can do it."

"There is nothing to worry about."

1—"They have pretty stiff requirements."

"I don't think my grades are good enough."

"I think I could handle the work in college."

"I need good grades for that job."

"Grades won't matter for that job."

2—"My grades are good enough. I've always made the honor roll."

"I'll need an 80 average to get into college."

"I'll need above average grades in Math and Shop courses."

"I'll need at least a 90 average in all subjects to get a job like that."

(3) Knows what kinds of subjects are required or desirable for entrance into vocation, training, or college program.

0—"I'd like to take Math and English courses."

1—"I may have to take Math for that job."

"I'll need to take Social Studies."

"Business courses will help me qualify."

2—"I'll need six credits in Math and two credits in Science for that."

"You should have a year of shop training."

b. *Training and/or Education*

(1) Knows the type of, or content of, training involved.

0—"I don't want to go to college."

"My folks want me to go to college."

"I want to train to be a mechanic."

1—"There is a special college for shop teachers."

"You have to take an on-the-job training course."

"You have to go to a business school."

"I will have to take a conservation course."

"I'll learn more on the farm than I would at school."

"You have to go to a technical institute."

2—"I would have to go to college and then to a medical school."

"You'd have to take several college courses in Mathematics and Chemistry."

"I'd have to take courses in Mechanical Drawing and Auto Mechanics."

"I'd start out by feeding the cows and cleaning the barn and would learn to milk cows later."

(2) Knows the length or extent of training involved.

0—"I'd like to finish my training in a year or two."

1—"It wouldn't take long to complete the training."

"It would take quite a while to study for that."

"A dentist has to go to school for twelve years." (This statement is inaccurate but does indicate that the subject knows the training is quite lengthy.)

2—"You have to have an M.A. to teach high school in New York State."

"You have to serve as an apprentice for four years before you can get a job like that."

"After college you have to go to medical school for four more years."

"They have a two year course for television repairmen."

(3) Knows the location of training facilities.

0—"I don't know where I could train for that."

1—"There is an on-the-job training program here in town."

"There may be a course for that in New York City."

"There may be a course like that in the army."

"There is a two year school for that in New York, but I've forgotten the name of it."

2—"I'll go to school here. (The local community college)

"Columbia College has a course like that."

"The Air Force has a course like that at X Field."

"Factory where my uncle works trains men for that job."

c. *Economic Requirements*

(1) Knows how much capital is needed for the training or the business.

0—"You need the financial background for it."

1—"I don't think that I have enough money for college."

"A college education is expensive."

"Tools are expensive."

2—"A state teachers college is free. You only have to pay $15 for lab fees."

"X College charges $12.50 a point for tuition."

"The tools I would need cost $500."

"A farm like that would cost $...."

(2) Knows the cost of maintenance.

0—"I wouldn't want a business that costs a lot to run."

1—"A salesman uses a car and has other expenses while traveling."

"It costs a lot of money to live at college."

"Business rent is expensive."

"I'll lose the money I could earn if I didn't go to college."

2—"Room and board costs $... at Columbia College."

"Business space rents for $... per month."

"The union dues are $... per month."

"A salesman usually has to spend 4–5¢ per mile for transportation."

(3) Knows of facilities for financing training or business.

0—"I can handle the finances."

1—"If I save for a while I'll have enough to buy a farm."

"I can get money from the G. I. Bill."

"I can get a scholarship."

"I can work and save up for the training."

2—"My family will be able to pay one-half of the expenses, and I can earn $500 by working summers."

"I wouldn't be able to earn much as an apprentice but my folks would give me $50 a month for my living expenses."

"An athletic scholarship would pay for the tuition, and I could save for the rest by working summers."

"X College has a $350 scholarship that I could get."

(Mentions more than one source of financial help and/or states how much he expects to get from each.)

d. *Psychological Requirements*

(1) Knows what abilities are usually required by the vocation.

0—"I'm good at shop work."

"I write well."

1—"You have to be pretty good with your hands."

"You have to be good with figures."

"You have to be able to write."

"You have to know how to handle a gun."

"A teacher has to be able to handle a class."

2—"You have to be able to add long lists of numbers correctly."

"You have to be able to assemble small objects quickly."

"You must be able to write with good English and express yourself clearly."

"A teacher has to be able to control a class with fair but firm discipline."

(2) Knows what interests are usually demanded by a vocation, and/or knows which hobbies and activities are indicative of these interests.

0—"I like flying."

1—"I like to read about raising animals."

"You have to like to meet people for that job."

"You have to like to work with figures on a job like that."

"I became interested in that by watching men working at it."

"I like business. Even when I was a young boy I used to play with my father's cancelled checks."

2—"I became interested in aviation by working with models."

"I like to work with precise figures and come out exactly right."

"A doctor has to like to work with people who are sick and complaining."

"I enjoy taking care of animals and so I began thinking of becoming a veterinarian."

"I would like to work with athletics as a gym teacher does."

"I like to work with figures and I don't like to meet people, so that job would suit me."

(3) Knows what personality traits are usually important and/or why they are important.

0—"I'm friendly and I'm a hard worker."

"I get along well with people."

1—"You have to be able to stick with it until it's done."

"You have to be able to get along with people."

"A teacher has to be patient."

"You have to be a good leader on that job."

2—"You have to be able to think quickly in an emergency."

"You have to be liked by your customers if you are to make a lot of sales."

"You have to be able to take monotonous work, for you do the same thing day in and day out."

e. *Physical Requirements*

(1) Knows what the health requirements are and/or the reasons for these requirements.

0—"I'm in good health."

1—"You have to be healthy."

"You have to pass a physical examination."

2—"A doctor has to be able to withstand diseases."

3—"You can't afford to be sick very often when you have your own business."

"For safety reasons, a bus driver has to have a good heart."

"A teacher has to be healthy because she is often exposed to diseases carried by the children."

"You get paid by the day so you lose wages when you are sick."

(2) Knows what physical demands are usually involved and/or why they are demanded.

0—"I don't like to work too hard."

1—"You don't have to labor too hard on that job."

"You have to be pretty strong."

"You have to be able to see good."

2—"You need a lot of weight and strength to be able to move heavy furniture."

"You have to have 20/20 vision because of the small parts you work with."

(3) Knows the implications of age for the job.

0—"I want to be able to retire while I'm still young."

1—"An aviator may be grounded while still young."

"You are not supposed to work there until you are a certain age."

"A ballplayer can play at the game for a fairly long time."

2—"Lifting that much weight is all right now but will be too much for me when I am fifty."

"You can enlist in the army at sixteen if your parents will sign for you."

"People hesitate to go to a young doctor because they prefer an older, more experienced man."

"You have to be twenty-one to join the state police."

"A wrestler can't work very much after he's forty."

COMPONENT 2. DUTIES

a. *What is done*

(1) Knows typical tasks performed by workers.

0—"I would like to work around animals."

1—"I will play baseball."

"You help out around the farmhouse."

"You work around cars."

"You make drawings of machines."

"A doctor treats his patients."

2—"A catcher catches the pitches, plays home plate, and signals the pitcher about how to pitch."

"A teacher teaches by talking, demonstrating, and assigning lessons."

"A mechanic adjusts the carburetor and tunes up the engine by adjusting the tappets."

(Lists more than one duty and/or explains fully what one of the duties involves.)

(2) Knows what machines, tools, techniques, equipment, materials, animals, and/or special methods of working with people are used by the worker.

0—"I like to work with machine tools."

1—"An architect uses drawing tools."

"A television director works with scripts."

"You use machine tools for that."

"You use carpenters' tools."

"You try to serve the customers politely."

2—"He uses a hammer, saw, nails, etc."

"An x-ray camera is a special camera that can take pictures of the inside of the body."

"A teacher uses a lot of books and magazines."

(Mentions two or more tools used or describes and/or explains one tool fully.)

(3) Knows the setting in which the work is usually done. (See item 3*d*(3).

0—"I would like to work on a farm."

1—"I would work on a farm."

"I would have to work in an office."

"I would teach in a high school."

"You would drive a truck all day."

2—"Most of the time is spent in an office, but you have to visit factories in the field once a week."

"The teacher spends most of her time in a classroom, but does have to watch the children playing in the yard during some lunch hours."

*b. Why it is done*

(1) Relates the specific job to the procedure, product, or service as a whole.

0—"The teacher teaches."

1—"The teacher helps the students learn about things."

"The mechanic fixes a car so that it will work again."

"You feed the mink so that they won't go hungry."

(The subject has a limited perspective of the purpose for which the work is done.)

2—"The teacher tries to help students learn so that they will be prepared for a job and the responsibilities of an adult."

"The mechanic fixes a car so that it will run properly and efficiently and safely again."

"X kind of food is better for the mink because it gives it a glossier coat which will make it more attractive as a coat to wear."

(The subject has a broad perspective of the purpose for which the work is done.)

(2) Knows how and why the tools are used to implement tasks.

0—"You plane the sides of the box."

1—"Tools are used to shape the wood and work the metal."

"The architect uses tools to make his drawings."

2—"The level is used to make sure the layer of bricks is horizontal."

"The angle box is used to make sure the angle of cut is accurate."

"You use an x-ray camera to find out if an organ is diseased."

"There are fifty discs on the machine. You pull it behind a tractor and it makes lumps in the soil—cuts it all up."

"The architect uses his tools to draw straight lines, make correct angles, and to draw his diagrams to the proper scale."

This item should be carefully differentiated from item 2a(2). In that item, score is given for any description or explanation of the tools that are used. In the present item, score is given for any statement describing the function of the tools used.

(3) Knows why the work is or is not important to the community.

0—"I like to help people."

1—"The discoveries of science help people."

"You have to have plumbers."

"It's an important job."

"The town couldn't get along without it."

2—"A forest ranger prevents overcutting; this is done to prevent erosion, floods, and a scarcity of wood in the future."

"If you didn't have plumbers the town would be less sanitary and you might even have epidemics."

c. *How well it must be done*

(1) Knows what detail, work tolerance, care, and/or precision is required.

0—"You have to be good."

1—"You have to be pretty exact when making a tool."

"A pharmacist has to be careful."

2—"You have to be exact to the 1/1000 of an inch."

"A pharmacist has to mix the exact amounts of the right ingredients."

(2) Knows the consequences of mistakes or poor performance.

0—"I wouldn't feel right unless I could do a good job."

1—"If it's not good enough, you'll have to do it over."

"If it's not done right, the boss will be angry."

"A bad teacher can cause a lot of trouble."

2—"If it doesn't fit right, there will be too much friction and the other parts of the machine will wear too much."

"A careless worker can spoil a lot of expensive material."

"If you do good work you can build up a good business."

"You can waste a lot of time if you are not careful."

"The health and safety of a customer depend upon a pharmacist's carefulness."

"If you are not a good teacher, the pupils may lose interest in school and leave."

"If you work too slowly, you may hold up the whole assembly line."

(3) Knows the timing or pace of work involved.

0—"You have to work hard."

"It's pretty easy work."

1—"You can't let up for a minute on that job."
"A doctor leads a busy life."
"You don't have to work fast on that job."
"You have to work fast on that job."
2—"A doctor works very hard all of the time and is often called out at night."
"You have to make three pieces a minute."
"That job is fairly slow except for Friday nights, when most of the customers come in."
"You are busy all of the time. You have no time to just stand around."

COMPONENT 3. CONDITIONS OF WORK

*a. Monetary Rewards*

(1) Knows what the basic wages are and how they are paid.
0—"I'd like a job with good pay."
1—"They pay pretty good."
"You can't earn much at that."
"A pilot is paid better than an airplane mechanic."
2—"You can earn one dollar an hour."
"You earn three cents a piece."
"You can earn $7,000 a year at that job."

(2) Knows of opportunities to supplement income.
0—"You can get a lot of extras on that job."
1—"You can work overtime and earn a lot of extra money."
"You have a car allowance on that kind of job."
"A teacher can earn extra money by working during the summer."
(Mention of expense account, discount privileges, bonuses, commission, etc., would also deserve credit.)
2—"If you work on Saturdays you earn time and one-half pay."
"You get two weeks of paid vacation."
"A sailor gets his meals, room, and clothes free. That is worth at least $60 a month."
"You can get a car allowance of $50 a month."
(Knows the approximate income and/or the benefits that can be received from the above.)

(3) Knows the starting salary, maximum salary, increments, and/or how they are determined.
0—"I wouldn't mind starting out with a low income if I were sure I could earn a good salary later."
1—"Your pay is poor at first but can become much greater."
2—"I would start at $1500 but the most I could earn at that would be $2500 a year."
"Teachers in some places can get increments of $100 a year until the maximum salary is reached."
This item should be carefully differentiated from item (1) above so that double credit is not given. Statements of salary are scored under (1) unless some reference is made to increments, maximum salary, etc.

*b. Hours*

(1) Knows how many hours are worked per day and/or per week.
0—"I wouldn't want to work more than fifty hours a week."

1—"You work about forty hours a week."

"You work a regular work week."

2—"Most workers work from eight to five for a five-day week, with an hour off for lunch each day."

"A teacher works from eight-thirty to four, with an hour off for lunch."

(2) Knows about overtime, shifts, irregular hours, etc.

0—"I wouldn't want to work at night."

1—"I may have to work overtime occasionally."

"I may have to work on the night shift."

"A doctor may be called out at night."

2—"Some salesmen have to work from nine to three on Saturdays."

"A teacher often has to attend meetings, mark papers, etc., after school hours."

"An obstetrician is called out at night several times a week."

(3) Knows how much time is available to spend away from the job.

0—"I'd like to have enough time to be with my family."

1—"You get a vacation every year."

"There may not be much time for home life."

2—"You couldn't have much night life because you have to get up at 5 A.M. for that job."

"You get two weeks off each year."

"You have your vacation early in July when the whole factory closes down."

"Since you have to go to work at 7 P.M., you don't have much time to see your family."

"The only time you would have for recreation would be on weekends."

"You have eighteen days off after you finish basic training."

c. *Security*

(1) Knows how secure his preferred occupation is re tenure, seasonality, etc.

0—"I want a steady, secure job."

1—"It's a fairly regular job."

"The job provides security for old age."

2—"After you have worked for a long time, you are hardly ever laid off."

"A ballplayer signs a yearly contract, so he is secure for at least that year."

"The carpet business is busy in summer but rather slow from November to April."

"A teacher on tenure can't be fired except for moral reasons."

(2) Knows about workman's compensation, unemployment, retirement, sick leave, and other special benefits.

0—"I want a job with compensation benefits."

1—"You get sick leave there."

"The army has retirement benefits."

2—"You get two weeks paid sick leave per year there."

"You can retire from the army after twenty years."

(3) Knows of his probable affiliation with unions, professional groups, etc., and/or how they may affect his job security.

0—"I don't want to join a union."

1—"I'd have to join a union."

"I won't have to join a union."

"I belong to the 4-H club. (Although this statement is quite specific, the 4-H club is not an adult group and for that reason cannot receive maximum credit.)

2—"I'd have to join the C.I.O., Local #... They stand up for the worker pretty well and give him many benefits."

"The school faculty can be active in securing higher salaries."

"I'd join the Rotary Club. You could make many business contacts there."

"I could join the Farmers Union."

*d. Physical Conditions*

(1) Knows of the hazards to health or injury involved in the job.

0—"If you smoke, you lose your breath fast and it's harder to run."

1—"The job is rather dangerous."

"Teaching is rough on the nerves."

"That job is rough on your eyes."

"That is a safe job."

2—"The workers are lazy and get on your nerves. My father has so much trouble with them that he gets very nervous and irritable."

"A carpenter can cut his hand on a saw."

"The kids make a lot of noise which irritates the teacher."

(2) Knows of precautions that can minimize the hazards.

0—"I wouldn't take a job that was dangerous."

1—"If you are careful you won't be hurt."

2—"The machines have guards to prevent injury."

"If you work with proper lighting you won't strain your eyes too much."

"The teacher has all summer to rest up and recover from nervous strain and get away from children."

(3) Knows of the usual situational conditions.

0—"I like a job that makes you travel a lot."

"The working conditions are good on that job."

1—"It is outside work."

"You move around a lot while you work."

2—"You spend most of your time outside, but you are indoors an average of three or four hours a week."

"Working in a store is nice clean work and you can wear a suit."

"In construction, you stay in one place for a while, but you have to move on eventually."

"A mailman is always on his feet and walks a long way every day."

"A traffic cop has to be out in all kinds of weather."

"A plumber has to get down on his hands and knees to do many parts of his job."

This item should be carefully differentiated from 2a(3) for that item refers to the setting in which the work is usually done. The present item is concerned with physical conditions like heat, dampness, exposure to elements, amount of moving around the job requires—as in the examples above.

 e. *Psychosocial Conditions*

   (1) Knows what challenge, variety, and/or routine the vocation usually offers.

   0—"I want an exciting job."

   1—"I want to play baseball for the sport of it."

   "The job is exciting."

   "The job has a lot of variety."

   2—"Half of your time is spent with routine work, but the rest of the time is interesting."

   "You meet many different people, which offers a lot of variety."

   (2) Knows what kind of customers or associates he will work with, the general public contact he will have, and/or the kind of relationships he may have with them.

   0—"You work with eight men."

   1—"I know someone fairly well who works at that."

   "You have a chance to develop friendships with people."

   2—"The workers you can hire are careless and hard to work with, but they are hard to replace, so you have to put up with them."

   "I would spend most of my time working with school-aged children."

   "You work with college men."

   "Truck drivers are a rough crowd."

   "I know some persons who work at the job and I would enjoy working with them."

   "I would be closely supervised on that job."

   "I would have a chance to develop leadership on that job."

   (3) Knows what prestige the job has.

   0—"I want to be a common man."

   1—"People usually look down on that kind of work."

   "That is a respectable job."

   "The prestige of that job is pretty good."

   2—"You can get to be pretty famous as a ballplayer."

   "You can be somebody big at that job."

   "The job has as much respect as a doctor's job."

   "Very few people like that work, because it is so dirty."

COMPONENT 4. OPPORTUNITIES

 a. *Entry*

   (1) Knows how a job in the field can be obtained.

   0—"I'd like to have my father get a job for me."

   1—"A friend of mine may know where I could get a job like that."

   "I could get a job through the want ads."

   2—"My uncle knows the foreman who is hiring men for that, and he may be able to put in a good word for me."

   "X agency often advertises jobs like that."

   "The school placement man often has leads for this kind of work."

   (2) Knows the usual entry job, or jobs, and the relative merits of each,

and/or knows of a similar or related job he might apply for in the armed services.

0—"I'd like to get a job on the farm."

1—"I could work on a farm during the summer to get experience."

"They use a lot of mechanics in the army, so I might be able to get a job like that."

"You usually have to start with a job like copy boy."

2—"You could train for the job in the Air Force and then transfer to a commercial job."

"I could try to get into radar, communication, or some other branch of the army offering jobs in electronics."

"It might be better to work your way up from the bottom in a business, because you would learn more about it."

"I could work as a foreman at the shop until my father gives the firm to me."

(3) Knows how applicants are selected for entry jobs.

0—"They would select men for the job."

1—"They would hire the best man."

"You have to take a test."

2—"They hire the man with the most experience."

"The man with the best training would get the job."

"The one with the highest mark on the test would get the job."

"They would hire the man with the best appearance and diction."

b. *Supply and demand*

(1) Knows local employment prospects (including the New York City area).

0—"I don't think there is much opportunity around here."

1—"A large company is more likely to have a job open."

"I've heard that they are hiring men at the mill."

"I may be able to get a job at X factory."

"There is a shortage of mechanics now."

2—"I've heard that they are hiring mechanics at the mill."

"My father will give his business to me."

"I would have to move to get a job, because there aren't any openings here."

"There are five men working at that here. One of them is sixty-four and will retire soon."

"They have been hiring one new worker a year."

"The boss told my brother that he needs another man for that job."

"Several factories have opened up and they all need mechanics."

(2) Knows of the employment prospects nationally and in different industries.

0—"I'd go where I could get the most work."

1—"Most small cities have veterinarians."

"The long range trend is for a greater number of workers to be employed in the electronics trades."

"Most factories have mechanics."

"It's not too easy to get into the Federal Bureau of Investigation."

"You can get a job as a carpenter anywhere these days."

"You can use forestry training in government service work or in private industry."

2—"There are five thousand men doing that in the U. S. now, but there will soon be a demand for twice as many."

"I could get a job like that in Wisconsin or in Minnesota."

(3) Knows how his vocation might be affected by economic trends, war, depression, or technological change.

0—"They will always need engineers."

1—"Engineers would be in demand if there were a war."

"Laborers are among the first to lose their jobs when there is a depression."

2—"If there were a war, engineers would be needed in the army, in defense plants, etc."

"Once the construction boom ends, carpenters might not have it so easy."

c. *Advancement and Transfer*

(1) Knows the lines and limits of advancement.

0—"I'd like a job with a chance for advancement."

1—"You have a better chance for advancement in a large company."

"The more you know about your job, the more chance you have to be advanced."

"With my background I can only go so far."

2—"After getting some experience I may be promoted to an X, the next highest job."

"After a year I may get a raise of $5.00 a week."

"After working as a personnel clerk I could be advanced to an interviewer."

(2) Knows how advancement is earned.

0—"I'd have to work my way up."

1—"If you do a good job with a farm you can build it up."

"Advancement comes with greater experience."

"You can get a better job once you have a little more seniority."

"To get a better job I would have to meet special requirements."

"I'd have to pass a special test."

2—"With greater seniority as a motorman you would have a better selection of hours of work to choose from."

"After getting further training in night school I might be advanced to an X."

"I could become a foreman after I have two years of experience."

"I would have to pass a civil service test to get that better job."

(3) Knows the requirements and/or the conditions of jobs to which he could transfer.

0—"I could get a good job when I get out of the F.B.I."

1—"I could become a private detective with the training I had in the F.B.I." (Statement about transfer job)

2—"Detective work wouldn't be as respectable, but I would be able to earn as much money."

A score of two would be given if any of the duties, requirements, conditions of work, etc., were mentioned in connection with the transfer job.

## INDEX IIB. SPECIFICITY OF PLANNING FOR THE PREFERRED OCCUPATION [5]

*General Directions*

This index consists of nine components, each rated on a scale of 0 to 3. The maximum score per component is three. The sum of the component T-scores constitutes the Index score. Each of the four interviews should be carefully read. Particular attention should be paid to the fourth interview for it usually contains most of the scorable material.

No credit or penalty will be given for statements containing misinformation. When two or more statements apply to a component, record the highest score.

A statement should be scored only if it is in direct reference to the given preference or in the context of a discussion about that preference. If the boy is merely repeating his parent's opinion or if it is not clear what he is talking about, do not score.

COMPONENT 1. STEPS TAKEN TO OBTAIN INFORMATION FOR HIGH SCHOOL PLANNING

0—No mention

1—Has discussed his plans with (presumably) uninformed persons; no other resources (such as reading, school handbook, etc.) explored.

"I've talked to some of my friends about the courses I would need to be a surveyor, but they don't know very much about it."

2—Has discussed plans with uninformed persons but has explored other resources; *or* has discussed plans with informed persons without an exploration of other resources; *or* has explored resources without discussion with anybody.

"I haven't had a chance yet to talk to the counselor, but I have studied the school handbook pretty carefully."

"My friends weren't able to tell me anything useful, so I went to the principal's office and got some printed information."

"I talked to the math teacher about what I would need for engineering, but I haven't been able to read the pamphlet he recommended."

3—Has discussed his plans with informed persons and has explored other resources.

"I spoke to my uncle who is an engineer and then got some pamphlets from the counselor so that I would know what courses I should be taking."

COMPONENT 2. SPECIFICITY OF HIGH SCHOOL PLANS

0—No mention *or* mentions plans that are clearly inappropriate to his occupational objective.

1—Mentions general broad relationship of high school course(s) to his occupational plans.

"I want to be an engineer, so I guess I'll be taking the college prep course."

[5] W. P. Wolk. Some correlates of vocational planning in ninth-grade boys. Unpublished doctoral dissertation, Teachers Coll., Columbia Univer., 1958. Pp. 62–68. See also pp. 14–21.

"I want to work in an office, so I'll take some commercial courses."
2—Mentions more specific relationship of high school courses to his occupational plans.
"To get into engineering school I'll have to take at least three years of math and science."
"I plan to take bookkeeping—I want to be an accountant."
3—Mentions relevance of other high school courses to his plans than those mentioned in 2 above.
"I want to fit in a course in shop because it's an advantage if an engineer can make his own models."
"I'm taking the agriculture course, but I also want to take bookkeeping because a farmer has to know how to keep records."

COMPONENT 3. SPECIFICITY OF ALTERNATIVE HIGH SCHOOL PLANS [6]
0—No mention of an alternative plan.
1—Indicates he has an alternative plan.
"If I can't get a course in poultry farming, there's plenty of other courses I could take that would help me in farming."
2—Describes the general nature of the alternative plan (which is appropriate to the alternative objective).
"I could take the general Ag. course, for example."
3—Describes the specific nature of the alternative plan.
"I would take general Ag. for two years, and also biology, shop work and perhaps some bookkeeping. These are good things for a farmer to know."

COMPONENT 4. STEPS TAKEN TO OBTAIN INFORMATION FOR POST-HIGH SCHOOL PLANNING
0—No mention.
1—Has discussed plans with (presumably) uninformed persons without exploration of other resources.
"I've talked to some of the guys about medicine, but they don't know much more than I do, because I haven't read up on it either."
2—Has discussed plans with uninformed persons but has explored other resources; or has discussed plans with informed persons without an exploration of other resources; or has explored resources without discussion with anybody.
"I talked to my dad about becoming a doctor, but since he isn't in medicine I didn't get much from him. So I went on one of those guided tours they give at the hospital and read some magazine articles."
"I've talked to my dad about medicine because he's a doctor, but I haven't had a chance to do anything else."
3—Has discussed his plans with an informed person and has explored other resources.
"I've talked to the guidance teacher about engineering and read some pamphlets."

COMPONENT 5. POST-HIGH SCHOOL PLANS
0—No mention or mentions plans that are clearly inappropriate to his occupational objective.
1—Mentions general sponsorship and/or general nature of the training.
"I want to be an apprentice carpenter so I can learn the trade."

---

[6] There were no scores above zero on this component, so it was not used.

"If I'm going to become an engineer, I'll have to go to college."

2—Mentions particular sponsorship and general nature of the training.

"To be a carpenter I'll have to spend a couple of years as an apprentice with a construction company."

"I want to go to MIT and become an engineer."

3—Mentions particular sponsorpship and specific nature of training.

"I'd like to go to MIT for four years and take a course in engineering which would include structural design, calculus, physics, and chemistry."

"To be a carpenter I'll have to spend two years as an apprentice with a construction company. The first few months I'll just be carrying tools and doing simple clean-up jobs, but then I'll gradually learn to make simple joints, put up siding, etc., and eventually be able to work from blueprints."

COMPONENT 6. ALTERNATIVE POST-HIGH SCHOOL PLANS

0—No mention.

1—Indicates he has an alternative plan.

"If I can't get into college, I can always go into my father's business."

2—Describes the general nature of an alternative plan.

"If I can't get into college, I can go to the N. Y. Technical School for TV technicians and then go into my father's business."

3—Describes the specific nature of an alternative plan.

"If I can't get into college, I can go to the N. Y. Technical Institute for two years. Then I can come back and get practical experience from my father so that I can take over on my own later on."

COMPONENT 7. ENTRY PLANS

0—No mention of planning for entry.

"I'll worry about getting started later."

"I shouldn't have trouble getting a job."

1—Mentions general plan(s) for entry.

"I'll try one of the local factories."

"During my last year at college I'll register with the college placement office."

2—Gives more specific plans for entry.

"When I finish college, I'm going to apply for a junior engineering or drafting job with some of the large electrical manufacturing concerns. That's how you usually start."

"The big engineering companies often send people to interview college seniors, and if I'm good I may get a beginning job that way."

3—Mentions possible alternatives to, or outcomes of, plans for entry.

"When I finish college, I'm going to apply for a junior engineering or drafting job with some of the large electrical manufacturing firms. If I don't get a job with a big company, I'll try for a beginning job with some of the smaller outfits. I can always shift to a larger company later if I want to."

"The big engineering companies often send people to interview college seniors, and if I'm good I may get a beginning job that way. If I don't I'll still try the college placement office, send out applications, and maybe try another employment office."

COMPONENT 8. PLANNING TO FACILITATE ENTRY

0—No mention.

1—Mentions general step(s) to facilitate entry.

"In getting started it's important to have a recommendation from your school."

"If you have any contacts in the field it's easier to get started."

2—Gives specific details of steps.

"I'm going to do a good job in college. It helps in getting a recommendation when you apply for a job later."

"While I'm in school I'm going to try to get some part-time jobs with companies that use engineers. It's good experience and may help you get a job later."

3—Mentions alternative plans to facilitate entry.

"If I can't get a job in this area, I'll apply to some out-of-town companies. Once I'm started I may be able to come back this way if I want to."

"Sometimes you can get a beginning union job out of town and then you may be able to transfer to one of the local unions."

COMPONENT 9. PLANNING FOR ADVANCEMENT IN THE OCCUPATION

0—No mention.

1—Has general plans for preparing for promotion or wage increases or expansion of business.

"I'm going to take some business courses in my spare time so as to improve my chances of promotion."

"Whatever money I make I'm going to use to improve my farm."

2—Mentions specific plans for preparing for promotion, wage increases, or business expansion.

"I'm going to take some courses in business methods and accounting so that I can be promoted to a grade 1 clerk."

"As soon as I can establish credit at the bank, I'll buy some pedigreed stock so that I can increase my milk yield."

3—Mentions alternative advancement plans.

"If the courses at the technical institute don't help then I'll go into business myself."


## INDEX IIC. THE EXTENT OF PLANNING ACTIVITY [7]

This measure consists of a scale from 0 to 3, for the rating of discussion of plans with members of the family and with outside persons, reading of printed materials, and use of other non-personal resources, non-mention being given the lowest rating and emphasis on the use of authoritative sources outside of

[7] This vocational maturity index was developed and scored by David Cohen. It was originally intended for use as part of the index Independence of Work Experience, but was dropped from that measure because of its failure to correlate significantly with the five components that were retained. Extent of Planning Activity was used as an index of Dimension II, Information and Planning about the Preferred Occupation, in the first intercorrelational analysis (Chapter III) and in the factor analysis (Chapter IV). It was later combined with components of Index IIB, Specificity of Planning (Chapter VI).

the home receiving the highest rating. Sample excerpts from interviews illustrate the descriptive statements. The interview analyst reads interviews and makes excerpts of relevant statements, and assigns a rating based on the highest-rated behavior manifested by the boy. When combined with other components to constitute Index IIB, the rating is converted to a T-score and the sum of the component T-scores becomes the index score.

0—Does not mention discussion of plans or use of resources.
1—Discusses plans with members of the family only. There is no use of outside resources.
   "I talked with Dad about engineering and he thinks it's a good field."
2—Discusses plans with members of the family and also makes use of outside resources.
   "I talked with Dad about engineering and I also spoke about it with our school counselor."
3—Makes use of outside resources primarily in planning. Any discussion of plans with members of the family is secondary in importance.
   "I've been reading about engineering in the school library since I talked with our school counselor. I mentioned it at home, and Dad said it would be up to me."

## INDEX IIIA. CONSISTENCY OF VOCATIONAL PREFERENCES WITHIN FIELDS [8]

Vocational preferences were elicited in the last interview of the series of interviews with the boys, in response to the question: "We've talked about school, your activities outside of school, and your family. This time let's talk about your plans for the future. What would you like to be by the time you're thirty?" (Super et al., 1957, p. 122) These preferences were ranked according to the sequence in which they were elicited in the interview, with the preference stated first designated as the preferred occupation. A few exceptions were made (when a boy stated that the preference mentioned first was not his first choice). When the boy's description of his preferred occupation made it very clear that the job title the boy had given it was incorrect, the preference was assigned the correct job title for the job description.

Only preferences mentioned by the boy were considered; comments by interviewers were omitted except when they were attempting to classify the job title from the description given by the boy.

Each boy's interview-derived preferences, up to four, were classified as to occupational field, using the modification of Roe's occupational classification by Moser, Dubin, and Shelsky (1956).

The sum of the number of different fields preferred was obtained for each boy. This sum minus 1 was his score on the index. A boy with only one preference received a score of 0, no discrepancy.

[8] This index was developed and scored by Helen P. Moser.

### INDEX IIIB. CONSISTENCY OF VOCATIONAL PREFERENCES WITHIN LEVELS [9]

Vocational preferences were obtained from interviews, as described in the preceding section on Index IIIA.

Each boy's interview-derived preferences, up to four, were classified as to occupational level, using the modification of Roe's occupational classification by Moser, Dubin, and Shelsky (1956). The levels of this scale range from one (Professional and Higher Managerial) through six (Unskilled).

To obtain a score for this index, the level number of the highest-level preference was subtracted from the level number of the lowest-level preference. A boy with only one preference received a score of 0, no discrepancy.

### INDEX IIIC. CONSISTENCY OF VOCATIONAL PREFERENCES WITHIN FAMILIES [10]

Vocational preferences were obtained from interviews, as described in the section on Index IIIA.

Each boy's score on Index IIIA and his score on Index IIIB were summed. The total was his score on Index IIIC.

### INDEX IVA. DEGREE OF PATTERNING OF MEASURED INTERESTS [11]

Using Darley's (1941) method, each boy's profile on the Career Pattern Study modification of the Strong Vocational Interest Blank was categorized as to possession of a primary, secondary, tertiary, or no interest pattern.

### INDEX IVB. INTEREST MATURITY

Each boy's score on this index was the standard score he received on the Interest Maturity scale of the Career Pattern Study modification of the Strong Vocational Interest Blank.

[9] This index was developed and scored by Helen P. Moser.
[10] This index was developed and scored by Helen P. Moser.
[11] This index was developed and scored by Helen P. Moser. Some pertinent work was also done by Perin M. Mehenti (Perin M. Mehenti. Agreement between vocational preferences and inventoried interest in relation to some presumed indices of vocational maturity. Unpublished doctoral dissertation, Teachers Coll., Columbia Univer., 1954. Pp. 22–23).

## INDEX IVC. LIKING FOR WORK [12]

The fourth interview will be carefully read and only those statements made with reference to the global concept of work will be scored according to the manual.

Scoring is based on the interview statements. All the relevant statements are read carefully and a global judgment is made as to the liking score to be assigned to any particular boy. Sample statements are given to serve as guides. If no statements are made by the boy, he is assigned to the "no mention group."

If the statements made by any boy cannot be scored on the scale, he is put into the "unscorable group."

1–Strong liking.
"I love to work; I would never like to stop working."
"I would like to go to work every day and work hard. I feel fine that way."
"Work is something I really love to do."

2–Mild liking.
"I would rather work than stay home."
"Sometimes I feel I would like to work."
"Work doesn't hurt; there are some good things to be gotten from it."

3–Neither like nor dislike.
"Everybody works; I will work too."
"One has to work in order to eat."

4–Mild disliking.
"There is not much good working."
"I am not eager to work."
"I wish I didn't have to work."

5–Strong disliking.
"I hate to work; there is no good working at all."
"I can never like the idea of working. It's of no use."
"There is nothing to gain in work; I would never work."

[12] M. Yoganarasimhiah. Some factors related to work attitudes in ninth grade boys. Unpublished doctoral dissertation, Teachers Coll., Columbia Univer., 1957. Pp. 42–43. See also pp. 19–24.

## INDEX IVD. DEGREE OF PATTERNING OF WORK VALUES [13]

The Work Values Inventory [14] was used in this index. Scores of 20 and above or of 8 and below on any of the fifteen values assessed by the inventory are beyond the 5 per cent confidence level. The number of such scores was summed for each boy, to obtain his score on index IVD.

## INDEX IVE. EXTENT OF DISCUSSION ABOUT
## REWARDS OF WORK [15]

The fourth interview will be carefully read and only those statements made with reference to the global concept of work will be scored according to the manual.

Scoring is based on the interview statements. All the relevant statements are read carefully and a global judgment is made as to the "discussion" score to be assigned to any particular boy. Sample statements are given to serve as guides. If no statements are made by the boy, he is assigned to the "no mention group."

If the statements made by any boy cannot be scored on the scale, he is put into the "unscorable group."

    1—Mentions one reward.
        "I wish to become famous in my work."
        "I want to achieve something."
        "I want to enjoy my work."
    2—Enumerates several rewards.
        "A good boss and a lot of money is all I want."
        "I wish I could become famous and earn money."
        "I guess you have to have money and like work too."
    3—Mentions more details and interrelationships.
        "I like to have a house, car, and plenty of things. I have to earn money for that. But liking work is really what matters. I don't think money can make it up."
        "But for money, there is no good working at all. I work because I'll need money to buy things and to have a good life. To save money for retirement. If I had as much money as I wanted, I don't think I would work."
        "I want to make a living first. But I also like to be helpful to others.

[13] This index was developed and scored by Helen P. Moser.

[14] The Work Values Inventory is a test about attitudes toward work. It was prepared for use in the Career Pattern Study by Donald E. Super, Junius A. Davis, Charles F. Warnath, and Attia M. Hana. It is a paired-comparison inventory designed to measure the relative strength of fifteen presumed values (creative, aesthetic, planning, theoretical, variety, independence, supervision, work conditions, associations, way of life, social welfare, security, material, prestige, mastery).

[15] M. Yoganarasimhiah. Some factors related to work attitudes in ninth grade boys. Unpublished doctoral dissertation, Teachers Coll., Columbia Univer., 1957. Pp. 42–45. See also pp. 19–24.

I must help others, because they help me earn a living. I want to be famous, too. If I help a lot of people, I'll be widely known."

## INDEX IVF. ACCEPTANCE OF RESPONSIBILITY FOR CHOICE AND PLANNING [16]

*General Directions*

This index attempts to assess three components, Acceptance of Responsibility for Choice, Acceptance of Responsibility for Educational Plans, and Acceptance of Responsibility for Occupational Plans. These are rated on scales of from four to six points each. In each of the three components, action is considered more mature than inaction, acceptance of responsibility is considered more mature than rejection of responsibility, and the use of competent help is considered more mature than completely independent action.

Ratings are based on the reading of relevant excerpts from the interviews, the highest-rated excerpt determining the final rating for each component. Component scores are converted to T-scores, and these are summed to provide the index score.

COMPONENT 1. ACCEPTANCE OF RESPONSIBILITY FOR CHOICE

0—Non-acceptance (rejection) of responsibility.
  "Next year there's a choice between college prep and other courses. It'll be up to my Dad to decide that."
1—No mention of acceptance or rejection.
  "Next year there's a choice between college prep and other courses."
  "You can take Ag. here."
2—Mentions responsibility for choice but expects others to carry it.
  "Parents should help a boy choose his career—they know best."
  "I could take the Ag. course—that's what my Dad advises."
3—Mentions acceptance of responsibility for choice.
  "*I'll* have to decide between college prep and Ag."
  "I'll have to decide for myself. Nobody else'll do it for you!"
4—Mentions acceptance of responsibility for choice with attitude that this is good.
  "Parents should let a fellow choose what he wants to do—and be happy."
  "The school can tell you about admission requirements, but you should make your own decision."
5—Mentions acceptance of responsibility for choice and desire for help in exercising it.

[16] Component 1 of this index was developed by David Cohen and Max Dubrow. It was scored independently by each of them. See: D. Cohen. The relation of independence of work experience to general adolescent independence and certain indices of vocational maturity. Unpublished doctoral dissertation, Teachers Coll., Columbia Univer., 1958. Pp. 39–44; and M. Dubrow. Factors related to the vocational readiness of adolescent boys. Unpublished doctoral dissertation, Teachers Coll., Columbia Univer., 1959. Pp. 76–77, and pp. 20–26.
Components 2 and 3 of this index were developed and scored by Helen P. Moser.

"I think you should choose yourself. Talk it over with parents but only to get their help and backing."

"I'm going to talk it over with my counselor before I decide—if it still looks good I'll take Ag."

Note:—A rating on this scale may be based upon statements made by the boy and/or inferences which can be made from the boy's behavior.

COMPONENT 2. ACCEPTANCE OF RESPONSIBILITY FOR EDUCATIONAL PLANS
   0—Absence or rejection of plan-making.
   1—Little acceptance of plan-making as evidenced by plans made entirely by boy or by parents. No evidence of cooperative planning.
   2—Some evidence of acceptance of plan-making; some cooperative planning, but still primarily by boy or by others.
   3—Much evidence of acceptance of plan-making. Cooperative planning by boy and others.

COMPONENT 3. ACCEPTANCE OF RESPONSIBILITY FOR OCCUPATIONAL PLANS
   0—Absence or rejection of plan-making.
   1—Little acceptance of plan-making as evidenced by plans made entirely by boy or by parents. No evidence of cooperative planning.
   2—Some evidence of acceptance of plan-making; some cooperative planning, but still primarily by boy or by others.
   3—Much evidence of acceptance of plan-making. Cooperative planning by boy and others.


## INDEX VA. INDEPENDENCE OF WORK EXPERIENCE [17]

*Directions for Scoring*

For this scale, independence of work experience is defined operationally as vocational activities free from immediate parental supervision. The measurement of independence of work experience is based upon an analysis of the recorded interviews with the boys and the information provided by each boy in his Personal Data Blank (CPS) and in his Interest Essay (CPS Revision). The recorded parent interviews will be used only as necessary to obtain factual information for elements in the scale where such information is not available in the boys' interviews. The scale is a measure of independence of vocational behavior through a consideration of the chores, and part-time and summer jobs in which a boy may have participated and for which he received some form of remuneration.

Independence of work experience for an early adolescent population may be broken down into the following components: 1) Source of work, 2) Auspices of work, 3) Supervision on the job, 4) The nature of responsibility exercised on the job, 5) The extent of paid experience. Each component is scaled to reflect less to more vocational independence. On each component a boy receives the

[17] D. Cohen. The relation of independence of work experience to general adolescent independence and certain indices of vocational maturity. Unpublished doctoral dissertation, Teachers Coll., Columbia Univer., 1958. Pp. 78–81. See also pp. 39–44.

highest score warranted by the applicable data. Since the scales for measuring each component are ordinal in nature, with the distances between points unknown, each component scale will be transformed into a T-score scale when the group has been scored. A boy's score for independence of work experience is the sum of his scores (T-scores) on the five components. In this scale, all references to employment mean paid employment. Paid employment includes chores for which pay is received. An allowance which is based in whole or in part upon the performance of certain chores is considered to be pay.

Following are the component scales upon which the boy is to be scored, together with sample statements to serve as guides where necessary and individual scoring directions.

COMPONENT 1. SOURCE OF WORK (How the job was secured)

    0—No paid employment
    1—Family
    2—Friends
    3—Self or strangers

A bonus of one point is added to the boy's score if there is evidence which indicates that the boy initiated the effort to get the job. For example, the boy's father may have secured the job for him, but this may have been done at the request of and on the initiative of the boy. This would entitle him to the extra credit.

Note: If a boy has had paid employment, but the data do not reveal information sufficient to warrant a score on this component, it will not be scored. The boy's total score for vocational independence will, however, be prorated on the basis of scores received on 4 out of 5 components. Example: If the total score for the 4 components (exclusive of Component 1) equals 192 (T-score), the boy's score for independence of work experience equals 240 (5/4 192).

    Range of scores: 0 to 4

COMPONENT 2. AUSPICES OF WORK (The employer)

    0—No paid employment
    1—Family
    2—Friends
    3—Strangers
    4—Self
    Range of scores: 0 to 4

COMPONENT 3. SUPERVISION ON THE JOB

    0—No paid employment
    1—Receives close supervision

        The supervisor (boss, owner, manager, etc.) is present all or most of the time to observe and direct the job. He may even work along with his employee(s).

    2—Receives moderate supervision

        The employee is usually given his instructions and then performs on his own with occasional check by the supervisor.

    3—Receives no supervision

        Works independently or supervision is so remote that the employee can be considered to be on his own.

    Range of scores: 0 to 3

COMPONENT 4. THE NATURE OF RESPONSIBILITY EXERCISED ON THE JOB

0—No paid employment

1—Responsibility primarily for self

This is an elemental type of responsibility which the worker is expected to assume on any job. It involves responsibility for his own safety and well-being on the job to the extent that this lies within his own control. A boy would receive a score of 1 if this is the primary element of responsibility required by the job. Jobs such as "cleaning the church grounds" or "washing windows," where there are essentially no materials or equipment involved, are samples of jobs which would warrant a score of 1.

2—(a) Responsibility for materials and/or equipment, *or*
(b) Responsibility for the satisfaction of persons other than the employer *or*
(c) Responsibility for money

Responsibility for any of these three areas goes beyond the basic responsibility for self required by all jobs. They involve alertness, judgment, and the use of tact. The boy would receive a score of 2 if the job requires the exercise of *any one* of the three types of responsibility. Examples of jobs which might qualify for such a score are (a) apprentice machinist, (b) mowing lawns, (c) truck helper.

3—Responsibility for *any two* of the areas qualifying for a score of 2

Examples of jobs which might qualify for a score of 3 are

(a) The grocery clerk who handles stock and also waits on customers.
(b) The caddy who handles equipment and satisfies people.
(c) The pinboy who handles equipment and satisfies people.

4—Responsibility for *all three* of the areas qualifying for a score of 2

Examples of jobs which might qualify for a score of 4 are

(a) The store clerk who handles materials, waits on customers, and takes cash.
(b) The gas station attendant who handles materials, waits on customers, and takes cash.
(c) The newspaper boy who serves people, handles materials, and takes cash.

5—Responsibility for the safety and welfare of others

This is considered to be the highest level of responsibility, since it involves the health and welfare and possibly the life of another person. Examples of jobs qualifying for a score of 5 are (a) baby sitter, (b) lifeguard.

Range of scores: 0 to 5

COMPONENT 5. THE EXTENT OF PAID EXPERIENCE

0—No paid employment

1—Casual paid employment

A casual job is one which is performed for a single employer for less than 2 months if part-time in nature, and for less than 1 month if full-time in nature. Casual jobs are generally characterized by their irregularity as to employer and schedule and their short duration.

2—Part-time paid employment

A part-time job is one which is performed for a single employer on

a regularly scheduled part-time basis for a period of at least 2 months.
3—Full-time summer paid employment
   A full-time job is one which is performed for a single employer on a regularly scheduled full-time basis for at least 1 month.
A bonus of *one point* is added to the boy's score on this component in the following cases:
   (a) Two or more jobs qualifying for a score of two: Score three.
   (b) One job qualifying for a score of three and at least one job qualifying for a score of two: Score four.
A bonus of *two points* is added to the score of the boy who has had two or more jobs qualifying for a score of three: Score five.

A part-time job which becomes full-time during the summer for the same employer is counted as two jobs if they meet the indicated criteria for part-time and full-time jobs. A part-time job which continues into the summer for the same employer is still considered as one part-time job.

Range of scores: 0 to 5

## INDEX VIA. AGREEMENT BETWEEN ABILITY AND PREFERENCE [18]

General mental ability was measured by the Otis Quick-Scoring Mental Ability Test, Gamma, Form C (Otis, 1939). The boy's preferred occupation was ascertained from the fourth interview, as described in the scoring instructions for Index IIIA. Agreement between ability and preference was assessed by determining whether the individual's tested intelligence exceeded that of the bottom quarter of individuals in his preferred occupation.

In Table II of the Army General Classification Test manual (1947, p. 8) ranges of AGCT scores for various civilian occupations are reported. The boy's preferred occupation was matched to occupations in this table. In the case of occupations not listed in the table, two judges selected a listed occupation which they deemed similar in terms of mental ability.

The Otis Gamma IQ's were converted into Army General Classification Test score equivalents by using the means and standard deviations of both tests.[19] A score of plus was given if the boy's converted Otis score fell above the twenty-fifth percentile on the AGCT for the corresponding occupation in Table II of the AGCT manual. A score of minus was given if the boy's converted Otis score fell below the twenty-fifth percentile on the AGCT for the corresponding occupation.

[18] This index was developed by Patricia A. Gross and other Career Pattern Study staff members, based on previous work by Helen P. Moser. Scoring was done by Patricia Gross.
[19] The value for the standard deviation of the Otis test was obtained from Dr. Roger Lennon of the World Book Company.

## INDEX VIB. AGREEMENT BETWEEN MEASURED INTERESTS AND PREFERENCE [20]

Interests were measured by the Career Pattern Study modification of the Strong Vocational Interest Blank. The boy's preferred occupation was ascertained from the fourth interview, as described in the instructions for scoring index IIIA. Agreement between measured interests and the preferred occupation was evaluated by determining the degree of patterning of the boy's interest test scores within the occupational group to which his preferred occupation was assigned. The scoring procedure is described in the following paragraphs.

The preferred occupation was assigned to one of the eleven occupational groupings shown on the Strong profile sheet. When there was no comparable occupation, two judges determined the best placement. (Judged placement in such instances was considered preferable to using a filler score. However, filler scores were used when it was impossible to assign a particular preference, such as wrestler or baseball player, to any of the groups on the profile.)

The degree of patterning of the boy's measured interests (primary, secondary, tertiary, or none) in the Strong group assigned for his preferred occupation was determined.[21]

Numerical scores were given according to the following criteria: A score of 4 indicated a primary interest pattern in the group to which the preferred occupation had been assigned; a score of 3 indicated a secondary interest pattern in the group to which the preferred occupation had been assigned; a score of 2 indicated a tertiary interest pattern in the group to which the preferred occupation had been assigned; a score of 1 indicated no interest pattern in the group to which the preferred occupation had been assigned.

## INDEX VIC. AGREEMENT BETWEEN MEASURED INTERESTS AND FANTASY PREFERENCE [22]

Interests were measured by the Career Pattern Study modification of the Strong Vocational Interest Blank. Fantasy preference was defined as the boy's

[20] This index was developed by Patricia A. Gross and other Career Pattern Study staff members, based on previous work by Helen P. Moser. Scoring was done by Patricia Gross.

[21] Interest patterns were classified as primary, secondary, and so forth, by David Cohen (1958), using Darley's (1941) method.

[22] This index was developed by Helen P. Moser, based on previous work by Perin M. Mehenti (Perin M. Mehenti. Agreement between vocational preference and inventoried interest in relation to some presumed indices of vocational maturity. Unpublished doctoral dissertation, Teachers Coll., Columbia Univer., 1954.)

first response to the following question in the Life Planning Questionnaire: [23]

"If you had the chance to go into any kind of work you wanted as an adult, say 15 years from now, what occupation would you choose? Think only of what you would *like* to do, what you would be *happy* at. Do not think about the abilities required or the training which is necessary to get into this kind of work. Just write down the name of the occupation you would *like* to be in. If you want more than one, write these down, but put your favorite one first."

An A or B+ on the Strong scale for the occupation which was the same as or judged to be similar to the fantasy preference was scored 2.

A score below B+ on the Strong scale which was the same as or similar to the fantasy preference was scored 1.

When no Strong scale was the same as or similar to the fantasy preference, no score could be given.

## INDEX VIID. AGREEMENT BETWEEN OCCUPATIONAL LEVEL OF MEASURED INTERESTS AND LEVEL OF PREFERENCE [24]

The occupational level of the boy's measured interests was assessed by his score on the Occupational Level scale of the Strong Vocational Interest Blank (Career Pattern Study modification). His preferred occupation was ascertained from the fourth interview, as described in the scoring instructions for Index IIIA. The occupational level of the boy's preferred occupation was determined and was then compared with his actual Occupational Level score on the Strong Blank. The scoring procedure is described in the following paragraphs.

The occupational level of the preferred occupation was determined by use of Table 50 (Mean Scores of Occupations on Occupational-Level Scale) in *Vocational Interests of Men and Women* (Strong, 1943, p. 192). When a particular preferred occupation was not listed in the table, a listed occupation judged to correspond most closely to it was used. No score could be given, however, when a preference did not correspond to any of the occupations in the table.

Means and standard deviations of Occupational Level scores of various occupations are given in Table 50. One standard deviation below the mean of the appropriate occupation was taken as a cut-off point in determining agreement between levels of interest and preference. If the individual had an actual Occupational Level score that was equal to or above the cut-off point for the occupation corresponding to his preference (that is, the mean OL score of the occupation minus one standard deviation), he received a plus. If his actual Occupational Level score fell below the cut-off point, he received a minus. For example:

[23] For details concerning the Life Planning Questionnaire, see Hamburger (1958), pp. 21–24, and pp. 82–88.
[24] This index was developed and scored by Helen P. Moser.

Boy's actual OL score = 50
Boy's preference = pilot
Mean OL score for aviator = 54.3, with a standard deviation of 6.4
Mean OL minus one standard deviation = 47.9 (cut-off)
Boy's score of 50 is above the cut-off point; therefore, he receives a plus.

## INDEX VIE. SOCIOECONOMIC ACCESSIBILITY
## OF PREFERENCE [25]

Socioeconomic accessibility of preference was defined as the discrepancy between socioeconomic level of the parental occupation and socioeconomic level of the boy's preferred occupation. The boy's preferred occupation was ascertained from the fourth interview, as described in the instructions for Index IIIA.

Parental occupational level was rated by use of Hamburger's revision (1958) of the occupational rating scale from the Index of Status Characteristics (Warner, Meeker, & Eells, 1949). The occupation of the primary breadwinner in the family (usually the father) was rated. All ratings were based on the pooled judgment of two judges. [26]

The boy's preferred occupation was rated on the same scale. Any questions concerning the ratings to be assigned were settled by discussion between the judges.

The difference between the level of the boy's preferred occupation and the level of his parent's occupation was ascertained. The amount of discrepancy between the two, without regard to sign, was used as the score for the index. For example:

Level of boy's preferred occupation = 4
Level of parental occupation = 6
Socioeconomic accessibility score = 2

[25] This index was developed by Helen P. Moser, based on previous work by Perin M. Mehenti (1954). Scoring was done by William Dubin.
[26] The judges were William Dubin and Martin Hamburger.

LIST OF VOCATIONAL MATURITY MEASURES FOR WHICH
FILLER SCORES WERE USED IN STATISTICAL COMPUTATION

| *Measure* | *Number of Filler Scores Used* |
|---|---|
| Use of Resources in Orientation | 4 |
| Liking for Work | 7 |
| Degree of Patterning of Work Values | 16 |
| Extent of Discussion about Rewards of Work | 3 |
| Acceptance of Responsibility for Choice and Planning: Educational Plans | 12 |
| Acceptance of Responsibility for Choice and Planning: Occupational Plans | 12 |
| Agreement between Measured Interests and Preference | 9 |
| Agreement between Measured Interests and Fantasy Preference | 19 |
| Agreement between Occupational Level of Measured Interests and Level of Preference | 7 |

# Additional Material on Correlates

## CAREER PATTERN STUDY PROCEDURE FOR SCORING THE THEMATIC APPERCEPTION TEST [1, 2]

Each of the fifteen TAT cards used with the subjects is assigned a score, according to the rules listed below. The total score on the test is the sum of the separate scores assigned each card. If a card was not given or is not scorable, the total score should be prorated.

Emphasis in scoring is given to the over-all quality of affect in the story. The general scoring instructions for all cards are as follows.

> *Score 5* (Severe maladjustment)
> Refusals.
> Stories of violence (death, including suicide; serious crime), severe guilt, strong fear.
> *Score 4* (Maladjustment and conflict, not severe)
> Milder negative emotions, such as disagreement, anger (not out of control), failure (not crushing).
> *Score 3* (Neutral)
> Descriptions with no story.
> Stories which are primarily descriptive and in which neither positive nor negative affect is very much apparent.
> A balance of positive and negative affect if the story itself is not extreme.

[1] This scoring procedure was developed by Phoebe L. Overstreet. Use was made of ideas suggested by Dymond's procedure for rating the TAT (Rogers & Dymond, 1954, Ch. 8) and Rotter's method of scoring the Incomplete Sentences Blank (Rotter & Rafferty, 1950).

[2] Excerpts from the Career Pattern Study scoring manual are shown here, not the complete manual.

*Score 2* (Adequate adjustment)

Stories with minimum conflict, adequately handled, only mild problems. Stories showing independence and effectiveness in handling situations, with little conflict.

*Score 1* (Well adjusted)

Happy, positive stories, with good interpersonal relationships, love, a logical happy outcome (that is, the happy outcome does not seem contrived or incongruent with the story).

Specific scoring suggestions for each card: [3, 4]

*Card 1.* Score in the positive direction if the hero likes playing the violin. Score in the negative direction if the hero is forced to play the violin against his will.

*Card 2.* Score in the positive direction stories about the girl helping her parents, or the farmer getting a good crop. Score in the negative direction stories of jealousy, or of conflict between parents and daughter.

*Card 3BM.* Score in the positive direction stories in which the individual gets over his negative affect in a convincing, non-contrived manner (if the negative affect is not too serious). Score in the negative direction stories of death, grief, punishment, rejection.

*Card 4.* Score in the positive direction if a positive interpersonal relationship is established after not too strong a conflict. Score in the negative direction stories of anger, revenge, physical violence, quarrels.

*Card 5.* Score in the positive direction if a pleasant interpretation (such as a nice surprise) is made of the picture. Score in the negative direction stories of spying, being caught, punishment, rejection, violence.

*Card 6BM.* Score in the positive direction stories of consent being given for marriage; son going to war, becoming a hero, and returning safely. Score in a negative direction stories of parental conflict, death of a family member or close friend, son in trouble and rejected by mother.

*Card 7BM.* Score in the positive direction stories depicting a good father-son relationship, such as father perceived as helpful to son. Score in the negative direction stories of quarrels, anger, marked disagreement.

*Card 8BM.* Score in the positive direction if the hero takes a helpful role, such as getting help if an accident occurs, or becoming a doctor. Score in the negative direction for shooting or operation stories without mitigating circumstances.

*Card 9BM.* Score in the positive direction if success theme is developed. Score as neutral stories of hoboes without any particular affect, or stories of being tired and resting. Score in the negative direction stories indicating fear of the men, aggression, punishment.

*Card 10.* Score in the positive direction stories of happy reunions, people in love. Score as neutral stories of greeting or parting without any particular emotion involved. Score in the negative direction stories of grief or reluctant parting.

*Card 12BG.* Score in the positive direction stories of having fun boating or fishing, or stories of successful rescue. Score as neutral stories of

---

[3] Scoring examples taken from test protocols are given in the complete Career Pattern Study manual.

[4] The card numbers follow the listing given in Murray (1943, pp. 18–20).

water sports with no particular affect. Score in the negative direction
stories of drowning, fleeing criminals, pursuit.

*Card 13B.* Score in the positive direction stories of play or of nurturance.
Score in the negative direction stories of loneliness, death of parents, or
poverty which causes hero discomfort or suffering.

*Card 14.* Score in the positive direction stories of dreaming about a
future which is eventually attained, or of enjoyment in looking out the
window. Score in the negative direction stories of suicide, pursuit,
robbery, loneliness.

*Card 16.* No specific scoring suggestions other than the general rules may
be made for this card, because the stories are so varied.

*Card 17BM.* Score in the positive direction stories with a success theme,
such as winning a contest. Score in the negative direction stories of
accidents, escape (if situation is made too unpleasant), and other kinds
of violence.

## SCORING MANUAL FOR SCALE ASSESSING INTRINSIC VERSUS EXTRINSIC WORK VALUES (REWARDS FROM WORK)[5]

The fourth interview will be carefully read and only those statements made
with reference to the global concept of work will be scored according to the
manual.

Scoring is based on the interview statements. All the relevant statements
are read carefully and a global judgment is made as to the score to be assigned
to any particular boy. Sample statements are given to serve as guides. If no
statements are made by the boy, he is assigned to the "no mention group."

If the statements made by any boy cannot be scored on the scale, he is put
into the "unscorable group."

Definitions: *Intrinsic rewards* are those that result from factors inherent
in the work itself, e.g., enjoyment of work activity, creativity, challenging
tasks, etc. *Extrinsic rewards* are those that result from factors external to the
tasks that comprise work, e.g., monetary rewards, prestige, working conditions,
etc.

1—Mentions intrinsic rewards only.
"The biggest thing about work is the pleasure of doing it."
"I want to be real good at my job and like it very much."
"Just the satisfaction of working, that's all."
2—Emphasizes intrinsic rewards more than extrinsic rewards.
"Enjoying work is important; money can't make it up."
"If I had all the money, I still would work. I like it."
"I guess you have to have money and like the work too. Liking work
is what I enjoy most."

[5] M. Yoganarasimhiah. Some factors related to work attitudes in ninth grade
boys. Unpublished doctoral dissertation, Teachers Coll., Columbia Univer., 1957.
Pp. 42–44. See also pp. 19–24.

3—Mentions intrinsic as well as extrinsic rewards.

"Enjoying work is as important as earning money."

"I like good company to work with; I also want to enjoy my work."

"Good working conditions are as important as likable work."

4—Emphasizes extrinsic rewards more than intrinsic rewards.

"Even if I don't like the work, if I can make money, it's fine with me."

"A good boss and lot of money would make me happy in any kind of work—good or bad."

"I would like a respectable job and money; that will make me like my work."

5—Mentions extrinsic rewards only.

"I want to earn a living."

"I wish to become famous in my work."

"Money is most important in any work."

## List of Correlates for Which Filler Scores Were Used in Statistical Computation

| Correlate | Number of Filler Scores Used |
|---|---|
| Father's Educational Level | 6* |
| Mother's Educational Level | 5† |
| Cultural Stimulation | 3 |
| Family Cohesiveness | 3 |
| Father Identification | 12 |
| Agreement between Levels of Vocational Aspiration and Expectation | 2 |
| Presence of Parental Vocational Aspiration for Boy | 7 |
| Parental Mobility | 9‡ |
| Social Mobility of Family | 3 |
| Thematic Apperception Test | 10 |
| Incomplete Sentences Blank | 12 |
| Adolescent Independence | 3 |
| School Achievement versus Underachievement | 3 |
| Religious Affiliation | 2 |
| Intrinsic–Extrinsic Work Values | 3 |

* In addition to the 6 filler scores, 7 best estimates were used.

† In addition to the 5 filler scores, 8 best estimates were used.

‡ In addition to the 9 filler scores, the level of the grandparental occupation was indeterminate in 34 cases, necessitating arbitrary decisions concerning level. The scores assigned these cases were, therefore, estimates.

# References

Anderson, J. E. Dynamics of development: system in process. In D. B. Harris (Ed.), *The concept of development*. Minneapolis: Univer. of Minnesota Press, 1957. Pp. 25–46.

Bell, H. M. *Youth tell their story*. Washington: American Council on Education, 1938.

Bernstein, A. J. Absence of primary interest patterns in adolescent boys. Unpublished doctoral dissertation, Teachers Coll., Columbia Univer., 1953.

Blau, P. M., Gustad, J. W., Jessor, R., Parnes, H. S., & Wilcock, R. C. Occupational choice: a conceptual framework. *Industr. Labor Relat. Rev.,* 1956, 9, 531–543.

*The Blue Book*. Middletown High School, Middletown, New York. 1951–1952. Middletown, N. Y.: The Student Council, 1951.

Buehler, Charlotte. *Der menschliche Lebenslauf als psychologisches Problem*. Leipzig: Hirzel, 1933.

Caplow, T. *The sociology of work*. Minneapolis: Univer. of Minnesota Press, 1954.

Cattell, R. B. *Factor analysis*. New York: Harper, 1952.

Cohen, D. The relation of independence of work experience to general adolescent independence and certain indices of vocational maturity. Unpublished doctoral dissertation, Teachers Coll., Columbia Univer., 1958.

Committee on Technical Recommendations for Psychological Tests and Diagnostic Techniques. Technical recommendations for psychological tests and diagnostic techniques. *Psychol. Bull. Suppl.,* 1954, 51, No. 2, Part 2.

Craven, Ethel C. Social concomitants of interest. Unpublished doctoral dissertation, Teachers Coll., Columbia Univer., 1958.

Cronbach, L. J. Test "reliability": its meaning and determination. *Psychometrika*, 12, 1947, 1–16.

Darley, J. G. *Clinical aspects and interpretation of the Strong Vocational Interest Blank*. New York: Psychological Corporation, 1941.

Darley, J. G., & Hagenah, Theda. *Vocational interest measurement*. Minneapolis: Univer. of Minnesota Press, 1955.

Dubrow, M. Factors related to the vocational readiness of adolescent boys. Unpublished doctoral dissertation, Teachers Coll., Columbia Univer., 1959.

Dysinger, W. S. Maturation and vocational guidance. *Occupations*, 1950, 29, 198–201.

*Examiner manual for the Army General Classification Test. First Civilian Edition*. (Revised November, 1948) Chicago: Science Research Associates, 1947.

Gesell, A., Ilg, Frances L., & Ames, Louise B. *Youth: the years from ten to sixteen*. New York: Harper, 1956.

Ginzberg, E., Ginsburg, S. W., Axelrad, S., & Herma, J. L. *Occupational choice.* New York: Columbia Univer. Press, 1951.

*Golden Jubilee, 1888–1938.* Middletown, N. Y. (undated).

Grace, A. G. The relationship of mental ability to occupational choices of adults. *Voc. Guid. Mag.,* 1931, 10, 354–358.

Hamburger, M. Realism and consistency in early adolescent aspirations and expectations. Unpublished doctoral dissertation, Teachers Coll., Columbia Univer., 1958.

Hana, A. M. Work values in relation to age, intelligence, socio-economic level, and occupational interest level. Unpublished doctoral dissertation, Teachers Coll., Columbia Univer., 1954.

Havighurst, R. J. *Human development and education.* New York: Longmans, Green, 1953.

Henderson, H. L. The relationship between interests of fathers and sons and sons' identification with fathers. Unpublished doctoral dissertation, Teachers Coll., Columbia Univer., 1958.

Heyde, Martha B. Certain factors related to parental vocational and educational aspirations for boys. Unpublished doctoral dissertation, Teachers Coll., Columbia Univer., 1959.

Hollingshead, A. B. *Elmtown's youth.* New York: Wiley, 1949.

Hudson, G. R. Some factors related to the use of community organizations by ninth grade boys. Unpublished doctoral dissertation, Teachers Coll., Columbia Univer., 1953.

Jersild, A. T. *The psychology of adolescence.* New York: Macmillan, 1957.

Kluckhohn, Florence R. Dominant and substitute profiles of cultural orientation: their significance for the analysis of social stratification. *Social Forces,* 1950, 28, 376–393.

McNemar, Q. *Psychological statistics.* New York: Wiley, 1949.

Mehenti, Perin M. Agreement between vocational preference and inventoried interest in relation to some presumed indices of vocational maturity. Unpublished doctoral dissertation, Teachers Coll., Columbia Univer., 1954.

*Middletown, N. Y., Wallkill, Goshen Directory, 1956.* New Haven: Price & Lee, 1956.

Miller, D. C., & Form, W. H. *Industrial sociology.* New York: Harper, 1951.

Moser, Helen P., Dubin, W., & Shelsky, I. M. A proposed modification of the Roe occupational classification. *J. counsel. Psychol.,* 1956, 1, 27–31.

Murray, H. A. *Thematic Apperception Test manual.* Cambridge, Mass.: Harvard Univer. Printing Office, 1943.

National Opinion Research Center. Jobs and occupations: a popular evaluation. *Opinion News,* 1947, 9, 3–13.

Neuhaus, J. O., & Wrigley, C. F. The quartimax method: an analytic approach to orthogonal simple structure. *Brit. J. stat. Psychol.,* 1954, 7, 81–91.

New York State Department of Commerce. *New York State business facts. Mid-Hudson area. 1954 Supplement.* Albany, N. Y.: New York State Department of Commerce, 1954.

Nicholas, C. S. Parent-son participation in vocational planning. Unpublished doctoral dissertation, Teachers Coll., Columbia Univer., 1958.

Nolte, H. W. The relationship of information regarding preferred occupations to intelligence, experience and other factors. Unpublished doctoral dissertation, Teachers Coll., Columbia Univer., 1956.

Norton, J. L. Patterns of vocational interest development and actual job choice. *J. genet. Psychol.,* 1953, 82, 235–262. (a)

Norton, J. L. General motives and influences in vocational development. *J. genet. Psychol.,* 1953, 82, 263–278. (b)

Otis, A. S. *Otis Quick-Scoring Mental Ability Tests. Manual of directions for Gamma Test, Forms C and D.* Yonkers, N. Y.: World Book Co., 1939.

Reynolds, L. G., & Shister, J. *Job horizons.* New York: Harper, 1949.

Roe, Anne. *The making of a scientist.* New York: Dodd, Mead, 1953.

Roe, Anne. *The psychology of occupations.* New York: Wiley, 1956.

Rogers, C. R., & Dymond, Rosalind F. *Psychotherapy and personality change.* Chicago: Univer. of Chicago Press, 1954.

Rotter, J. B., & Rafferty, Janet E. *Manual, the Rotter Incomplete Sentences Blank, College Form.* New York: Psychological Corporation, 1950.

Rotter, J. B., Rafferty, Janet E., & Lotsof, Antoinette B. The validity of the Rotter Incomplete Sentences Blank: High School Form. *J. consult. Psychol.,* 1954, 18, 105–111.

Schmidt, J. L., & Rothney, J. W. M. Variability of vocational choices of high school students. *Personnel Guid. J.,* 1955, 34, 142–146.

Schoeppe, Aileen, & Havighurst, R. J. A validation of development and adjustment hypotheses of adolescence. *J. educ. Psychol.,* 1952, 339–353.

Sears, R. R. Identification as a form of behavioral development. In D. B. Harris (Ed.), *The concept of development.* Minneapolis: Univer. of Minnesota Press, 1957. Pp. 149–161.

Sparling, E. *Do college students choose vocations wisely?* Contributions to Education, No. 561. New York: Bureau of Publications, Teachers College, Columbia University, 1933.

Strong, E. K., Jr. *Vocational interests of men and women.* Stanford, Calif.: Stanford Univer. Press, 1943.

Stubbins, J. The relation between level of vocational aspiration and certain personal data. *Genet. Psychol. Monogr.,* 1950, 41, 327–408.

Sturm, J. Awareness of need to choose an occupation in relation to home and economic independence factors. Unpublished doctoral dissertation, Teachers Coll., Columbia Univer., 1958.

Super, D. E. *Appraising vocational fitness.* New York: Harper, 1949.

Super, D. E. A theory of vocational development. *Amer. Psychologist,* 1953, 8, 185–190.

Super, D. E. Career patterns as a basis for vocational counseling. *J. counsel. Psychol.,* 1954, 1, 12–20.

Super, D. E. Dimensions and measurement of vocational maturity. *Teachers Coll. Rec.,* 1955, 57, 151–163.

Super, D. E. *The psychology of careers.* New York: Harper, 1957.

Super, D. E., & Bachrach, P. B. *Scientific careers and vocational development theory.* New York: Bureau of Publications, Teachers Coll., Columbia Univer., 1957.

Super, D. E., Crites, J. O., Hummel, R. C., Moser, Helen P., Overstreet, Phoebe L., & Warnath, C. F. *Vocational development: a framework for research.* New York: Bureau of Publications, Teachers Coll., Columbia Univer., 1957.

Super, D. E., & Luntz, L. Some uses of biographical inventories in describing adjustment and predicting success. Office for Social Science Programs, Air Force Personnel and Training Research Center, Technical Memorandum 57–1.

Taylor, Katherine von F. Reliability and permanence of vocational interests of adolescents. *J. exp. Educ.,* 1942, 11, 81–87.

Terman, L. M., & Oden, Melita H. *The gifted child grows up.* Stanford, Calif.: Stanford Univer. Press, 1947.

Thomas, L. G. *The occupational structure and education.* Englewood Cliffs, N. J.: Prentice-Hall, 1956.

Thorndike, E. L. *144 smaller cities.* New York: Harcourt, Brace, 1940.

Torrance, E. P. Some practical uses of a knowledge of self-concepts in counseling and guidance. *Educ. psychol. Measmt.,* 1954, 14, 120–127.

United States Department of Commerce, Bureau of the Census. *Census of population: 1950.* Vol. 2. *Characteristics of the population.* Part 1. *United States summary.* Washington: U. S. Government Printing Office, 1953.

United States Department of Commerce, Bureau of the Census. *Census of population: 1950.* Vol. 2. *Characteristics of the population.* Part 32. *New York.* Washington: U. S. Government Printing Office, 1953.

Warner, W. L., Meeker, Marchia, & Eells, K. *Social class in America.* Chicago: Science Research Associates, 1949.

Wolk, W. P. Some correlates of vocational planning in ninth grade boys. Unpublished doctoral dissertation, Teachers Coll., Columbia Univer., 1958.

Wrenn, C. G. Intelligence and the vocational choices of college students. *Educ. Rec.,* 1935, 16, 217–219.

Yoganarasimhiah, M. Some factors related to work attitudes in ninth grade boys. Unpublished doctoral dissertation, Teachers Coll., Columbia Univer., 1957.

# Index

## TOPICS

## NAMES